TABERNACLES IN THE WILDERNESS

INTERPRETING THE CIVIL WAR
Texts and Contexts

EDITOR
Angela M. Zombek
University of North Carolina, Wilmington

Aaron Astor
Maryville College

Wiliam B. Kurtz
University of Virginia

Joseph M. Beilein Jr.
Pennsylvania State University

Brian Craig Miller
Mission College

Douglas R. Egerton
Le Moyne College

Jennifer M. Murray
Oklahoma State University

J. Matthew Gallman
University of Florida

Jonathan W. White
Christopher Newport University

Hilary N. Green
University of Alabama

Timothy Williams
University of Oregon

The **Interpreting the Civil War** series focuses on America's long Civil War era, from the rise of antebellum sectional tensions through Reconstruction.

These studies, which include both critical monographs and edited compilations, bring new social, political, economic, or cultural perspectives to our understanding of sectional tensions, the war years, Reconstruction, and memory. Studies reflect a broad, national perspective; the vantage point of local history; or the direct experiences of individuals through annotated primary source collections.

TABERNACLES

in the

WILDERNESS

The US Christian Commission
on the Civil War Battlefront

✣ ✣ ✣

RACHEL WILLIAMS

The Kent State University Press   *Kent, Ohio*

© 2024 by The Kent State University Press, Kent, Ohio 44242
All rights reserved
ISBN 978-1-60635-473-5
Published in the United States of America

No part of this book may be used or reproduced, in any manner whatsoever, without written permission from the Publisher, except in the case of short quotations in critical reviews or articles.

Cataloging information for this title is available at the Library of Congress.

28 27 26 25 24   5 4 3 2 1

CONTENTS

✢ ✢ ✢

Acknowledgments   vii

Introduction: "God Has Commanded Us to Go Forward"   1

1 Christian Manliness and the Volunteer Delegate System   18

2 Female War Work and the Christian Commission   38

3 Evangelization and the Printed Word   60

4 Preaching and Praying   77

5 Clothing the Union Soldier's Body   95

6 The Gospel of the Loaf   110

7 Death, Salvation, and the Christian Commission   128

Epilogue: "See What the Lord Hath Wrought"   144

Notes   151

Bibliography   179

Index   195

ACKNOWLEDGMENTS

This project was made possible by the generous sponsorship of the Arts and Humanities Research Council, and by the academic and pastoral support of my colleagues in the School of Cultures, Languages, and Area Studies at the University of Nottingham, United Kingdom. In particular, my thanks go to John Ashworth and Vivien Miller for their unfailing and invaluable guidance, and to Hannah Hawkins, Dan King, Stephanie Lewthwaite, Ben Offiler, Matthew Pethers, Christopher Phelps, Benjamin Pickford, and Robin Vandome for their mentorship, critical insights, and excellent company as I conducted the bulk of this research. At the University of Hull, Amanda Capern, Kevin Corstorphine, David Eldridge, Barnaby Haran, Jo Metcalf, Stewart Mottram, and Charles Prior have all given generously of their time and expertise as I prepared this manuscript for publication. It is a privilege and a pleasure to be a part of such a supportive and collaborative academic community.

I also owe a great debt to the archivists and librarians who supported my research and pointed me along likely avenues of exploration, in particular DeAnne Blanton and Timothy Duskin at the National Archives, and Ryan Bean and David Klaassen at the University of Minnesota. I am grateful to members of the association of British American Nineteenth Century Historians (BrANCH) and the Center for Civil War Research at the University of Mississippi for frank and useful feedback on my work, and for stimulating, enjoyable academic discussions. Kristen Brill offered eagle-eyed and helpful readings of various drafts, and Richard Carwardine made valuable and generous suggestions for expanding the archival research. At the Kent State University Press, Clara Totten and

Angie Zombek have championed this project with kindness, enthusiasm, and patience, and their support—along with the generous and helpful reports of two anonymous reviewers—have made this book tighter and richer.

I would not have been able to overcome the isolation and frustration that frequently accompanies academic research without the friendship of Patrick and Christine Budd, Helena Chadderton, Ella Davies, Alys Donnelly, Bethany Kirby, Suzanne Mosely, Alasdair Parkes, Lorna Severn, Meghna Sridhar, Gareth Stockey, and Bernard Wood. I remember with fondness Brett Gemlo and Elizabeth Snelson's hospitality while in Minneapolis. Thanks in particular to Elizabeth Davies for her much-appreciated company in Eastern Market; to Diletta De Cristofaro for worrying about the apocalypse with me; and to Rachel Sykes—for everything.

Finally, thanks always to my parents, Graham and Angela, and my sisters, Kathleen and Rebecca, for their love.

INTRODUCTION

"God Has Commanded Us to Go Forward"

Throughout May 1864, Gen. William Tecumseh Sherman's troops burned through Georgia, dogged in their pursuit of Gen. Joseph E. Johnston. After short, bloody encounters at Resaca and Adairsville, they pressed southwards, reaching Kingston on May 19. Sherman's forces paused less than a week in the small city before continuing their pursuit, driving the Army of Tennessee into the Allatoona Mountains and engaging in fierce fighting at New Hope Church. As they left town, they left behind the wounded who would drain resources and slow the Union whirlwind. By May 23, the makeshift hospitals in Kingston—a hotel near the railroad depot, a farmhouse and its outbuildings, hastily commandeered and superficially outfitted a few days earlier—were all but abandoned, most of the wounded evacuated to hospitals behind the line. Where just a few days previously they were filled with the groans of the dying and the stench of gangrenous flesh, now the wards lay empty but for the final few cases too critically wounded to be moved. The harried medical and nursing personnel had decamped, following Sherman across the Etowah River toward Dallas. The abandoned hospitals were left with a skeleton staff.

On his way to Chattanooga from the front, Rev. Edward Parmelee Smith, a prominent member of an organization known as the United States Christian Commission, stopped at Kingston to offer what help and succor he could to the stricken patients. He was acutely aware that no chaplains remained to minister to the last few hopeless cases in their final moments. "I knew it must be time for many of the wounded to die," he would later recall, "and they must not die alone." Some were unconscious or too delirious to notice his presence at their bedsides.

Others consented to pray with him and entrusted him with tokens and messages to convey to absent family. But one stuck out in Smith's recollections—a fair-haired Indiana lad of eighteen, his leg blown off by a cannonball, close to death and frantic for his mother. Smith sat with him into the early hours of the morning, promising to pass on his final words and his memorandum book and rings to his mother and sister. It took the boy all night to die. Smith prayed with him and reassured him with words of comfort that he would find eternal life in heaven. He watched as the boy pulled out ambrotypes of his family and kissed them each in turn, weeping as he did so. Finally, with nurses and fellow patients gathered around the deathbed, Smith and the dying boy, at last calm and accepting of his fate, sang together William Cowper's 1779 hymn: "There is a fountain filled with blood / drawn from Emmanuel's veins; / and sinners washed beneath the flood / lose all their guilty stains." Then the boy lapsed into unconsciousness and finally slipped away. Smith was deeply affected by this death—months later, as he tried to sum up his experiences for the benefit of the men who sent him to Georgia in pursuit of the army, he would write, "that midnight scene cannot be described . . . [it fills] a blessed page in my memory, but I cannot transfer it to you."[1]

Versions of this tragic scene played out in hospitals and camps throughout the South. Volunteer workers of the Christian Commission prayed and sang with dying men, offering spiritual guidance and reassurance and bearing witness to the final moments of countless Union soldiers. Yet, although these workers were scattered across the theaters of war, separated by time and distance, drawn from different denominations and walks of life, they turned time and time again to the words of Cowper's hymn—and to the "fountain filled with blood"—to soothe the souls of the dying and to turn their thoughts heavenwards as they died. Their motivations were various. On the face of it, the ready extension of spiritual comfort to dying, frightened men was simply time-worn Good Samaritanism. For others, however, evangelizing to dying Union soldiers was part of a bigger, more urgent project.

In the eyes of the most committed evangelical foot soldiers, the Civil War represented a final cataclysm that might hasten the Second Coming of Christ. They were as a result inclined to interpret Union deaths as sacrifices almost commensurate with Christ's on the cross. The blood of Union soldiers and, as Smith said of the Indiana youth, "the consecration unto death on the altar of country," contributed to a national process of cleansing, atonement, and regeneration which would culminate in the salvation of the world. The act of singing Cowper's hymn with and to men dying of wounds sustained in the service of the Union blurred and even erased the lines between the atoning blood of Christ and the blood of mortal humans, and tied individual—often ignominious, pain-

INTRODUCTION 3

ful, lonely—deaths into a wider, apocalyptic narrative that imbued the work of the Christian Commission with an almost unbearably solemn significance.

A civilian relief agency organized in late 1861 by evangelical Protestants, the United States Christian Commission set out to minister to the spiritual and physical needs of the Union Army and Navy during the American Civil War. The vigils that men like Smith kept at the bedsides of dying men were the starkest realization of the Commission's work, the apotheosis of the organization's self-appointed evangelical, benevolent mission. They were, however, only one small part of a raft of battlefront and home front activities initiated by Commission members during the conflict. Operating from a central office in Philadelphia and relying on funds raised and supplies donated by civilians on the home front, the organization sent thousands of volunteer delegates to the field of war to distribute food, clothing, medicine, and religious literature to troops, and to organize Christian worship, converse with men on spiritual matters, and—as we have already seen—comfort them as they died.

To justify this work, the founders of the Commission developed a complex and powerful theological interpretation of the Civil War, one that the ordinary men and women associated with it often helped to articulate and enact. Along with many American evangelicals, leading members of the Christian Commission interpreted the Civil War both as a wrathful judgment from God for the sins of the American nation and as a sign that the long-awaited millennium of peace and prosperity that would precede the Second Coming of Christ— and which human beings, through their actions and faith, could have a role in bringing about—was finally at hand. The nation, and the evangelical Protestants who had appointed themselves gatekeepers of morality and piety, had a duty to atone, through immediate, universal repentance, and through blood sacrifice, for squandering the utopian potential of the Revolution. This interpretation of the sectional conflict lent the Commission's proselytizing mission great urgency: the Federal Army, at the vanguard of the earthly battle to rescue the American Union (a political compact supposedly blessed by God), would also become the front line of the spiritual battle for the soul of America. Lemuel Moss's letter of encouragement to his colleague Annie Wittenmyer epitomized this mind-set: "[God] has commanded us to go forward, + we shall see his salvation," he wrote. "He will triumph gloriously. The news is encouraging from all parts of the army."[2] Fervent in their belief that America was the "New Israel"—the redeemer nation that would inspire and lead the moral and spiritual regeneration of the globe—many Christian Commission representatives instilled their work with a nationalist, apocalyptic significance which, in their view, transcended mere charity.

The Christian Commission counted among its workers Methodists, Baptists, Congregationalists, Presbyterians, Episcopalians, and more from across the spectrum of American evangelicalism. Each of these denominations brought its own doctrinal and ritual idiosyncrasies to the USCC, but no matter what else they disagreed upon, Commission members, regardless of confessional identity, were united in their evangelical commitment to concerted, aggressive, and urgent proselytizing and to aiding sinners toward the ultimate signal of salvation: a conversion experience. We will discuss the gamut of American evangelicalism and its preoccupations at greater length in chapter 3. For now, suffice it to say the Commission delegates, drawn from evangelical congregations from across the North, were tasked (or, indeed, tasked themselves) with saving the immortal souls of the men they encountered by converting them to their brand of Christianity. To that end, the Commission devised methods that encouraged men to earnestly consider spiritual matters. Many USCC personnel took this a step further, developing and articulating a powerful evangelical rhetoric that linked the fate of the individual soul to the fate of the American Union.

Tabernacles in the Wilderness explores how the workers of the Christian Commission put these ideas into action, zealously embracing the task of saving souls and attempting to enact that task in whatever small corner of the war to which they were assigned. Along the way, they faced frustration, calumny, disillusionment, and even physical danger—and yet, as a group, they persisted and remained convinced of the necessity of their work until the Commission formally wrapped up its affairs in early 1866. Preachers who left their hometown congregations to travel to the battlefields, theological students looking to cut their teeth, women seeking an outlet for their patriotism, little children diligently making sewing kits: the Christian Commission drew in a vast and varied constituency of participants and supporters. Its work spanned the globe, linking eager donors as far afield as California, Europe, and Hawaii to the men suffering on the battlefields. During its lifetime, according to its own exhaustive records, the Christian Commission received over $6 million in donations comprised of cash, publications, food, clothing, and services (such as railroad and telegraph fares). It commissioned nearly 5,000 volunteer delegates, who between them preached 58,308 sermons and held 77,744 prayer meetings.[3] It was a large, well-funded organization that commanded considerable public support and respect and, once fully operational, maintained a constant presence on the battlefront.

Yet, despite its financial clout and public profile, the role of the Christian Commission in Civil War relief work remains relatively unknown, consistently overshadowed by scholarly interest in the larger, richer United States Sanitary

Commission, which sought to increase the efficiency of the Union Army by introducing "sanitary" measures (such as better-ventilated pavilion hospitals) and coordinated systems of supply distribution. In many respects, the two commissions saw themselves as ideological and financial rivals during the conflict. The Christian Commission dismissed the Sanitarians as uncaring bureaucrats with a tendency to treat the Union soldier as a cog in a machine. Bernice Ames, urging the citizens of Rutland, Vermont, to send donations to the Christian Commission instead of the USSC, smugly reported, "the soldiers have a saying that Sanitary is for the officers, but Christian is for the boys."[4] Harper Bois, a delegate stationed at City Point, was even more blunt, claiming that the common refrain from the rank and file regarding the USSC was: "The Sanitary Com is a great humbug."[5] The Sanitary Commission likewise expressed disdain for the USCC's "amateurish lack of emphasis on rules, systems or organization."[6] Delivering a speech in California, it was abundantly clear who USSC President Henry Whitney Bellows was talking about when he sniped "[We do] not stop to ask whether a contributor or a soldier is a Christian or not . . . There is no nasty, narrow spirit of sectarianism about the [Sanitary] Commission."[7] Competing for funds and support from the same, or very similar, constituencies among the Northern citizenry, the commissions were obliged to justify their respective remits and to enter into expensive publicity campaigns to prevent their rival from gaining the upper hand, and to demonstrate the relevance and righteousness of their particular interpretation of the sectional conflict, of the purpose of philanthropy, and of the future direction of America.[8]

The Sanitary Commission won the propaganda war. Its strident derision of the Christian Commission still influences scholarly accounts of Civil War philanthropy, which too often reduce the work of the USCC to the well-meaning but haphazard distribution of tracts and Bibles or the functional provision of hot coffee and fresh vegetables.[9] Rather than treat the organization as a counterpoint to the Sanitary Commission, however, this book posits that the Christian Commission is worthy of examination in its own right. An example of civilian war relief distinct from its more famous contemporary by virtue of its explicitly religious purview, the Commission can help us better understand the development of American philanthropy in the nineteenth century and the role of the Civil War in shaping this development. This has often been framed as a straightforward story of steadily increasing bureaucratization, professionalization, and secularization that would eventually spawn the big foundations of the early twentieth century, yet the Christian Commission demonstrates that antebellum voluntarism and Christian sentimentalism persisted in American philanthropic activity through and beyond the Civil War, finding new expression (even via direct continuity of personnel) in the Social Gospel and other movements of the later nineteenth century.[10]

Moreover, the Christian Commission occupies an important place in theological and intellectual histories of the Civil War.[11] By examining the activities of Christian Commission delegates, and how they articulated and understood these activities, we gain better insights into the "lived religion" of the Civil War battlefront. That is, we better understand what David Hall, probably the foremost scholar of lived religion, called "the everyday thinking and doing of lay men and women."[12] The actions and methods of Christian Commission delegates reveal the importance of material items as vessels of religious meaning and tools of evangelism, and the value of shared ritual as channels of sentiment and collective identity. In the speeches, sermons, and editorials of its leaders, and in the diary entries, exit reports, and postwar recollections of its workers, Christian Commission workers across the evangelical spectrum grappled publicly and privately with pressing and difficult spiritual questions: Was the war a savage curse from God, or a chance to cleanse and reform America? Could dying for the Union guarantee a man eternal life? Were the souls of Union and Confederate soldiers equally worth saving? They translated their sometimes jumbled, unsophisticated, and internally inconsistent interpretations of the sectional conflict into what they hoped would be real and useful action.

ESTABLISHING THE USCC

The outbreak of the Civil War heralded a flurry of civilian relief activity in the North as loyal citizens sought to demonstrate their patriotism and enthusiasm for the war to crush the rebellion. As has been well documented, Northern communities set up soldiers' aid societies, often led by women, that sent supplies to the front and engaged civilians in public, political acts of production and fundraising.[13] Evangelical Christians across the North also threw themselves into this whirlwind of home front organizing, motivated by their anxieties about the souls of the departing armies. Much of the early evangelizing work that would pave the way for the Christian Commission was undertaken by individuals responding ad hoc to local circumstances. In Washington, Young Men's Christian Association worker William Ballantyne distributed old *Christian Almanacs* to regiments gathering around the city, while in Philadelphia, John Patterson, motivated by the need for ministry he observed while visiting the army, set up an Army Committee to send goods and reading material to

INTRODUCTION 7

the troops. Dwight L. Moody and B. F. Jacobs, prominent Chicago evangelists, travelled to Cairo, Illinois, to set up prayer meetings and distribute hymn books among mustered troops. In New York City, the artist Vincent Colyer began conversing with troops on religious matters, enlisting his YMCA colleagues to help write letters and distribute what supplies he could muster.[14] Efforts were scattershot and localized to begin with, but the dawning realization that the Federal government was unprepared for a protracted, bloody war on its own turf, and that many of the soldiers' needs—not only clothing, food, and medical care, but also spiritual instruction and support—were being neglected intensified this activity, and led civic leaders and seasoned philanthropists to consider a more organized civilian response.

These impulses swiftly bore fruit in the shape of several centralized civilian relief agencies, including the Women's Central Relief Association (which would later become, to cut a long and somewhat contentious story short, the United States Sanitary Commission), the Western Sanitary Commission, and, eventually, the United States Christian Commission, the only agency explicitly devoted to the religious life and health of the armies. It was Colyer who first proposed to fellow Young Men's Christian Association workers across the Northeast that a coordinated evangelical response to the crisis was required to prevent the moral decay of the thousands of young men leaving home to fight for the Union.[15] Having secured the approval and authority of various YMCA branches in and around New York, Colyer formed a National Committee in September 1861 to review and advise on the spiritual state of the armies. Assessing the situation as bleak, this National Committee advised the creation of a national body to oversee evangelical ministry to the armies, and on October 18, 1861, representatives of fourteen YMCA branches met in New York to form a "Christian Commission." They appointed an Executive Committee of twelve prominent evangelical clergymen and laymen, with Philadelphia dry goods merchant and Sunday School leader George Hay Stuart as president, a position he would occupy until the Commission disbanded in 1866.[16]

Despite this apparent appetite for coordinated action to save the souls of Union troops, the Christian Commission's work ground to a fairly complete halt shortly after its official foundation and initially achieved little of substance. Over the first seven months of its existence, several members of the original committee resigned and were replaced, meetings were sporadic, the Commission headquarters moved from New York to Philadelphia, and fundraising was uncoordinated. Some clergymen travelled to Union camps to provide ministry to troops but were largely left to their own devices, without support or guidance.[17] This all changed in May 1862. It was then that the volunteer delegate system (discussed in greater

George H. Stuart, circa 1865. (Library Company of Philadelphia; photographer unknown)

detail in the first chapter) was formulated and tested, and the USCC quickly began sending unpaid clergy and laity to the armies for six-week stints to distribute religious reading material, food, and clothing among those in need, and to organize and lead the men in worship and prayer, with the ultimate aim of converting the Union armies to evangelical Protestantism. By early 1863, this delegate system was well established, and the Commission had succeeded in securing the public (if sometimes slightly baffled and lukewarm) approval of prominent politicians and officers, including Abraham Lincoln and George McClellan.[18] Field agents were appointed to oversee operations in the fields of war, and a network of branches was established in major Northern cities to collect goods and funds, with a steady stream of applicants ready to fill the places of returning delegates. Their record-keeping system was now more thorough than it had been at the outset, too, with secretaries carefully recording every detail pertaining to money, supplies, personnel, and home front support and engaging in regular and lengthy communication with the growing network of USCC branches across the North.[19] Therefore, the work of the Christian Commission began in earnest in early 1863, and despite peaks and troughs in its financial fortunes and public popularity,

INTRODUCTION 9

maintained a stream of supplies and personnel to the front for the remainder of the war, expanding its fundraising operations further afield, and establishing a growing presence in the Union armies.[20]

ANTEBELLUM ORIGINS

Vincent Colyer, Dwight L. Moody, and the other pioneers who created the Christian Commission were hardly novices in the fields of Christian lay ministry and charitable work. Their commitment to addressing the spiritual needs of the hundreds of thousands of young men suddenly faced with mortal peril was built on decades spent engaged in determined and well-resourced evangelical reform activity. That is to say, the work of the Christian Commission was part of a longer continuum of religious thought and labor, which merits some examination here. Broadly put, antebellum theological and eschatological realignments which promised human beings greater control over their spiritual fates drove the Christian Commission's commitment to conversion, while the industrious and ever-evolving activities of revivalists and reformers before the Civil War provided well-established working models of how to put these ideas into practice and bring people to God.

In the early nineteenth century, Calvinist orthodoxy, which insisted that the elect, bound for heaven after death, were predestined and that human beings could do nothing to influence the spiritual fates of their souls, eventually ceded ground to the New Haven theology of Nathaniel William Taylor and, later, Charles Grandison Finney.[21] Crucially, these radical theologians, while maintaining a belief in human depravity, claimed that people not only had the ability to choose to obey God's law but also to seek, and ultimately to accept, God's saving grace.[22] If the soul could be perfected, and if, theoretically, *everyone* could be saved, then it was the duty of American evangelicals to capitalize on this and to lead as many souls as possible to God. This sense of urgent mission found expression in the activities of the so-called "Benevolent Empire."[23] This cluster of national evangelical endeavors, which were at their most active in the 1820s and 1830s, encompassed huge moral reform organizations such as the American Tract Society (established in 1825), the American Bible Society (1816), and the American Sunday School Union (1824), each with its own individual aims and ideas about how America was to be redeemed, but all contributing to what Clifford Griffin once called "a general crusade against evil."[24]

These benevolent reform movements, spearheaded by evangelicals convinced that creating a godly society based on biblical example and yearning for salvation would eventually prepare the way for the Second Coming of Christ, did not exist in a vacuum. Rather, they were informed by Christian anxieties about socioeconomic changes (especially in the Northern states), which significantly altered the relationship between the community and the individual. Increasing rates of migration (both rising rates of immigration, especially from Europe, and internal migration involving the movement of would-be settlers westwards and streams of people moving from the countryside to the growing cities) were perceived not only to disrupt the close-knit generational bonds that sustained small towns and villages but to bring an alarming ethnic and religious (read: Catholic) diversity to larger cities too.[25] As the antebellum population boomed, and cities swelled, so did anxieties about urban poverty, vice and crime, and disease. Rather than embracing the values and behaviors that would eventually reform the world and make it fit to welcome Jesus again, America, evangelicals feared, seemed to be going in the opposite direction. By the 1850s, marshalling their resources to combat sinfulness and godlessness, evangelicals redoubled their efforts, moving beyond promoting general moral uplift through the distribution of Bibles and the establishment of Sunday schools, and instead targeting what they saw as specific social ills such as drunkenness, prostitution, and Sabbath-breaking.[26]

One of the most prominent and long-lasting organizations established to tackle the perceived dangers of mid-century urban dwelling was the Young Men's Christian Association. Inspired by the example of British draper George Williams, who had established a group designed to bring young male workers together in prayer and moral community in London in 1844, American Christians began establishing associations in their own cities in the early 1850s. These new American YMCAs were deeply concerned with the streams of rural migrants, many of them single young men, flooding into the cities in search of employment.[27] Evangelical reformers involved in the YMCA considered this young new workforce particularly vulnerable to the temptations and dangers of urban living, from drink and prostitution to gambling and financial irresponsibility.[28] City life, it was supposed, ran counter to the participatory, communal ethos of the small town or village, leaving new arrivals "isolated from the traditional influences of church and family."[29] In response to these perceived threats, the various YMCAs sought to prevent the spiritual and physical ruin of susceptible young men, and to promote Christian fellowship and cooperation in God's work.[30] Dedicated to replicating the moral surveillance and guidance of the village within the faceless metropolis, the YMCA envisaged itself as a surrogate family for men separated from the stability of home and the moral guidance of mother, and attempted to provide friendship and advice for those new to the city.[31] In order to achieve this, YMCAs held lecture series and sermons to offer advice to the potentially vulnerable, and to provide a meeting point for like-minded Christian young men.[32] They developed library facilities, distributed religious publications, and set up employment and accommodation schemes to help men find their feet in an alien locale. YMCA members sought out new arrivals to the city, encouraged them to teach Sunday school, helped them to find board and work, and introduced them to a respectable, Christian group of friends.[33] As the president of the Washington YMCA Zalmon Richards said eighteen months into his branch's work, "our Christian combination can work, in attracting to the paths of virtue and safety those noble, yet deluded youth, whom the temptations and corrupting influences of city life may have [caught]."[34]

Many of the concerns of the YMCAs were intensified by the outbreak of the Civil War. The immorality and anonymity of the late antebellum city was nothing, in the eyes of evangelical reformers, compared to the vice and sin that stalked the crowded army camps. Fear for the souls of young men thrust with little preparation into the tumult of military life motivated representatives of several YMCA branches, as we have already seen, to transplant their ministry into the army camps, and eventually spawned the Christian Commission. Vincent Colyer surveyed the spiritual state of the troops he encountered around Washington, DC, in the aftermath of the First Battle of Bull Run with dismay:

> These young men are risking their lives for their country, exposed to constant hardships, and subjected to all the temptations and debasing influences of camp life. They are liable to sickness and prolonged suffering from wounds in hospital, and to sudden death upon the battle-field. To meet the great wants of these young men, under circumstances which so urgently call upon our Christian sympathies and gratitude, (for they are assembled in defense of our homes, our rights, and our government!) no adequate exertion has yet been made. . . . I need not urge the necessity of prompt as well as decisive action—for it must be apparent to everyone, that whatever is done effectively in this army work must be done quickly. At any moment, here, a terrible battle may take place, and all along our lines, (in the West particularly,) engagements are daily occurring; besides, the troops are continually in motion, and the habits of the men are forming daily, either for good or evil.[35]

Initially dedicated mostly to the distribution among Union troops of whatever religious literature local YMCA branches had to hand, the USCC eventually expanded and solidified its operations into a centralized agency for providing spiritual and bodily relief. Despite this expansion, its roots in the YMCA remained evident; the local YMCAs provided important networks of communication and cooperation, which were fully exploited by the USCC during the war. Several men prominent in the leadership of the antebellum YMCAs, many of them up-and-coming businessmen, manufacturers, and bankers, went on to play important roles in the USCC, and the basic profile (discussed at greater length in the first chapter) of the typical USCC delegate—young, male, and member of an evangelical congregation—was the same as that of the typical YMCA visitor.[36] More importantly, the USCC stayed committed to the eradication of vice and immorality in the army camps and employed many of the same techniques as the YMCAs—distribution of religious literature, personal conversation, and provision of dedicated meeting rooms—to protect the souls of vulnerable young men from the temptations and dangers in their paths.

The emergence and proliferation of the YMCAs was not the only development of the 1850s that directly informed the work and thought of the Christian Commission. Between 1857 and 1858, a spike in religious revivals swept across much of the nation, packing churches and meeting halls with penitent sinners communally praying and urgently seeking grace.[37] This so-called "Businessman's Revival" was a boon for the YMCAs. New branches opened up across urban areas in the North, and the dense concentration of potential converts crowding into the lunchtime prayer meetings provided the perfect opportunity for YMCA workers from New York to Cleveland to Philadelphia to distribute pamphlets and even to organize revival meetings of their own.[38] During and after the Civil War, Christian Commission leaders themselves stressed their indebtedness to this period of religious activity on the eve of the conflict. "It was the preparation of the nation and the church for the hour of trial," Lemuel Moss, Commission secretary, wrote. "All denominations were at work, and all classes of people were interested."[39] The 1857–58 Revival was crucial to the Christian Commission in several respects. Not only did it attract a new generation of YMCA leaders and evangelists, but it demonstrated the efficacy and potency of certain new worship methods that would soon become staples of the USCC arsenal. Commission leaders were particularly keen to point out the prominent role of laypeople in leading prayer meetings and the apparently harmonious and spontaneous evaporation of interdenominational infighting and rivalry during the revival. In their estimation these characteristics were wholeheartedly inherited and embraced by the men and women of the USCC.

This revival moment was far from unique in American history, however. Just as the YMCAs were part of a longer story of philanthropic evolution across the antebellum period, the 1857–58 Revival was built upon historic waves of religious enthusiasm and existing patterns of evangelical worship. In the first decades of

INTRODUCTION

the nineteenth century, the religious revivals of the Second Great Awakening regenerated existing congregations and catalyzed the formation of new ones.[40] These lengthy, rowdy, emotional mass gatherings of men and women, all throwing themselves (both metaphorically and physically) before God and publicly seeking salvation, temporarily erased—or at least minimized—sectarian differences and brought the postmillennial, perfectionist theology that drove evangelical reform into the mainstream, making it accessible and "socially constructive" to ordinary people.[41] Revivals, by demanding the urgent reformation of converts' souls, encouraged communities to live biblically and to embody Christ's example in their everyday lives. This impetus nourished the reform programs of the Benevolent Empire and later movements, as communities "burned over" by revivals formed local auxiliaries or sent donations to national benevolent societies and moral crusades to demonstrate their reinvigorated piety. In short, as William McLoughlin claims, revivals were "the most powerful engine in the processes of American church growth, frontier acculturation, and benevolent reform" in the antebellum period, not only shoring up the social and political clout of the evangelical churches but also revolutionizing worship techniques to exert maximum pressure on the souls of would-be converts.[42]

The antebellum theological transformations explained earlier went hand in hand with these new ways of worshipping and new ways of winning converts to God. As we will examine further in chapter 3, more sedate, reserved worship styles, largely associated with the well-established Presbyterian and Congregational churches, dominated the early nineteenth century. These soon gave way, however, to populist, democratized models of revivalism which were already finding expression at the turn of the century.[43] These new revival techniques, fueled in no small part by the exponential growth of Methodism, focused, according to Nathan Hatch, on "the primacy of the individual conscience."[44] That is, revivalists believed that individuals were free moral agents with the mental and spiritual capacity to search for salvation themselves and that emotional pressure was more effective in assisting this process than was complex theological argumentation. This focus on emotionality rather than doctrine and on individual rather than communal responses diminished the importance of denominational identity and elevated the laity to new levels of prominence and participation.[45]

This democratization was accompanied by innovations in revival techniques that emphasized emotionality and spontaneity, such as protracted prayer meetings during which congregations prayed for anxious sinners by name, and the groans and spasms of attendees were interpreted as indications that the Holy Spirit was present. Speakers at revival meetings often used colorful, coarse language to rouse their audiences, and meetings often featured lively folk music (this period was notable for the development of the gospel style, which was heavily influenced by slave spirituals). The popularization of revivalism made prayer a social experience, transforming conversion from a private experience predicated on arbitrary grace or intellectual puzzling into a deliberately intense and public process based on "purposive encounters between people."[46] While revivals were still seen as evidence of divine blessing by the mid-nineteenth century, they were no longer understood as solely the work of the Holy Spirit; rather than divine miracles, they were seen as humanly constructed means for encouraging receptivity to the Holy Spirit. In short, the preachers and laypeople who employed these new and often controversial methods were actively coaxing their congregations toward a closer individual relationship with God and attempting to boost church membership.[47] The sense of immediacy and urgency generated by revival measures transformed the conversion process, which had previously been a protracted and private struggle between the congregant and God, into a deliberately public spectacle. For many, this highly visible process compressed the struggle to believe and to accept salvation into a much shorter period of time, and fueled the sense of impending millennium.[48]

While the intensity of the Second Great Awakening had begun to fade by the 1840s, its brief resurgence in the late 1850s underlined the continuing potential for evangelicals to generate, sustain, and capitalize upon burgeoning religious enthusiasm. In many respects, the nature of the 1857–58 Revival reflected the evolution of American society. Instead of the lengthy Southern tent meetings of the earlier antebellum period, now many prayer meetings were held at noon to cater to the working hours of an emerging class of office and factory workers. These meetings were loosely structured and open to all to bring testimony, lead prayers, and sing together. The increasing focus on experience and emotion, and not on doctrinal exactitude, meant the previous animosity between denominations broke down. The revival was by no means a purely metropolitan phenomenon, but urban congregations near each other often joined together to organize gatherings and conventions not just in churches but in theaters, and meeting halls, traditionally secular spaces repurposed for the work of piety.[49] The 1857–58 Revival also witnessed increased lay involvement in prayer meetings, public speaking, and organization, breaking down the deferential relationship between priest and convert and emphasizing instead the equality of all people in the sight of God.[50] From the point of view of the Christian Commission leaders who were so inspired by this brief flare of religious fervor, the revival was significant not only for its role in renewing public interest in the YMCAs, but also for the impact it wrought on the way ordinary American Christians practiced their religion, the links it strengthened between religion and reform, and the experience it provided in organization, communication, and ministration for the laymen and clergy who would later serve as USCC delegates.

The Christian Commission came into being as a result of these developments in the 1850s: with YMCA membership on the up after a mid-decade slump and evangelical lay leaders freshly energized by the 1857–58 Revival, when war broke out in April 1861 these enthusiasts were well placed to confront the perceived spiritual crisis facing the nation with concerted and vigorous evangelizing. The workers of the Christian Commission put into practice their experience as revivalists and reformers, adapting well-established methods and mobilizing existing networks to tackle their wartime mission. They labored in challenging circumstances to reconcile their desire to alleviate the physical suffering they encountered with their deeply held religious convictions and their commitment to evangelize to men in peril. As we will see, the task of saving souls and repairing bodies frequently chafed against the realities of improvising worship, prayer, and pastoral guidance on the battlefront. Skeptical officers, indifferent troops, supply problems, even interpersonal incompatibilities: all hindered what USCC personnel saw as God's work on Earth.

This workforce was drawn from evangelical congregations across the North and involved both volunteer delegates (almost without exception men) stationed in army camps and military hospitals, and civilian supporters on the home front, many of them women crafting a model of pious patriotism through their public support of the Christian Commission. The first two chapters of the book address these two groups, focusing on the gendered parameters of war work during the Civil War. Chapter 1 considers the volunteer delegate system that formed the bedrock of the USCC's operations in the theater of war. It explores how the Commission sought to create an "army" of Christian workers whose physical strength and vigor exploded antebellum suspicions of the effeminacy of the clergy, equating the fight for the Union with the fight for the soul of America. Chapter 2, meanwhile, focuses on the role of women in the Christian Commission. Motivated by concerns of respectability, the USCC crafted a powerful rhetoric of female virtue and patriotism to justify the roles it created for women. However, the lived operations of the Ladies Christian Commissions and the special diet kitchens established in military hospitals frequently chafed against this conservative narrative and allowed women to exercise a public voice, gain new business and management skills, and forge new alliances that would help shape postwar women's activism.

A central concern of this book is the emphasis that Commission workers placed on both the bodies and the souls of the men they encountered and on the vital link between the two. Delegates used the body as a conduit to the soul and saw physical health and cleanliness as indications of internal spiritual renewal. The work for the body and the work for the soul were not two separate branches of the Christian Commission's work but—as the remaining chapters of the book demonstrate—were directed toward the same goal: reforming and redeeming Americans. The methods the Commission devised to target both souls and bodies and the beliefs and preoccupations of the workers who employed these varied ministries all contributed to the urgent evangelicalism of the Commission. The work drew together not only proselytizing words and rituals, but a wealth of material objects circulated by Commission workers and intended to convey spiritual meaning, comfort, and even protection. Examining the uses of this spiritually redolent material culture within the contours of battlefront life bring us closer to an appreciation of the rhythms and variations of Civil War lived religion.

Chapters 3 and 4 explore the centrality of conversion to the work of the Christian Commission. Commission workers devised and adapted methods to target men's souls directly, both on an individual and collective level. Foremost among these methods was the distribution of religious literature, the subject of chapter 3. Here I discuss how the Commission encouraged deep spiritual reflection and moral regeneration by distributing religious reading material such as Bibles, tracts, and newspapers, demonstrating a dedication both to literacy and to the agency of the individual in seeking salvation. This was not the only means of conveying spiritual information and guidance. As chapter 4 discusses, the Commission also employed the spoken and sung word, drawing upon the expertise of its workforce of lay preachers to extemporize sermons, lead prayer meetings and hymn-singing, and engage in private conversation, to create a dynamic communal worship experience and encourage spiritual contemplation, crisis, and ultimately resolution.

Though preaching, praying, and distributing religious literature occupied a considerable part of a delegate's working day and accounted for much of the Commission's financial outlay, bodily ministry was equally important to the mission. As I discuss in chapters 5 and 6, the USCC sought to minister to soldiers' bodies, not only as a demonstration of Christian charity but as a conduit to the soul and thus, an aid to conversion. Chapter 5 explores the distribution of clothing by Christian Commission delegates and the ways in which this clothing sought to remake damaged bodies—both individual and national—by restoring uniforms symbolic of the righteous, God-given Union cause to wholeness and cleanliness. Yet, as chapter 6 demonstrates, the Commission's bodily ministry was internal as well as external, resting upon the power of food and drink to heal ailing bodies, bring about repentance, and lead men to Christ. The work of ordinary delegates in distributing food and drink and organizing special meals or luxury items, as well as the work of the diet kitchens in encouraging physical and emotional recuperation and spiritual reflection, underlined the Commissioners' faith that "the way to a hungry man's soul is through his mouth."[51]

I conclude in chapter 7 by analyzing the work of the USCC among the dead and dying. In no other sphere of the Commission's work was the link between the body and soul clearer or more vital. Considering the role of Christian Commission delegates in conversing with those on their deathbeds, witnessing and reporting deaths, conducting or observing funerals, and creating graves and memorials for the dead, I show how the USCC cast dead Union soldiers as Christian martyrs sacrificed for the sake of the salvation of America and, by extension, the world. This created a powerful compound of piety and patriotism used by the USCC to enhance and justify its work.

CHAPTER ONE

Christian Manliness and the Volunteer Delegate System

The founding goal of the United States Christian Commission was simple but ambitious: to minister to the spiritual needs of the entire Union Army and thereby bring about such a wave of religious fervor that the morals of the entire nation would be reformed and the souls of the unregenerate saved. This daunting task would require the concerted and organized efforts of a great number of people both on the home front and the battlefront. To fulfill their mission, the Executive Committee devised a network of roles to maximize the reach of the Commission's efforts and to ensure no soul was left untouched. Foremost among these roles was the "volunteer delegate." Over the course of the Commission's existence, several thousand delegates traveled south, usually for a period of six weeks at a time, to minister to the wants of the Union Army wherever the physical and spiritual need was perceived to be greatest.[1] "Whatever of efficiency the Commission attained," Lemuel Moss, Commission secretary, later wrote, "must be referred mainly to the labors of these volunteer Delegates and the manner in which their labors were directed."[2] As we will see in this chapter, the Commission intended that these delegates would subscribe to and further the evangelical ideology of the USCC by conforming to an ideal of Christian manliness that combined physical vigor and energy with moral uprightness and compassion. The duties and traits expected of delegates, and their precarious status as noncombatant civilians in battle spaces, illustrate that Northern ideas about manliness and labor were multiple and malleable in the middle decades of the nineteenth century and were complicated by the circumstances of war.

The temporary and voluntary nature of delegate labor—delegates claimed reasonable travel and living expenses but did not draw a wage—set the system apart from the rival Sanitary Commission's workforce of paid, permanent agents.[3] Reflecting the increasing move toward the bureaucratization and professionalization of philanthropy in the mid-nineteenth century, the Sanitary Commission believed that voluntarism led inevitably and deleteriously to zealotry, idealism, and incompetence, and considered their paid employees to be more efficient and dispassionate. Conversely, the Christian Commission deemed the volunteer delegate system the best way to harness the enthusiasm and generosity of the Northern public. As a result, the only Christian Commission workers who drew a regular wage were a small number of permanent "field agents," who oversaw operations in assigned geographical areas and maintained continuity in the face of rapid volunteer turnover, and the diet kitchen "lady managers," about whom there will be more in the following chapter.[4] The volunteer delegates, that is to say, constituted the largest part of the Commission's workforce on the battlefront.

Volunteering to become a Christian Commission delegate was relatively straightforward. Applications (consisting of a letter of interest along with two letters of references testifying to the man's integrity and evangelical piety) were vetted either by the head office in Philadelphia or by the local branch to which the prospective delegate applied. Successful applicants were then obliged to present themselves at the head office to receive their badge and commission, along with any supplies they were asked to transport south. The paper commission, which delegates carried with them at all times, bore the delegate's pledge to uphold the values of the USCC and to obey and respect military and medical officers at all times.[5] It also doubled as a pass, entitling the bearer to free or discounted rail travel on lines run by companies friendly to the USCC. Once sworn in, delegates were assigned to a Christian Commission station. These stations were primarily established at supply centers, regimental camps, large hospitals, and other points at which large numbers of soldiers might be expected to gather. Station apparatus varied but often consisted—in deliberate homage to the YMCA rooms of the 1850s—of a storeroom, reading room, quarters for workers, and space that could be used for worship (a tent or otherwise improvised structure). Experienced delegates who had served on multiple occasions or had particular business skills, were appointed to the position of station agent and were responsible for coordinating religious services, allocating the delegates under their charge to the various duties within the station (such as visiting patients, leading prayers, helping the army chaplain, and fetching supplies), and dutifully filling out the weekly and monthly reports.[6]

The names, hometowns, and dates of service of each man, along with his commission number, were recorded in ledgers kept at the Philadelphia office. These ledgers contain the names of over five thousand men who served as delegates, many of them serving on multiple occasions. Once the delegate system took off in earnest, and until the end of the war, there were at any one time no fewer than three hundred delegates in the field. These volunteer delegates were recruited by posters and newspaper advertisements, by individual appeals from existing members of the Commission, and by local congregations anxious to be represented on the battlefront. A circular sent to all Philadelphia clergymen, for example, encouraged them to help recruit volunteers, as "not less than One hundred Delegates are imperatively demanded . . . the testimony [from the front] is that the harvest is ripe as well as great, and the sickle should be vigorously thrust in with the least possible delay."[7]

The delegate recruitment process was designed to prove to the Northern public that the USCC was a useful, moral, respectable organization worthy of support. This drove the Commission leadership to place particular constraints on the sorts of people they recruited. Wary of public opprobrium, the Commission confined delegate service to men. We will examine in chapter 2 how and why the Commission created restricted and heavily prescribed roles for women that were deliberately distinct from delegate service. Not only was the delegate workforce almost entirely male, as far as I have been able to ascertain, it was also entirely white. This was indicative of the organization's ambivalence toward issues of race and racism. The Commission contained in its ranks many veterans of antebellum antislavery organizations and broadly considered the persistence of American slavery a key obstacle to the perfection of the nation in God's image. After the war, Commission elders hailed the Emancipation Proclamation for giving "definitiveness and character to the contest."[8] Edward Parmelee Smith went so far as to call the war "the death grapple with slavery and rebellion."[9]

But these unequivocal pronouncements were rare—and usually retrospective. The Commission did not systematically seek to attack the peculiar institution, nor to prioritize aiding freed people or Black soldiers. This is not to say that Commission workers were indifferent to the challenges of navigating emancipation. Delegates devoted considerable energy to education schemes for Black troops, and the USCC struck up partnerships with the American Bible Society to distribute religious texts and workbooks to freed people.[10] Notwithstanding the residue of paternalism that suffused accounts of interactions between USCC delegates and freed people, delegates seem not to have discriminated in offering their aid and comfort to African American soldiers and refugees who fell under their purview.[11] Some effusively praised Black troops as "pious, zealous, and devotional people," and expressed admiration for "the bravery with which they threw themselves into the heart of the battle in every engagement."[12] Commission personnel also frequently identified the education and support of formerly enslaved people as the most pressing priority as the war drew to a close. "It is to the great work of improving their condition physically, socially, morally, and intellectually, that the energies of the country should now be, in a great measure, directed," George Stuart wrote in October 1865: "This is a duty which we owe to them—a debt which it is obligatory for us to pay. . . . They stand before us to-day with the chains of slavery broken. They demand as a right, in the name of justice and humanity, that we do something to destroy the effects of their long and bitter years of oppression and bondage fastened upon them by unholy legislation. We shall be recreant in our duty to God and our country if this appeal is despised."[13] Yet while Richard Levine's offhand comment that the USCC was "unconcerned with slavery" might not carry water, it is nonetheless clear that a general animus toward slavery, overall admiration (often inflected with a tone of surprise) for the comportment and competence of the USCT, and a vaguely expressed concern for the spiritual and material futures of freed people were not enough to overcome worries that commissioning Black delegates, or prioritizing work undertaken with and for formerly enslaved people, would damage the public appeal of the Christian Commission for white donors across the North.[14]

With public respectability and appeal of paramount concern, then, the white men who were sent to the army under the USCC's banner had to demonstrate to the government and to the army officials with whom they interacted daily that the work of the USCC was necessary and valuable to the Union cause. In some cases, the Executive Committee was able to secure letters of commendation and praise, good wishes for a prosperous and blessed endeavor, and, most importantly, permission from various dignitaries, including the president, the secretary of the navy, the surgeon general, and even the postmaster general.[15] Ulysses S. Grant also lent his practical support, issuing orders to ensure "permission will at all times be granted by the proper military authorities to such delegates to pass to all parts within the lines, without hindrance or molestation."[16] These endorsements were widely published in official reports, commemorative volumes, and in religious newspapers friendly to the Commission. Other high-ranking officials were less enthusiastic, however; some were apt to look upon the USCC as overzealous busybodies likely to get in the way rather than contribute tangibly to the war effort. General Sherman's curt reply to a request that two delegates join his army in Chattanooga was not unusual. "Certainly not," Sherman responded by letter. "There is more need of gunpowder and oats than any moral or religious instruction."[17]

Sherman's unequivocal rejection was representative of a wider public suspicion surrounding the motivations and competence of noncombatants on the battlefront. Widespread negativity toward the position of army chaplain was a case in point. This role was ambiguous, precarious, and often maligned. Reflecting the queasiness of the federal government surrounding the religious welfare of its troops, thorny questions concerning the status of chaplains as officers, their place in the army chain of command, and their entitlement to military pensions were not formally settled until April 1864.[18] There were only thirty regular army chaplains in the Union Army at the outbreak of the Civil War, and although the Civil War precipitated a rapid expansion of the army chaplaincy—over two thousand men were appointed to the role by 1865—the system could not cater for the sheer volume of troops fighting for the Union.[19] There was a chronic shortage of applicants throughout the war, and many regiments were left without a chaplain for the duration of the conflict.[20] Even where army chaplains were appointed, their presence was not always welcome, and the office attracted frequent ire and derision. Worries abounded that chaplains were being overpaid, and that applicants to the chaplaincy were nothing more than cynical mercenaries.[21] The shortage of applicants and the haphazard approach to their appointment meant men of varying degrees of piety, moral strength, and ability made it onto the roster. Some were discredited for stealing, desertion, or drunkenness, while others were deficient in temperament or ability, preaching dull sermons or suffering from exhaustion, which impeded their work.[22]

In reality, Christian Commission delegates often worked well with chaplains, sharing resources, setting up interdenominational prayer meetings and Bible study groups, and striking up friendships with their religious coworkers. Benjamin Waddle, for instance, praised the chaplains he encountered at Warrenton Junction as "worthy and faithful men," while G. H. Hall called his colleagues "a noble band of laborers and Christian gentlemen" remarkable for their "faithfulness and efficiency."[23] But while actual instances of hostility were few and far between, and for the most part delegates and chaplains muddled along together cordially and to mutual benefit, USCC leaders remained concerned that the negative reputation of the chaplaincy as a whole would rub off on the delegate system, and were keen to distinguish firmly between chaplains and delegates. "[The chaplain's] position is at best embarrassing and is rarely filled with comfort and satisfaction to all concerned," one delegate concluded.[24] Undeniably, like the army chaplaincy, the Commission attracted volunteers of wildly varying quality. The sheer number of delegates in the field, and the attendant difficulty of overseeing and directing their actions, despite the Commission's extensive system of paperwork, meant it was impossible to control every aspect of the delegates' lives and behavior or to fully predict their suitability for the work. As one public defense of the Commission put it, "in the large number of agents necessarily sent out by the Commission almost inevitably some will prove inefficient, some will fail in tact or good judgement, and some will even betray the cause."[25]

Sure enough, the Commission was frequently forced to counter instances of delegate incompetence and disobedience. Some delegates merely tended to daydream or forget tasks or took a lax approach to paperwork. W. L. Tisdale at Fortress Monroe despaired of the "negligent" delegates who consistently failed to invoice goods orders correctly, while in the Shenandoah Valley, J. R. Miller dismissed three delegates from Michigan "on account of the fact that they were rather difficult to manage and keep in appropriate places."[26] The unethical behavior of some delegates, however, had greater potential to damage the reputation and public standing of the Commission.[27] There were several instances of petty pilfering and of unscrupulous delegates selling donated USCC supplies for a profit. Hearing alarming reports of delegates running small private businesses fencing supplies, Stuart immediately and forcefully decreed that "the Christian Commission never sells any hospital stores of any kind under any circumstances to soldiers. If any agent has done so . . . we shall dismiss him immediately."[28] Two men went so far as to pose as USCC fundraisers, touring various neighborhoods and defrauding unsuspecting civilians by asking for cash donations.[29]

The Commission's concern about public reputation was reflected in its insistence that delegates cooperate productively with other bodies and authorities on the battlefront. Anxious to preserve the trust of the government and military authorities, the Executive Committee instructed all delegates to cooperate with and yield to the authority of all government representatives, be they officers, surgeons, or army chaplains. The paper commission with which each delegate was issued upon his departure to the front contained a pledge to this effect: "He is strictly enjoined, if with our forces when a battle is approaching, passing, or passed, to abstain from reporting anything on the subject not authorized by the commanding officer, and in general strictly to observe all Army and Navy regulations, and abstain from casting reflections upon the authorities, military, medical, and clerical."[30] Instructions issued to delegates embarking on service were laden with advice on cooperating with and deferring to army officers, surgeons, and other government personnel. "It is always desirable to see first the commanding officer of the regiment, brigade, division, or corps, in which [the work] is to be done, and explain it to him," one passage read, "and also see and explain to such other officers as may be convenient and expedient." The same set of instructions urged delegates to commend themselves to military personnel through their "gentlemanly Christian courtesy," in order to maintain good working relationships.[31] This deference to military hierarchy could reap rewards: officers frequently welcomed and supported USCC delegates in their work. George Downey recalled with pleasure the "kindness of Capt. Newton in showing and explaining" the heavy artillery held at Fort Totten where he was distributing reading materials.[32] Not all relations between delegates and officers were so cordial, however. With the delineation of the delegate's place and status at the bottom of the army hierarchy made abundantly clear and fearing that insubordination and aggravation might lead to vital privileges being revoked across the armies, the Executive Committee dealt harshly with any delegates threatening to defy these rules. J. E. Hall, for instance, was dismissed from the Commission's service because of his "forgetfulness of relations to the authorities."[33]

Nonetheless, the public ambivalence toward chaplains and other civilian noncombatants placed pressure upon the Christian Commission to prove the indispensability and worthiness of the delegates. The leaders of the Commission expended significant amounts of energy defining their ideal delegate and his contribution to the Union war effort. These ideal delegates were, it was claimed, akin to Christ's disciples: "men full of faith and the Holy Ghost, men so loving the world as to be willing to leave their homes and go without fee or reward to bear the glad tidings of a Saviour to the lost."[34] Published pamphlets and information booklets listed desirable characteristics and attitudes, outlining a narrow and explicitly, consciously gendered ideal of moral, spiritual, and physical strength intended to successfully execute the USCC's mission and uphold its reputation and appeal. "Four things are indispensable in all," one circular read. "Piety and patriotism, good common sense and energy."[35] In short, the USCC set out in these publications their blueprint for how to be a good Christian man in the United States in the midst of war. The language they used to articulate these expectations demonstrated the mutability of ideas about manhood and manliness during the Civil War.[36] A body of scholarship on the construction and evolution of masculinity, most closely associated with the work of Anthony Rotundo, has often identified a shift from a version of Northern manhood that, in the earlier decades of the nineteenth century, expected and rewarded self-control and selflessness, toward a more aggressive, virile model of masculine behavior by the turn of the twentieth century, one epitomized by the emergence of athletic competition and organized sports, including the YMCA's increasing preoccupation with physical activities.[37] While some of these impulses were channeled in secular directions and were even hostile to religion, by contrast the so-called "muscular Christianity" movement, which reached its height in the last decade of the nineteenth century, considered a combination of athleticism and religion the natural antidote to the perceived fragmentation and feminization of American society, and placed a premium on action, competition, and physical prowess as markers of mental strength and moral discipline.[38] Whether the evolution of American models of masculinity was as smooth or universal as this narrative suggests is another matter, however. Rather, throughout the century, a range of what Amy Greenberg calls "practices of manhood" jostled for attention and primacy, a consensus rarely, if ever, winning out.[39]

For the Christian Commission, the question was not simply how to be a man but how to be a *Christian* man. In his 1985 book *The Sinews of the Spirit,* Norman Vance explored how English novelists Charles Kingsley and Thomas Hughes created Victorian heroes whose lives fused physical prowess and manly adventure with self-discipline and, ultimately, a willingness to submit to God's will.[40] He called this (sometimes uneasy) combination "Christian manliness." This remains a useful concept for understanding the expectations the Christian Commission placed upon its male volunteers. In a succinct appraisal of the requisite criteria for delegate duty, G. R. Bent, a field agent with the Army of the Potomac, wrote to George Stuart, Commission president, that "we need men of judgement (who understand men), we want men of enterprise, strong men, physically, and men of good common sense, men full of faith and of the Holy Ghost."[41] Bent's assessment emphasizes that the crux of true manhood—without which all the physical strength and business acumen in the world was useless—was the moral incorruptibility and evangelizing vigor possible only through belief and trust in God.

Unsurprisingly, therefore, the most important criterion upon which the USCC insisted was the Christian identity of the delegates. The Christian Commission stipulated that delegates belong to a recognized evangelical denomination and that they be professing members of a specific congregation. Applicants who failed to supply two references, at least one of which came from a minister confirming church membership and Christian character, were rejected outright.[42] As we will explore in greater detail in subsequent chapters, the evangelical denominations, despite their practical and doctrinal differences, were united by their emphasis on a crisis-like conversion experience, and by their commitment to converting the world.[43] The insistence on evangelical membership, therefore, emphasizes how the USCC remained devoted to its founding mission; no matter how involved with physical welfare (as demonstrated by its widespread distribution of food, medicine, and clothing) it became as the war progressed, its main focus as conceived by the Executive Committee remained the conversion of souls to Christ. Although the Commission required proof of evangelical church membership, it remained resolutely interdenominational in character, welcoming delegates from across the ecclesiastical spectrum. "The Commission is anti-sectarian," one pamphlet read. "Episcopalians, Methodists, Baptists, Presbyterians, Congregationalists,

Lutherans, German Reformed, etc. all meet here, and forgetting everything that has divided them at home, join hearts and hands in the great work of doing good and glorifying God."[44] Interdenominationality was a prominent feature of many of the reform movements that had flourished in the antebellum period, fostering coordinated actions in an attempt to spread religious and moral ideas as far as possible.[45] Amid bloody sectional strife (which had, of course, torn apart evangelical denominations in the years before war broke out), Commission leaders were similarly anxious to emphasize points of commonality rather than divergence.[46] "Often in a company of Delegates there were as many Christian denominations represented as there were men," one worker recalled, "yet they came together without knowing or caring to know their several distinctive names. They were unanimous in their prayers, their aims, their labors; and that was sufficient for the time being—ecclesiastical relations, by no means unimportant in themselves, were unimportant there."[47]

These noble sentiments notwithstanding, interdenominationality was, on occasion, difficult to maintain. Some delegates found it difficult to suspend or forget the confessional identity that had first qualified them for delegate service. This was particularly problematic when it came to Holy Communion and baptism, rituals that generated considerable conflict over their theological meaning and the correct method of observance. Despite guidance to the contrary, in March 1864, Henry Safford baptized four soldiers in a stream near his station, while K. Atkinson conducted several mass baptisms by total immersion and also sprinkled others with water to renew their infant baptism.[48] Baptism was not the only contentious rite performed by Atkinson: he also reported that on one evening at Camp Convalescent, "a crowded house rec'd the Sac[rament] Of the Lord's Supper."[49] These denominationally specific rites threatened to compromise the impartiality and broad appeal of the USCC, and Commission leaders were anxious to distance themselves from these actions and to reinforce the ecumenical image of the organization, not least to avoid alienating its donor base, which was as denominationally diverse as its workforce. When a delegate named A. K. Potter complained about delegates administering Communion, Lemuel Moss apologized on behalf of the disobedient delegates, stressing "all questions of ecclesiastical organization + ordinances + discipline are foreign from [the Commission's] province + work."[50] Likewise, in response to George Nair's request for permission to baptize soldiers, William Boardman replied, "the Commission is not an ecclesiastical body but a spiritual one. We have no power to form churches, receive members to the church, baptize or perform or authorize any ecclesiastical act or function."[51] J. J. Abbott, Nair's field agent, also rebuked the delegate and halted the proposed baptisms, an action that Boardman ap-

CHRISTIAN MANLINESS AND THE VOLUNTEER DELEGATE SYSTEM   27

plauded. "Being an agency of all denominations," Boardman wrote to Abbott, "[the Commission] is bound to prevent anything being done by its delegates conflicting with the public sentiment."[52]

"HARD WORK"

Verifying the prospective delegate's credentials as an evangelical Christian was merely a starting point, however. Commission leaders held strong views on the personal attributes expected of would-be delegates. Foremost among the desirable attributes were youth and energy. The USCC insisted that the men they engaged as delegates be physically fit and in good health. This was, in part, a practical consideration: due to the arduous nature of the work undertaken by USCC delegates, the Executive Committee attempted to ensure that those commissioned were physically capable of performing their duties. From day to day, men could be expected to carry heavy boxes of supplies, move wounded soldiers, stay awake through the night with the dying, fill out vast amounts of paperwork in their free time, and travel around their district to the stations that needed them. Far from trying to disguise this fact, the Commission took pride in it. The First Annual Report contained a section plainly called "Hard Work," which explained: "men do not volunteer as delegates of the Commission because the work is easy, and a pleasant recreation. Never was there a service requiring or exciting more self-denying and ceaseless toil."[53] Sure enough, delegate reports reveal the detrimental effects Christian Commission work could have on the health of even the previously fit and strong. "After I had been in the field for nearly four weeks I was taken sick and . . . was advised by the surgeon to return home as soon as possible," wrote J. P. Kennedy, whose service with the Second Army Corps was curtailed by illness.[54] James Patton, too, was forced to leave the service early, a shortage of workers at City Point having led him and several colleagues to overwork themselves.[55] Even when sickness did not bring a delegate's service to an end entirely, it could cause severe disruption to the work. A. W. Knowlton, stationed at Alexandria, deeply regretted that, due to poor health, he had not been able to do as much as he wished—"But God be praised that I have been able to do any thing," he added at the end of one weekly report.[56] On rare occasion, the rigors of delegate service proved fatal; six delegates died during the war, five of them from apparent fatigue and overwork, and one, J. W. Leighton, was killed by enemy fire at Chattanooga.[57] Anxious to avoid increasing the army's workload by diverting medical care to sick or feeble delegates unable to perform their duties, the Executive Committee decreed, "we have to receive from each applicant credentials as to ... bodily strength to endure fatigue, general fitness for the work of exhortation and teaching."[58] For instance, the Committee turned down a Mr. Hill in April 1864, convinced that although he was intellectually and spiritually qualified, he was not physically strong enough.[59]

Although some found the physical challenges posed by the work overwhelming, others found the opposite to be true. Field Agent J. R. Miller found the work exhausting but ultimately galvanizing: "All the Delegates are in the best of spirits, and *all are hard workers.* At night all are weary, and sleep is welcome, but morning finds all refreshed, and ready and anxious to begin a new day's labors."[60] The invigorating impact of battlefront ministry on both physical and spiritual well-being was not lost on the Executive Committee, who used this to entice ministers to take a leave of absence from their home congregations and join the Commission: "the change is often very beneficial to the health of the Delegate—it ... quickens his zeal for the salvation of men."[61] Notably, they were confident these benefits could be experienced by all, regardless of age. While recruitment propaganda disseminated by the Commission emphasized the importance of physical strength and bodily health to successful delegate service, there were no consistent stipulations made as to age, and old age did not always prove an impediment. Indeed, in some cases, delegate service gave older men a new lease on life. One journalist who dined with several old USCC delegates in Culpepper praised his companions as "jolly, cheery, enthusiastic, delighted with their work, and triumphing with an easy laugh over what are real hardships to men past middle age."[62]

Christian Commission leaders were ambivalent about the age of the ideal delegate. After all, what Paul Ringel calls "cultural presumptions about youth" suggested that, while younger men might be stronger and fitter, youth also presented considerable challenges.[63] A flourishing industry of advice literature and the emergence of organizations like the Young Men's Christian Associations in the decades before the war advanced the premise that the minds and souls of young men—in particular, those navigating the perilous seas between childhood and full maturity—were acutely malleable and receptive to outside influences, both good and bad.[64] The Christian Commission, building on this tradition, harbored its own anxieties about the susceptibility of young soldiers to vice and temptation. Yet despite these misgivings, their calls for volunteers, by emphasizing values of athleticism and strength, tacitly suggested that younger men, in theory, made better delegates.

The question of whether youth was a hindrance or a help was particularly pertinent because a significant number of Christian Commission delegates were college students. Northern institutions of higher education faced considerable

CHRISTIAN MANLINESS AND THE VOLUNTEER DELEGATE SYSTEM   29

upheaval during the Civil War.[65] College students were statistically more likely to enlist than the overall white male population. Enrollments at many institutions plummeted as students suspended their studies to join up.[66] Still accessible only to a tiny elite (roughly 2 percent of the college-age white male population), a college education was designed not only to channel men into respectable professions but also to instill in them standards of gentlemanly behavior that fit them for political and civic leadership. Colleges (in theory) trained young men out of the worst traits associated with youth, replacing recklessness and frivolity with sobriety and industry. The Civil War naturally presented students with the opportunity to test their skills in the fire of battle. Yet, while college students joined the armies in disproportionate numbers, many likewise chose not to enlist or found alternative ways to offer their service to the Union.[67] This included, in numerous cases, volunteering for the US Christian Commission.

Among the delegate rolls were at least 118 students of colleges and theological seminaries. These student delegates hailed both from well-established institutions like Yale and from smaller, newer colleges, such as Olivet College, Michigan. Andover Theological Seminary, a Massachusetts institution with a history of abolitionism and benevolent reform that dated back almost as far as its foundation in 1807, was particularly well represented, with thirty-six students joining the USCC over the course of the war.[68] Institutions like Andover were filled with young men anxious to demonstrate both their piety and patriotism by volunteering for the Christian Commission. Over the course of the war, the Commission found these students' youth and energy to be both a blessing and a curse. In many cases, student delegates acquitted themselves well and were roundly praised in official USCC publications for their commitment, enthusiasm, and resourcefulness. Near Cave City, Kentucky, in March 1865, G. W. R. Scott, an Andover student, having run out of bandages, tore up his own shirt to dress patients' wounds.[69] John Calhoun Chamberlain (brother of Joshua), who suspended his studies at Bangor Theological Seminary to join the USCC, was lifted up as an example of tireless service when he walked ten miles at night, crossing a dangerous and swollen stream, to fetch supplies for a hospital outside Gettysburg.[70]

Most significant of these exemplary student delegates was James Russell Miller, a Presbyterian from Pennsylvania who began his ministerial training at Allegheny Theological Seminary in 1862. As the war intensified, Miller—who, in his later career, would become both editorial superintendent of the Presbyterian Board of Publications and a popular Christian author—first volunteered as an ordinary six-week delegate for the Christian Commission in March 1863, at the age of twenty-three. He acquitted his work so well that his colleagues convinced him to accept a paid position as a field agent, a post he took up just in time to

James Russell Miller, n.d. (Presbyterian Historical Society, Philadelphia, Pennsylvania; photographer unknown)

take charge of operations at Gettysburg.[71] This protracted service threatened Miller's studies at Allegheny. William Boardman, USCC secretary, wrote to the seminary's board of directors to impress upon them Miller's importance to the war effort and justify the prolonged suspension of his studies.[72] "Under ordinary circumstances we would not encourage candidates for the ministry to turn aside for a day," Boardman wrote. "In his case however the case is different. The army is a missionary field white for the harvest. The world presents no other like it. Mr Miller has experience[,] talent and adaptation to aid and direct the labors as a Field Agent which render his services of special value to the work."[73] Miller was granted permission to continue his work with the Christian Commission, remaining with the USCC until July 1865. In the best of cases, therefore, by training students "to act with knowledge [and] confront challenges," delegate service performed a similar didactic function to a college education.[74] Those held up as exemplary embodied the ideal of Christian manliness prized by the Christian Commission: active, intelligent, compassionate, and at their very best, capable of outstanding logistical and moral leadership.

This was not always the case, however. Youth could be a drawback, too. It was not only lofty idealism that accounted for the rush of applications from students. Some young men were motivated to apply by a yearning for (relatively danger-free) adventure, and by the short period of service. This was a source of constant frustration for the USCC, especially for the field agents who had to deal with these new recruits. John Cole, field agent for the Army of the Potomac, found the student delegates under his supervision inexperienced and frivolous. Ironically, given that he himself was only twenty-four, Cole wrote several times to the Executive Committee on the subject, dismissing them as "college boys," and complaining that they were prone to absconding before their agreed period of service had expired.[75] Delegate A. D. Morton also encountered students who took a slapdash approach to their work, exhorting the Executive Committee to remind young volunteers that they were "more than mere colporteurs."[76] Frustrating, too, was the rush of applications that accompanied the start of the summer vacation period, overwhelming the workforce (while leaving the USCC understaffed at other times of the year); as George Stuart lamented to one disappointed applicant, "the college vacations have thrown so many students into the ranks of our delegates that we are compelled to limit the number of that class accepted."[77] At best, therefore, student delegates were dedicated, able young men who readily pledged themselves to the cause, but at worst, they were reckless tourists anxious for a sanitized adventure, who lent legitimacy to the suspicion that young men were incapable of self-discipline and restraint. The mixed experiences and abilities of college students suggest that although youth and physical fitness were desirable attributes for Christian Commission delegates, they were by no means guarantees of aptitude for the work. Steven Woodworth argues that the role of army chaplain "required the stamina, flexibility, and robust health of a young man, but also the wisdom and maturity of an older one": the same might easily be said of the combined physical and emotional demands placed upon delegates.[78]

SOLDIERS FOR CHRIST

Beyond the obvious practical benefits, asserting the physicality of the USCC delegate had a symbolic significance. Naturally, ensuring that delegates were capable of "Hard Work" was important to maintaining the efficiency of the Commission, but the figure of the young, strong, healthy delegate, laboring manually and gladly for the Lord, was also central to the evangelical ideology of the Christian Commission.[79] Over the course of the nineteenth century, religious leaders feared that a perception of the clergy as effeminate and unfit for the macho competition of the marketplace (a perception compounded by the prominent role of laywomen in religious life) was undermining the reputation of the ministry in American society, and diminishing the power of the churches.[80] In order to win the respect and attention of the men, therefore, USCC delegates also had to promote a physical, active masculinity that would cause the targets of their evangelization to perceive them as equal in manliness to those who fought in combat. The physical attributes of the ideal delegate, and the active labor expected of him, aimed to challenge popular perceptions of the ministry as sedentary and gentle—that is, as effeminate—and promoted a new model of clerical masculinity, one reconcilable with the aggression and individualism of the nineteenth-century public sphere.[81] According to Anthony Rotundo, this was a tactic also employed by antebellum ministers anxious to rid their profession of the taint of effeminacy. He argues that the revivals and reform movements of the period enabled ministers to "apply assertiveness, energy, even masculine hostility to the cause of Christian goodness," allowing the clergyman to express the action and aggression of the worldly marketplace "while pursuing the sacred goals of love and goodness that his culture linked to women."[82]

Christian Commission publications often used metaphors that cast delegates in active roles to valorize and legitimize the work. By encouraging volunteers with "fields white for the harvest" and exhortations to "thrust in the sickle without delay" (Revelation 14:19), the USCC cast its delegates as manual laborers using their hands and physical strength to reap converts for Christ. Even more telling was the use of deliberately militaristic language and imagery that cast the delegates not as farmers but as soldiers armed for a holy crusade. "They are Christian scouts," one pamphlet read, equating the work of delegates to reconnaissance and intelligence gathering, "always alert on the look-out in the advance, first at every place of suffering, keen to find every case of want."[83] An account of the USCC's work in Virginia following the Battle of Fredericksburg was peppered with military terminology:

> a "section" of delegates, under a captain, attended by a four-horse team and wagon loaded with stores, marched with each army corps, five in all, with one team extra as a reserve . . . a detachment of delegates came with the wounded to Fredericksburg, and served them there, while the teams went on to Belle Plain for supplies. A corps of minute men with ample supplies meanwhile came to Belle Plain, and were then in advance of all other relief to meet the wounded coming on from Fredericksburg.[84]

This passage drew repeated parallels between the soldiers and the delegates, blurring the distinctions between these positions. Military rhetoric also suffused the hymns collected in the hymnbooks distributed by the USCC; one book was prefaced by an index of subjects that included "Battle," "Christian warfare," and "Victory."[85] Hymn singing was an integral part of USCC prayer meetings, and leading the singing naturally fell to the delegate; thus, when soldiers and delegates participated in the shared act of singing lyrics like "soldiers of Christ, arise, / and put your armor on," or "sure I must fight, if I would reign / increase my courage, Lord," they conflated not only the acts of fighting for the Union and fighting for Christ, but also the roles of the soldier and the delegate.[86] The instructions included with each delegate's diary further equated these roles and the determination and bravery required of both: "A heroism not inferior to that which charges to the cannon's mouth to capture the battery, is required on the part of those who would conquer under the banner of the cross, and take captives for Jesus."[87]

The work of the Christian Commission delegate, then, was held up as conforming to the scriptural idea of the Christian soldier. This paradigm is most evident in the Pauline epistles. Paul commands the Ephesians to put on the "breastplate of righteousness," the "shield of faith," and the "helmet of salvation," and wield the "sword of the Spirit." "Put on the whole armor of God," Paul exhorts, "that ye may be able to stand against the wiles of the devil. For we wrestle not against flesh and blood, but against principalities, against powers, against the rulers of the darkness of this world, against spiritual wickedness in high places" (Ephesians 6:10–18). So, by commissioning the strong and healthy to perform active, strenuous tasks and employing military-religious language in doing so, the USCC cast its delegates as Christian soldiers in this biblical mold, clad in the "armor of God," and engaged in a cosmic war that reimagined and transcended the earthly conflict surrounding them.

The physical and moral attributes required of delegates, and the way these attributes fed each other, is abundantly evident in a sermon that was delivered by George Bringhurst. Bringhurst, an Episcopal minister in his mid-thirties from Moyamensing, Philadelphia, was the first delegate to be issued a commission, and he returned to the front several times throughout the war to preach and minister to Union troops.[88] His reliability as a worker and dedication to the cause of the Christian Commission meant he was invaluable as a home front ambassador for the organization. In order to maintain a steady flow of public donations to the Christian Commission's coffers and to ensure the military and political authorities remained favorable to the Commission's presence on the battlefront, delegates were encouraged to make speeches and even embark on lecture tours in their local areas, emphasizing the importance and vitality of the USCC. "Will you not now come up to the help of the Lord, and stir up all whom you know, to give liberally?" George Stuart asked in a direct appeal to returning delegates as the war drew to a close. "Will you see that meetings are held in every congregation and school district in your neighbourhood, and collections taken? . . . you can tell your story!"[89] Bringhurst was one of the delegates tasked with promoting the work of the Christian Commission; he transcribed the sermon he preached to his home congregation at All Saints Episcopal Church in Moyamensing upon his return from the front and sent it to the head office in Philadelphia for publication. Bringhurst took as his text Acts 4:20 ("we cannot but speak the things which we have seen and heard"), and set about captivating his audience with an exciting and lurid account of his adventures. His account of his service illustrates well how Christian manliness, as embodied by the USCC delegate, not only required decisive and aggressive action, athleticism, and strength but also obliged the delegate to demonstrate restraint, self-control, tenderness, and compassion.[90]

Bringhurst framed his service and the role of the Christian Commission delegate more generally as vital to the Union cause and as equivalent to military service. While paying homage to the young men who "bared their bosoms to the enemy's rage, to save our happy firesides and homes," Bringhurst at the same time emphasized that his own form of service was active, valorous, and manly. "We had no right to put down that sword," he claimed, explaining that his sense of duty drove him to volunteer for the "path" laid down before him by God. "There I want to walk until the monster is crushed," he told his audience, exhorting them to join him in supporting the Christian Commission and, by extension, the godly cause of the Union. He condemned the "faint hearts" and "timorous souls" who might give up in the face of adversity and suffering, suggesting that his own heart and soul were quite the opposite. Bringhurst cast himself and his fellow delegates as crusading Christian soldiers following God's call and contributing actively to the suppression of the rebellion and the restoration of the redeemer nation.

Throughout the sermon, Bringhurst's language, channeling the extemporized passion of the most spellbinding itinerant preachers of the Second Great Awakening, brought home the urgency and immediacy of the Christian Commission's work.[91] His use of the present tense sought to convey his audience to the very scene of battle, building an atmosphere of dread and anguish by his vivid portrayal of the adverse conditions in which he labored. Describing a stormy, desperate night at Belle Plain, he said, "Where there is so much distress, I scarcely know what to do! But this is no time to be idle— . . . that man must have some water; there is a man who has lost a leg, has been riding since early morning in the rain, with nothing to eat; I have some biscuit in my haversack, he must have them!" As the sermon progressed, Bringhurst dispensed with gram-

CHRISTIAN MANLINESS AND THE VOLUNTEER DELEGATE SYSTEM 35

mar altogether, descending into a staccato of fragmentary sentences—"start with a boat load of wounded soldiers for Washington. Wash, dress them, give them a good substantial meal. Write a number of letters. Reach Washington at 1 o'clock"—that mirrored the frenetic pace and variety of tasks that characterized a typical day in delegate service.

Bringhurst outlined at length the large and frequently unpredictable range of duties that his service required of him. According to his account, in addition to leading prayer meetings and hymn singing, preaching sermons, writing letters for the wounded and dying, distributing religious literature and material comforts such as food and clothing, and performing burial services, Christian Commission delegates might also be called upon to administer basic medical care, transport supplies, and direct the labors of other volunteers. Throughout, the resourcefulness, physical strength, and athleticism required of USCC volunteers was apparent. Bringhurst frequently detailed working late into the night, in all weathers, sleeping in makeshift and highly uncomfortable shelters, grabbing a bite to eat wherever he could, before waking early to walk vast distances— sometimes along stretches of road renowned for guerrilla attacks—to fetch supplies or reach stricken men. Bringhurst used his own body as a shield and a crutch, holding a gum blanket over one man to protect him from driving rain and propping up another as he helped him limp to a hospital ship. On one occasion, he and his fellow delegates put their hands to use tearing down some old buildings and fashioning crude beds from the lumber so that wounded soldiers would not have to lie on the bare ground.

Yet, importantly, Bringhurst's efforts were not solely manual. His sermon stressed the emotional perspicacity required of him and his fellow delegates. In his descriptions of bedside conversations with dying men, he emphasized the tenderness with which he touched and spoke to the men, recalling how one man "takes my hand and holds it upon his breast" and thanked God for the opportunity to "smooth the dying pillow" of countless men. He also reflected upon the impact of the work and the scenes he witnessed on his own emotions. While he expressed gratitude for the "sweet smiles" he received as remuneration for his efforts, the work was emotionally gruelling as well as rewarding, and he recalled to his audience that "the groans of the wounded are hard to bear." Most affecting of all were the burials Bringhurst oversaw—"we wrapped them in their blankets and strewed their forms with flowers," he wrote. "We caught the loving accents meant for loved ones, fond and dear. We bore them to their lowly graves, and shed a sacred tear." As scholars such as Glenn Hendler and Brian Roberts have demonstrated, crying was not inherently coded as unmanly in the mid-nineteenth century. From the reformed drunkard tearfully recounting his intemperate past to Gold Rush miners weeping over shared feelings of homesickness, men's tears could be heroic, passionate displays of emotion that helped to forge homosocial bonds or manifested an internal process of reformation and restoration externally.[92] Similarly, in his sermon Bringhurst presented his tears—the bodily expression of his grief—not as unbridled or effeminate but as a restrained and honorable response that married sentiment and morality and hence fit into the ideal of Christian manliness.[93]

All this suggests that delegate work was not solely about grit and strength. During their service, delegates forged relationships with soldiers that often involved caregiving and emotional support. As one delegate recalled after the war, "their hearts were warm. They had not become accustomed to the sad and necessary scenes of military life, and they were ready to sympathise with all who were in sorrow of body and mind."[94] There was often, in the ways delegates attempted to offer moral guidance or exercise control over soldiers' behavior, a parental undertone to these relationships, but this was neither straightforwardly paternal *nor* maternal. Some scholars have identified a relatively clear demarcation between roles ascribed to mothers and fathers in the antebellum North, with fathers disciplining and preparing their sons for the rigors and competition of the marketplace and mothers safeguarding Christian morality and raising virtuous, sober children.[95] Reid Mitchell imports this model to the Civil War army camp, suggesting that army officers frequently saw themselves as fathers, combining love for their men with firm, fair discipline, while female nurses and other female workers neatly occupied the role of surrogate mother.[96] As the figure of the male USCC delegate suggests, however, the reality of these interactions was less clear-cut. While his work might require him to employ skills coded as masculine by nineteenth-century society, such as public speaking, administrative and financial acumen, physical strength, and the ability to act as an authority figure, he might equally and even simultaneously adopt the roles of nurse, teacher, moral adviser, and confidant.

At several points in his sermon, Bringhurst embraced tasks that required emotional sensibility and tenderness, incorporating these elements into his framing of himself as a manly Christian soldier, apparently without consternation or fear of emasculation. Dipping into his haversack for supplies to feed a hungry young soldier, he reminded his audience of "the widow's meat and oil," drawing parallels between himself and the widow of Zarephath, whose service for the prophet Elijah in the face of her own deprivation and hardship was rewarded by God (1 Kings 17:8–16). The day before building bunks with his own hands, he busied himself making bouquets of wildflowers to cheer the bedsides of wounded soldiers. Bringhurst emphasized that his role called upon delegates to humble themselves in the face not only of God's will but also of the sacrifices made by countless young men. In a passage evocative of Christ washing the feet of his disciples (John 13:1–17), Bringhurst recalled tying the shoelaces of a soldier who had lost an arm: "I stooped to grant his request, and as I kneeled and tied those leathern strings, I deemed my position more honourable than the grandest and most magnificent this world could give." This submission was cast not as shameful or unmanly, but as an act of righteous Christian compassion. In fact, throughout the text, Bringhurst emphasized the morality of self-sacrifice and humility: "I am drenched," he wrote in one of several passages reflecting on the bodily discomfort he suffered as a delegate, "but these boys must be helped." This reflected another variation of mid-century manliness—while submitting (for instance, to a political rival or to a nagging wife) was seen by many as emasculating, for others, "self-denial and cosmic resignation were cardinal virtues" indicating qualities of forbearance and force of will.[97] God's role in Bringhurst's ability to adequately meet the physical and emotional challenges of delegate service was never in doubt: in the face of battle, Bringhurst claimed he "experienced no fear whatever." Puzzled by this, he later realized that the battle had taken place on a Sunday morning while his home congregation were at prayer, sustaining him from a distance.

The Christian Commission, as we have seen, recruited men to further the organization's evangelical mission and to conform to the USCC's image of a Christian soldier. They were charged with preserving the reputation of the Christian Commission in the field and on the home front, and with upholding its interdenominational, extragovernmental character. In particular, through their physical strength, vigor, and piety, delegates were intended to embody a spirit of Christian manliness that would inspire soldiers to consider the fates of their souls and would add weight to the evangelical message the delegates preached.

CHAPTER TWO

Female War Work and the Christian Commission

Men were not the only Northerners who volunteered to aid the Christian Commission in its mission. Evangelical women offered their assistance in large numbers and played important roles in the work of the organization. Yet, as with the challenges faced in commissioning delegates who conformed to the USCC's ideal of Christian manliness, employing the talents and energies of women in effective and socially appropriate ways posed difficult questions for the Commission. One commissioner predicted, "Nothing will be left undone, which Christian women can with propriety possibly do, to promote either the bodily welfare or religious benefit of those who fight the battles of our nation."[1] The writer perceived female piety and patriotism to be of great importance to the work of the Christian Commission but was equally keen to stress the limitations of female involvement by placing the caveat of "propriety" on women's actions. The implication was clear: the field of battle—an environment peopled almost exclusively by men perpetrating and enduring violence and suffering—was not considered suitable for the women who professed a desire to offer their services. The boundaries of female "propriety" were challenged by the tumult of war and the social realignments this precipitated, and the Christian Commission struggled to impose its own interpretations of these boundaries onto its prospective workforce.

The Executive Committee crafted two distinct roles for women within the Christian Commission: firstly, as organizers and members of the home front Ladies Christian Commissions (LCCs) and, secondly, as managers of special diet kitchens set up in military hospitals. The LCCs built on the operations of benevolent societies, while the diet kitchens sought to employ the skills of women as domestic managers and caregivers. Therefore, both roles were intended to make use of perceived female skills and virtues to further the Commission's evangelical mission—not by requiring women to proselytize directly to troops or engage in spiritual ministration but by raising funds and delivering care in ways considered acceptably feminine. As with the USCC's delegate recruitment policy, the USCC's policy toward these workers was shaped by concerns for the organization's reputation and the reputation of the women it employed and by prevailing middle-class gender expectations that valorized female virtue and piety. The work undertaken by women on behalf of the Christian Commission conformed to conservative interpretations of femininity by assigning women to domestic tasks (though often carried out in public spaces) that did not overtly compromise their expected roles as mothers, wives, and caregivers. While these roles inadvertently afforded individual women opportunities to accrue business, management, and communication skills, and to forge new networks and modes of female benevolent cooperation, ultimately both the LCCs and the diet kitchens channeled the wartime zeal and patriotism of female volunteers into activities that endorsed and upheld, for the most part, the persistent association of femininity and domesticity, albeit an association played out increasingly in the public sphere.

The position of women within the USCC drew upon a well-established tradition of female religious and charitable activity, a tradition that was at once liberating and limiting. As Mary Ryan, Nancy Cott, and others have demonstrated, involvement in church activities constituted one of the few forms of public participation viewed as appropriate and acceptable for middle-class white Northern women.[2] The Second Great Awakening boosted the numbers of women associated with evangelical churches, with some estimates suggesting new women converts outstripped men by a ratio of as much as two to one between 1790 and 1830.[3] Moreover, the growth of participatory, democratized Christian denominations with their dynamic worship practices and postmillennial theological urgency created new opportunities for women to practice and perform their faith, often in visible, collaborative, and communal ways.[4] As enthusiastic congregants, advocates of revivalism, founders of missionary and reform societies, Sunday School and Bible class teachers, members of maternal associations, subscribers to and writers for religious magazines, and as laywomen visiting the afflicted or raising funds for pious causes, Northern women played important social roles in antebellum church communities.[5] Yet these roles, multiple and flexible though they were, were policed by a pervasive and powerful cultural ideal of white womanhood built around the assumption that women were by nature pious, compassionate, self-sacrificing, and maternal. Convinced of the moral authority wielded by women over their husbands and children, ministers tasked female congregants with inculcating Christian values in their families and with placing pressure on them to seek salvation. Outside the home, too, whether collecting funds to support missionaries, taking charitable donations to needy neighbors, or penning religious poetry, women's religious contributions were framed as acceptable extensions of their domestic roles rather than unprecedented transgressions that would threaten middle-class gender norms.

The outbreak of the Civil War compelled many evangelical women to consider how they might employ their existing experiences of religious and charitable endeavor in service of the Union's righteous cause. Among them, numerous women swiftly and enthusiastically volunteered for delegate service with the Christian Commission. Frequently, in writing to offer their services, they took pains to stress the qualities—whether physical or moral—that made them well suited for the role. Mary Bingham, for instance, expressed her desire to serve as a delegate in a lengthy letter to George Stuart, stressing that she was both "brave" and "able to endure great fatigue."[6] Edward Clark, the pastor of the First Congregational Church in Bridgewater, Massachusetts, wrote to the Executive Committee on behalf of a female congregant, expressing her desire to labor for the USCC, and praising her as "a married lady of pleasing manners, gentle, earnest, and prudent"—that is, a perfect model of evangelical womanhood.[7] It bears noting that at least thirty-six women were issued commissions by the USCC. Most of these were relatives—usually wives—of male delegates.[8] Among them, for example, were Emma Revell Moody, the newlywed wife of prominent Chicago evangelist Dwight L. Moody, and Frances Jacobs, wife of Benjamin F. Jacobs, the secretary of the Chicago USCC. Emma Moody and Frances Jacobs accompanied their husbands as they toured major Christian Commission stations in the South. Charles P. Lyford and his wife Eliza undertook several joint trips to Philadelphia, Harpers Ferry, and Camp Convalescent and were instrumental in establishing the USCC in California in 1864, embarking on an exhausting tour of speeches, sermons, and fairs on the Pacific Coast to publicize the work of the Commission.

The thirty-six women who received official commissions were outliers, however. Most of the women volunteers—no matter their credentials—were rejected for delegate service by Executive Committee personnel because the duties typically associated with the position represented too great a departure from public activities deemed appropriate for evangelical women. As we have seen, the "Christian manliness" expected of delegates included space for expressions of emotion, tenderness, and self-sacrifice. Although in so doing, the role challenged narrow, exclusively macho ideas about masculinity, it did not upend and dispense with gender expectations altogether. Not only were the physical rigors expected of delegates considerable, but they were expected to evangelize energetically and loudly to the soldiers in the hospitals and camps to which they were assigned. To involve women in this project—and especially to require them to preach— would be to violate the conservative norms of the evangelical churches by placing women outside the roles they usually occupied in religious life. While women considerably outnumbered men in most antebellum congregations, and while their voluntarism fueled the social presence of the churches through their roles as charitable visitors, fundraisers, and Sunday School teachers, the pulpit largely remained the arena of men before the Civil War.[9] This is not to say that women preachers were entirely nonexistent. Prominent figures like Phoebe Palmer, Abigail Roberts, and Harriet Livermore gained considerable prestige and influence with their itinerant preaching tours and evangelical gatherings and, according to Elizabeth Elkin Grammar, women preachers were "unusual but not aberrant."[10] Despite this, however, women preachers faced considerable suspicion and condemnation from critics who considered their public evangelization a perverse and unseemly transgression of white, middle-class femininity.[11] What Lucretia Mott called the male "monopoly of the pulpit" was shored up in the antebellum era not only by popular expectations of female demureness but also by interpretations of biblical passages, which supposedly asserted that women should occupy subordinate—and preferably silent—positions in the church.[12]

The Commission's queasiness about the reputational damage that might ensue from requiring women to preach or otherwise evangelize in unfeminine ways was apparent in their repeated firm rejections of would-be female delegates. For instance, a woman named Miss Ball from Little Falls, New York, raised funds for the Christian Commission in her hometown—a role familiar to many evangelical women involved in charity and moral reform before the war—yet when she wrote to George Stuart to volunteer her services as a delegate on the battlefront, he expressed his gratitude for her past efforts but ultimately concluded, "I am sure you will not consider it as depreciating your influence if we are obliged to decline your request."[13] Hattie Jackson was similarly rebuffed. "It would hardly be proper or expedient to commission a lady," Lemuel Moss wrote in response to her offer of assistance.[14] Moss's letter demonstrated the Commission's concern with preserving both the reputations of the women who applied for delegate positions and the reputation of the USCC itself as a respectable institution—concerns that outstripped any fears about the physical dangers that might await women delegates on the battlefront.

The USCC's commitment to a model of Christian womanhood that emphasized piety and respectability was evident in the rhetoric they employed simultaneously to encourage and regulate women's contributions to the Commission.

Praise for women workers who conformed to the Commission's vision was none-too-subtly gendered, with one commissioner, for instance, lauding women's "quick sympathy and ready hands" and their "womanly affection and delicacy."[15] As well as its repeated use in official USCC publications, this rhetoric also suffused high-profile Commission events. At a large public gathering held in the Philadelphia Concert Hall on May 4, 1864, female representatives of 122 Philadelphia evangelical congregations gathered to hear male speakers urge them to contribute their money and labor to the USCC. The meeting promoted an ideology of pious female domesticity, valorizing women's war work but firmly outlining acceptable outlets for women's patriotic impulses. The keynote address at the Philadelphia meeting was delivered by the well-traveled evangelist Edward Norris Kirk, pastor of Mount Vernon Congregational Church in Boston and erstwhile mentor of the revivalist Dwight L. Moody. Kirk's speech encapsulated the USCC's perception of women as frail but virtuous moral guardians who could counteract the corruption of politics and the savagery of war with their soothing and pious influence. Kirk littered his speech with imperatives and biblical examples to illustrate the exact form this moral influence should take, commanding women to be humble and frugal in their lifestyles and self-sacrificing in their attempts to help the Union, "whatever station you occupy, however limited the gift entrusted to you by the Lord." Kirk argued that women, though barred from the active evangelization practiced by male USCC delegates, could play a role in saving America by demonstrating the godliness of the North and by nursing the beleaguered nation. "Humble yourselves in this day of your country's calamity," Kirk commanded. "If the Ninevites could consent to fast, and clothe themselves in sack-cloth at the call of a strange prophet, surely the Christian women of the Republic can consent to express a sympathy with their suffering and imperilled country, by self-denial in dress and food . . . to give outward and appropriate expression to their grief for sins which have so provoked their beloved Redeemer, and called forth from him such expressions of displeasure." Kirk's reference to the sinful city of Ninevah was a pointed one; by fasting and dressing in sackcloth, as commanded by the reluctant prophet Jonah, the Ninevites avoided divine punishment for their former wickedness (Jonah 3:10). America, a Ninevah for the nineteenth century, could also avoid the wrath of God if its citizens repented and rid the nation of the sins of slavery, materialism, and godlessness.

Women were central to this process of repentance as their behavior would influence that of their sons, husbands, and brothers. According to Kirk, the women of the South had whipped the men of the Confederacy into a frenzy of hatred that bubbled over into rebellion. The pious women of the North could, conversely, wield good and moral influence over their menfolk to resolve the

FEMALE WAR WORK AND THE CHRISTIAN COMMISSION 43

conflict in a manner pleasing to God. He entreated women to forgo extravagance and luxury for the greater good and to pray earnestly for the preservation of Northern troops and the restoration of the Union. His instructions to the gathered women on how to pray were indicative of traits associated with idealized middle-class Northern womanhood: "be simple, be earnest, be humble." Kirk further hallowed the work of women by casting female war workers as nurses to an ailing national body. "Love your country," he demanded. "Bear its sorrows on your heart. Regard it as you do a sick child, with a never interrupted sympathy, carrying its pain into your very sleep with you." A woman's patriotic duty, according to this rhetoric, was to conform to idealized standards of maternal nurture and love, subjugating her own needs to that of her male relatives and, by extension, her country.[16] This vision for the ideal of wartime womanhood—patriotic, useful Christians devoted to helping the sons of the Union, but not willing to compromise their virtue, their femininity, or their reputation to do so—shaped the versions of women's war work sanctioned by the USCC. Committed to this vision, the Executive Committee directed women volunteers toward two distinct and specific institutions that sought to uphold in different ways the association of female piety and social respectability: the Ladies Christian Commissions and the special diet kitchens.

THE LADIES CHRISTIAN COMMISSIONS

The Ladies Christian Commissions (LCCs) were not an unusual manifestation of women's war work on the Northern home front.[17] Aid societies established and run by women began proliferating across the North in the immediate aftermath of events at Fort Sumter in April 1861.[18] As Jeanie Attie and Judith Giesberg have explored, involvement in these aid societies was simultaneously a political and patriotic act. Many women who joined in raising funds or making havelocks, uniforms, and sewing kits for departing troops lamented that they were barred from military service because of their gender, and so the intensified production of foodstuffs and medical supplies became a battleground for women, where they could prove their dedication to the Union while at the same time testing the limitations of the private sphere.[19] Nevertheless, this war work, despite its sometimes public nature, took a sufficiently feminized form to preserve women's respectability and virtue in the eyes of men. This was also true of the activities of the Ladies Christian Commissions. An important branch of the USCC's operations, they channeled goods and cash from small communities or individual congregations on the home front to the Philadelphia headquarters and thence to the delegates of the USCC for distribution. They raised money through fairs, lecture series, door-to-door fundraising, subscription fees, and special collections and mobilized women to make and donate clothing, medical supplies, food, and drink. Many made use of existing networks of organization such as sewing circles, church-centered benevolent societies, and family or friendship groups.

Measuring the number, size, and contribution of the LCCs proved difficult even during the life span of the USCC. One report counted 266 separate LCCs by the end of the war, which had donated nearly $200,000 between them to the coffers of the USCC, but Lemuel Moss acknowledged ruefully that "it has not been possible to secure a complete record of each one of these organizations, and from many others of such societies, sending money and goods to the parent society, we have received no official records whatever."[20] Gaps and discrepancies in recording the LCCs occurred due to variation in their setup and operation. Individual branches frequently failed to submit reports of their activities and takings to the head office. Some aid societies regularly donated to the Christian Commission without ever officially affiliating themselves with the parent organization. Larger LCCs, such as the Buffalo chapter, collected donations and goods from "tributary" aid societies (the Buffalo LCC counted 139 such local groups under their aegis).[21] These inconsistencies meant drawing up an exhaustive list of LCCs proved impossible even for the meticulous record keepers of the USCC. It was not until June 1864 that the Executive Committee launched an ambitious attempt to establish a branch in every town in the North and to standardize their operations and membership subscriptions. Robert J. Parvin, the rector of St. Paul's Episcopal Church in Cheltenham, Philadelphia, was placed in charge of coordinating LCCs and administering funds received from them. To aid this project, the USCC printed practical guidelines for establishing LCCs in each parish, outlining the best methods of allocating committee posts, collecting yearly subscriptions (with a suggested spectrum of membership categories including "active," "associate," "honorary," and "youth"), and organizing manufacturing and fundraising activities.[22]

While many ladies' aid societies had been sending supplies and funds to the USCC headquarters on an ad hoc basis since the Commission's foundation, the number of societies formally identifying as "Ladies Christian Commissions," grew after this recruitment drive was launched in June 1864. The USCC also sent certain individuals on canvassing missions to promote and establish LCCs; George Wiswell, the pastor of Central Presbyterian in Wilmington, for example, was charged with securing the organization of LCCs in Delaware, and Mary Bannan, the wife of Schuylkill County conscription officer Benjamin

Bannan, was made responsible for establishing LCCs in and around Pottsville, carrying with her copies of the annual reports to aid in her publicity mission.[23] The aforementioned 1864 Philadelphia meeting at which Edward Norris Kirk spoke was explicitly designed to encourage women of the city to form LCCs. These efforts bore some fruit. By the end of that year, according to one ledger, sixty-nine LCCs were listed for Philadelphia alone, including the United LCC of Methodist Episcopal Churches of Philadelphia, which drew together the benevolent activities of fifteen separate congregations. A further eighty-four LCCs were listed for the rest of the country, the vast majority clustered in New York state and Pennsylvania, but also hailing from as far afield as Wisconsin, Michigan, Oregon, and Honolulu.[24]

On the West Coast, the Ladies Christian Commission established in San Francisco in 1864 was particularly active. Otherwise known as the Pacific Ladies Christian Commission, the branch was initially established by Elizabeth Bowman, the wife of Col. Samuel Bowman of the Eighty-Fourth Pennsylvania Volunteer Infantry. Well acquainted with the work of the USCC through her brother, Commission Secretary William Boardman, Bowman accompanied Executive Committee members Robert Patterson and George Mingins to California with a view to whipping up enthusiasm and support on the West Coast. There, she capitalized on the small but dedicated band of evangelical women in the city, led by Mary Keeney, to establish the "Pacific" LCC. Early scholarship characterizes Gold Rush California as an almost exclusively male society; the few women who feature in these accounts are invariably sex workers or immigrant laborers. This erases the determined and active contributions of middle-class women to civic life in the mid-nineteenth century. Protestant women in San Francisco were heavily involved in coordinated benevolent enterprises from as early as 1851, establishing, among other institutions, the San Francisco Ladies' Orphan Asylum Society and the San Francisco Ladies' Protection and Relief Society.[25] Indeed, as Mary Ann Irwin has suggested, because the rapid growth of the city overwhelmed its weak bureaucratic structures and outstripped the development of public welfare programs, women's charitable endeavors in San Francisco "provided badly needed services," accruing for their "lady managers" greater political power and legitimacy by dint of their necessity.[26] Establishing a Ladies Christian Commission among these seasoned philanthropists was thus a logical and relatively straightforward step.

Like other LCCs, the Pacific LCC eventually oversaw a network of smaller auxiliaries, coordinating funds and distributing literature to interested parties. The PLCC maintained a steady income, as did many LCCs back in the East, by regularly canvassing neighborhoods for donations and collecting membership fees from congregations, but its most high-profile success was the fair held in Union Hall, San Francisco, between August 24 and September 8, 1864. In the East, the Christian Commission often tried to discourage ladies' aid societies from organizing fairs, fearing that they were too much the preserve of the Sanitary Commission and that they gave rise to huge swells of public support followed by massive slumps. Anticipating difficulty establishing a foothold on the West Coast, however, USCC leaders were happy to encourage a more glitzy approach to fundraising in San Francisco. The 1864 fair raised over $25,000 for the coffers of the USCC, attracting an estimated three thousand visitors on the opening day alone and receiving extensive coverage in the *Daily Evening Bulletin* and other local newspapers. The event contained many features common to fundraising fairs before and during the Civil War, including demonstrations of cabinet-making, an art gallery, a museum containing Chinese and Japanese bronzes, various tableaux vivantes, a grotto, concerts, a photography studio, a man demonstrating novelty robotic figures, and a soda fountain, in addition to the usual panoply of stalls selling goods, antiques, memorabilia, and hardware for all purposes.[27] Visitors could also make donations toward subscription gifts—luxury personalized items that would then be presented to a politician or dignitary to demonstrate the fidelity and power of the Christian Commission—among them a Bible for President Lincoln; a new sewing machine for Mrs. Starr King, the wife of Thomas Starr King, the noted missionary; and a quilt for General Hooker, General Butler, or General Grant (the recipient to be decided by a vote).[28] This scheme, as well as the customary sale of novelties such as Washington's signature and drafts of Lincoln's speeches, did more than raise funds: it was an explicit statement of the patriotism of the women who organized the Union Hall fair.[29]

The fair, as Beverly Gordon has noted of other comparable examples, represented the commodification of domesticity in ways that at once preserved "conservative propriety" and allowed women, through the shared fellowship of organizing and hosting the event, to "demonstrate their competence and operate relatively independently of men."[30] The PLCC organizing committee took care to maintain their own virtuous reputations, ensuring that there were no raffles or other gambling-adjacent activities available ("much to the credit of the ladies," the *Evening Bulletin* noted approvingly).[31] At the same time, women unabashedly exercised their business acumen: "It was delightful to witness the glee with which the ladies took in the cash," the same newspaper reported without a trace of reproach. "Many ingenious and pleasant plans have been contrived for coaxing out a few more dollars."[32] That is to say, the activities of the Pacific Ladies Christian Commission provided women with a means of contributing publicly to the Union cause while testing, but not overstepping, the expected bounds of femininity.

The relative independence afforded to the women of the PLCC was not always replicated back in the East, where the men who led the Christian Commission sought more proactively to shape and oversee the operations of the women's auxiliary associations. Executive Committee interference in the running of the LCCs varied. For example, they sent speakers to address Ladies Christian Commissions; James Grant, who served as a delegate at Gettysburg, was sent to Washington, New Jersey, and Thomas Atkinson, a delegate with the Army of the Cumberland, visited Hartsville, Pennsylvania, to talk about his experiences with the USCC. "He has been a long time in our service," George Stuart explained to the president of the Hartsville Ladies Aid Society, Miss E. N. Davis, "and will have no idea of talking about anything save the Master's work in the Army."[33] These speeches served to generate interest in the cause of the USCC and helped civilians removed from the immediate carnage of war better visualize the ways in which their funds were put to use, thus encouraging a steady and growing stream of donations. After Atkinson's address, for instance, the Hartsville society reported "new interest in the spiritual and temporal welfare of our brave countrymen who were enduring the hardships of war in our defence."[34] The Christian Commission also distributed pamphlets (such as the annual reports and the monthly "Information" pamphlets), which kept members of the LCCs abreast of its activities in the armies.[35] Of particular use was the "Form of Constitution for Ladies' Christian Commissions," which contained suggestions for how money should be collected and sent to Philadelphia, and the protocol for using some funds for the LCC's own activities (such as renting rooms or buying supplies for manufacture).[36] This pamphlet emphasized that the most dependable and desirable source of funds was a membership fund, which could then be supplemented by other means, such as monthly collections, and by meeting regularly to make up clothing and other stores.[37]

The central office also engaged in regular correspondence with the presidents and secretaries of Ladies Christian Commissions and ladies' aid societies, providing advice and encouragement, and thanking them for donations to the central treasury, whether material or financial, all with the aim of securing their continuing allegiance and support. In some cases, this oversight proved beneficial: affiliation with the USCC meant volunteers could call upon the Executive Committee for assistance. Bernice Ames, for example, helped one Philadelphia LCC trace packages of stores that had gone astray at Fredericksburg and Chattanooga, sending a local field agent to locate the packages and negotiate with local officials.[38] Similarly, when the Crawford LCC complained to the Executive

48   TABERNACLES IN THE WILDERNESS

Committee that boxes of donations valued at $300 were being held by the Customs Department, George Stuart used his acquaintance with Edwin Stanton to ensure the packages would be transported to the army free of charge.[39]

However, affiliation with the USCC also came with increased supervision and regulation, as when the Philadelphia head office attempted to control the sorts of donations sent to them by female war workers. George Stuart advised Abbie Doates of York, Michigan, on the best nonperishable foodstuffs to send, instructing her society to collect "good books on History, Biography, Philosophy, and Criticism with the best authors—including Religious works."[40] The Commission frequently stressed that cash donations were preferred to stores, "as we always can buy at heavy discount, and thus save a great deal." Despite this, the Commission acknowledged that the communal act of collecting and manufacturing clothing and foodstuffs was vital to maintaining enthusiasm for the work.[41] "We would rather have money," Stuart wrote to Mrs. C. F. Maurice, president of the Sing Sing LCC, "but often such an interest is excited by the making up of clothing and the packing of boxes that we shall leave entirely the disposition of the matter to your own society."[42] Evaluating how the Lambertville, New Jersey, Ladies Aid Society met in a "united effort at a designated time and place" to brew blackberry wine, pickle fruit, and make up parcels, Lemuel Moss also recognized that communal labor could bring social and moral benefits that mere cash donations could not. "At the end of this work," he wrote, "they were vastly richer in experience and noble sentiment and hallowed memories than at the beginning."[43]

Maintaining a close relationship with the LCCs and affiliated ladies' aid societies was of paramount importance for the reputation of the USCC, which relied on home front support for its continuing survival. The Christian Commission was not alone in the appeals for aid it issued to the civilian population of the North; the Sanitary Commission was a key rival for the allegiance of local ladies' aid societies. Both organizations relied heavily on these societies for financial support and campaigned aggressively, urging the societies to affiliate with them, each emphasizing the characteristics that distinguished their work from the other and supposedly made it superior. Needless to say, the men who led the two commissions held rigid beliefs about the types of war work appropriate for women. The Sanitary Commission, concerned with efficiency and with avoiding the sentimentalization of benevolence, tried to convince Northern women that their war work would be wasted if not properly disciplined and regulated, and that the men of the USSC were (naturally) best placed to ascertain the precise needs of the army. "A large proportion of the gifts of the people to the army hitherto have been wasted, or worse than wasted, because directed without knowledge or discrimination," one early Sanitary Commission circular read, urging women to form aid societies in their local communities. "It is only through the Commission that such gifts can reach the army with a reasonable assurance that they will be received where they will do the most good and the least harm."[44]

The Christian Commission, on the other hand, emphasized the spiritual nature of its work and played on the moral concerns of evangelical women. While the Sanitary Commission offered centralized bureaucracy and the promise of efficient disbursement of supplies, the Christian Commission's strength on the home front derived, as Lori Ginzberg suggests, from "the continued grassroots respect accorded church-related organizations and the continuing power of the older ideology of benevolence."[45] Despite this, there was no clear winner in the battle between the USCC and the USSC for home front support. The USSC was initially far ahead of the USCC in these stakes, as its operations were established much earlier, and the Sanitarians set up a dedicated system for soliciting donations from aid societies in 1861, but from 1864 the USCC began to make serious inroads into Sanitary Commission support on the home front, with some ladies' aid societies previously loyal to the USSC switching allegiance between the two organizations. Bernice Ames, secretary of the USCC, was confident that this change was widespread: "the change from the Sanitary to the Christian Commission which your Society has made is being made extensively throughout the country," he wrote to Mary Rowe, president of the newly affiliated LCC of Hartford, Connecticut.[46]

Whether this assessment was an accurate one, however, is debatable. True, after three years of operations, the Sanitary Commission had begun to encounter some disgruntlement from aid societies resentful of the autonomy they had ceded to the Commission and suspicious of its operations and intentions. Jeanie Attie suggests that the "more religious, more conservative" Christian Commission offered a desirable alternative to the Sanitary Commission, which was dogged by allegations of corruption and fraud, and that switching allegiance "offered female volunteers a means of punishing the Sanitary Commission for its alleged misdeeds and at the same time exerting some measure of control over the products of their labor."[47] There is little evidence, however, that ladies' aid societies abandoned the USSC en masse in the latter stages of the war. Rather, the relationship of local groups such as ladies' aid societies to larger bureaucratic bodies like the two commissions remained fluid. Although the Christian Commission and Sanitary Commission considered their approaches and missions to be ideologically incompatible, their donors did not always see it this way: support for one commission did not necessarily preclude support for the other.[48] The final financial report of the Ladies Aid Society of Hartsville,

Pennsylvania, demonstrated this flexibility. Altogether, the women of Hartsville put together thirty-nine boxes of stores at an estimated value of $4,050. Eight of these were sent to the Christian Commission (the organization that received the largest number of boxes from the society), but two were sent to the Sanitary Commission, two to the Philadelphia Ladies' Aid Society, and several directly to the army and to various military hospitals.[49] In making donations to several different organizations at once, the Hartsville society's example suggests that the Christian Commission's goal of a coherent network of fully affiliated and uniformly structured Ladies Christian Commissions did not reflect the reality of female war work.

In fact, it is clear that women did not accept the USCC's model of female war work unquestioningly and passively; rather, they sought to exercise ownership and autonomy over their work, using the language of domesticity and female virtue to legitimize this autonomy. In the case of the women of Hartsville, they endorsed the idea that men and women were suited to separate but complementary roles by dint of their respective, innately gendered talents. As the society's president recalled, at the regular meetings held in the church's lecture room, "the gentlemen did not aid much with the sewing, but . . . were always ready where their services could be of avail—in forwarding boxes, collecting supplies, &c."[50] As this example suggests, women who raised funds and manufactured material donations for the Christian Commission did not depart dramatically from prevailing contemporary notions of female morality and virtue but were nevertheless able to use these notions to inform their pragmatic, critical approach to the way their war work was organized.

SPECIAL DIET KITCHENS

Despite the impossibility of exercising complete control over the affairs of home front ladies' aid societies, and perhaps because their attempts to do so were not as draconian as those made by the Sanitary Commission to regulate civilian war work, the Commission commanded sufficient loyalty to maintain a steady flow of donations from female workers anxious to demonstrate their piety and patriotism through their association with an explicitly evangelical relief agency. The Ladies Christian Commissions were not the only way in which women could work for the USCC, however. Activities such as manufacturing clothing, raising funds, and packing foodstuffs were confined to the home front and incorporated into the existing parameters of civilian life. The other role reserved for women by the Christian Commission—service in the diet kitchen

FEMALE WAR WORK AND THE CHRISTIAN COMMISSION   51

system—was drastically different, as it required women to travel from their homes to military hospitals on or close to the battlefront. At the same time, however, this role still relied upon the dominant cultural association of domesticity and femininity to maintain its legitimacy and protect the reputation of women who worked in the hospitals in the Commission's name.

Briefly put, the diet kitchen system catered to sick and wounded soldiers who were so weak that they could not tolerate the monotonous and heavy diet typically found in military hospitals. Each diet kitchen was run by a pair of paid "lady managers" who oversaw a team of cooks, usually made up of hospital stewards and convalescent soldiers, and provided meals individually tailored to the needs of the sickest and weakest patients. They differed from the Ladies Christian Commissions in two important respects: first, they involved women laboring on the battlefront rather than in their local communities, and second, whereas the LCCs were an evangelical variation of the widespread pattern of ladies' aid societies in the North, the diet kitchens were unique to the Christian Commission. While the LCCs, to a great extent, upheld dominant ideas about what constituted the appropriate involvement of women in the public sphere, the diet kitchens, although they drew on similar ideas about women's innate virtues and skills, by their existence in military spaces and their engagement with debates about professionalization and the remuneration of women's work, posed—albeit perhaps inadvertently—a greater challenge to the preservation of a gender ideology, which still associated femininity with domesticity and the home.

The diet kitchen scheme was the brainchild of Annie Wittenmyer of Keokuk, Iowa, a woman already well acquainted with civilian war work and the problems of operating within tangled and patriarchal bureaucracies. Involved with the Sunday School movement before the war, she was instrumental in founding the Keokuk Ladies' Soldiers' Aid Society (KLSAS). As its corresponding secretary, she was responsible for maintaining a network of aid societies across Iowa. She was also appointed Iowa State sanitary agent during the war, and as part of this work, she undertook tours of various battlefields, where she forged an acquaintance with Gen. Ulysses S. Grant. Eventually, however, offended by accusations that the KLSAS had sold (rather than distributed) supplies donated by the town's citizens and frustrated by her ongoing battle to maintain the autonomy of the KLSAS from the Sanitary Commission, Wittenmyer turned her attention to lobbying for federally funded orphan asylums and eventually to what would become the USCC diet kitchen system.[51]

"The plan of a system of special-diet kitchens," she wrote in her 1895 memoir *Under the Guns,* "came to me, clearly and definitely, as a flash from the skies, like a divine inspiration."[52] In a lengthy report penned for the USCC Executive

Committee at the end of the war, she was rather more prosaic, explaining that her battlefield tours had alerted her to the shortcomings of food supply and preparation in military hospitals. She lamented that cooking for sick men was often left to soldiers inexperienced in catering and incapable of showing the requisite compassionate and nurturing spirit believed innate to women. She acknowledged that medical officers and quartermasters were aware of the shortcomings of hospital kitchens but concluded that their efforts to remedy them, largely by delegating to overworked nurses were, for the most part, flawed and unsuccessful.[53] In response, Wittenmyer sketched out a basic plan for the diet kitchen system: the kitchens were to be established within army hospitals under the jurisdiction of the surgeon in chief, supplied by the hospital commissary, and supplemented when necessary by the stores and coffers of the USCC. The ward surgeons were responsible for drawing up specially tailored diet lists or bills of fare, which were then returned to the diet kitchen managers, whereupon the women would oversee the preparation of the food for the day.[54] The first diet kitchen was opened at the Cumberland Hospital in Nashville in the winter of 1863. Within twelve months, there were twenty-four kitchens in operation across the Western theater, and when the scheme was rolled out to the Eastern theater, this number swelled to nearly sixty, the largest being the kitchen at Point of Rocks on the Appomattox River, which catered daily for between sixteen hundred and eighteen hundred patients.[55] Wittenmyer used the network of governmental allies she had cemented while working as Iowa State sanitary agent to secure free transportation for diet kitchen staff and stores, and to gain approval and endorsement from high-up politicians such as Surgeon General J. K. Barnes, Assistant Surgeon General R. C. Wood, who described the scheme as "useful and practical," and even a short note from Lincoln commanding all officials to allow her unhindered passage to the army.[56]

Over one hundred women worked in the diet kitchens under the aegis of the USCC.[57] Like the LCCs, the diet kitchens drew upon Victorian concepts of domesticity and female virtue to legitimize their work. Their very existence depended on persuading military and hospital personnel—and the Northern public at large—that women were not only capable of war work on the battlefront, but that they were uniquely and innately suited to it. This was no mean feat. The seat of war was hardly considered an appropriate arena for women. Opposition to women wishing to help the war effort in a capacity beyond scraping lint or preserving fruit was widespread, both among the families against whose disapproval they rebelled and among the doctors and army officials reluctant to admit them.[58] The white, middle-class women who made up the bulk of female Civil War workers for whom records exist were considered by many to be too weak to cope with strenuous physical labor. The challenges posed by battlefront labor were not only manual but spiritual and emotional too: pious, respectable women, many believed, were ill equipped to deal with the traumatic sights and sounds common to military hospitals.

In the face of this skepticism, Annie Wittenmyer and the USCC were anxious to assure the Northern public that, although it would bring women face to face with the unvarnished horrors of war, diet kitchen work was appropriate and useful, and to convince grumpy surgeons in charge that these women would help, rather than hinder, the hospital work. The instructions issued to each manager emphasized this: "In their management, the Commission assumes a double responsibility: to the medical authorities of each hospital, for the character and efficiency of the ladies employed, and to the loyal, liberal men and women of the nation, who have placed in their hands so abundantly their good gifts, for the impartial, judicious, and economical use of the stores entrusted to them."[59] From the very beginning of the scheme, Wittenmyer emphasized the respectability of the women involved. This respectability, in her view, derived from their high-minded motivations and selflessness; that is, from the ways in which they embodied mid-century ideals of womanly virtue. Frequently, this led Wittenmyer to employ women already known to her or to Commission leaders. For example, Hannah, the wife of Edward Parmelee Smith, oversaw the kitchens in the Cumberland Department, while Iowa sisters Mary and Amanda Shelton had worked with Wittenmyer in earlier relief organizations. Beyond these personal connections and recommendations, Wittenmyer had a particular image of womanhood in mind for her cohort of "lady managers." They were expected to be neatly and demurely dressed.[60] A measure of selflessness was also encouraged. Wittenmyer claimed, "The ladies employed for this work were selected with great care, and with a view to Christian character and fitness, and were women of refinement and culture who came into the work from the highest motives or Christian love and duty."[61] Another writer praised those women "who sacrifice the peace and quiet of sweet homes and loved associations, to endure trials and hardships amid the desolating track of wasting armies."[62] In a string of miniature biographies of lady managers she prepared for the Philadelphia office, Wittenmyer singled out particular women for praise, hailing the virtues that fitted them for the position. Hannah Shaw, a single woman from Pittsburgh who eventually became general manager of the first diet kitchen at the Cumberland Hospital, was apparently "a young lady of great energy, goodness of heart, and sterling integrity." Similarly, Mrs. Dale and Miss Fanny Sage, based at the Washington Hospital, Memphis, were described as "ladies of culture, ability, and sweet, self-sacrificing Christian spirit," who, due to these qualities, "made their mission a success." These workers were deemed successful because of, rather than despite, the ways they conformed to prevailing expectations of their gender.

However, it was not only the moral irreproachability and Christian virtues of her team of managers that recommended them, in Wittenmyer's view. She also strove to rebuff critics of female war workers by highlighting women's unique practical skills and expertise, describing her workers as, for instance, "earnest," "zealous," "accomplished," and "efficient." As with the LCCs, which assumed that the women involved possessed not only the compassion and disinterestedness but also the skills and experience to raise funds and produce goods for the benefit of soldiers, the diet kitchen system also took for granted competencies that were culturally associated with middle-class womanhood. In particular, women were expected to be accomplished and unflappable managers of their own households. The idea that women were particularly well suited to manage domestic affairs was not new. Antebellum pioneers of household advice writing—most notably, Catharine Beecher, the author of manuals such as *A Treatise on Home Economy* (1841)—advanced the view that the home was the particular domain and responsibility of women, and that women's political power derived not from participation in the public sphere but from their efficient and morally unimpeachable management of domestic affairs. Creating and maintaining a harmonious, frugal, and welcoming home was the solemn duty of American women, through which they were to construct a bulwark for their husbands against the ruthless competition of the world of business and build a perfect environment for the raising of young Christian patriots.[63]

Wittenmyer's vision for the diet kitchen system endorsed the theory that cultivating domesticity required specialist skills and expertise, and that women were best equipped to develop and apply these skills. As is explored further in chapter 6, the diet kitchens drew inspiration from a range of existing intellectual strands, not least the dietetic theories of Sylvester Graham and others, who suggested that food and drink had an indelible impact on one's emotional, spiritual, and moral state. But Wittenmyer invoked most vocally the ideas of Florence Nightingale, famous on both sides of the Atlantic for her work in the Crimea and who had written at length about the physical and mental importance of diet in her influential *Notes on Nursing* (1859).[64] Quotes from this slim volume were peppered throughout the texts produced by the Christian Commission, especially when promoting and praising the diet kitchens. The frontispiece to the recipe book distributed to all diet kitchen managers, for instance, bore a quotation by Nightingale: "thousands of patients are annually starved in the midst of plenty, from want of attention to the ways which alone make it possible for them to take food."[65] In another passage quoted in the recipe book, Nightingale advanced the notion that each patient was different, and that individual appetite and taste were vital to patient care: "you cannot diet a patient from a book," she wrote. "You cannot make up the human body as you would make up a prescription . . . the patient's stomach must be its own chemist."[66] She was particularly concerned, as the diet kitchen managers would be in their turn, with maintaining variety of diet, and with using the best method of cooking "so as to secure the greatest digestibility and the greatest economy in nutritive value of food."[67] Nightingale thus placed great emphasis on diet as crucial to convalescence, and Wittenmyer employed Nightingale's profile as a respected expert to lend the diet kitchen scheme legitimacy and authority.[68]

In order to underline that the kitchen should remain the domain of women and that running a successful kitchen was no mean undertaking, Wittenmyer and her colleagues highlighted the apparently universal haplessness of men in the face of domestic tasks. For example, Wittenmyer lamented that before the establishment of the diet kitchens, cooking was largely left to convalescent soldiers. "Few of the men employed as cooks in these hospitals were trained or skilled," she recalled. "Most of them had obtained their knowledge of cookery after being assigned to duty, under most unfavorable circumstances."[69] The lack of experience among soldier-cooks was evident even to the surgeons forced, for want of better personnel, to employ them. "The great stumbling-block," one harried surgeon wrote, "has been the proper preparation of the food, so as to be palatable and nutritious to the sick. The men who were detailed for that purpose have been generally too careless and too little conversant with the arts of cooking to render just the service needed."[70] The diet kitchen system meant that cooking for the sick was instead entrusted to "experienced and competent Christian women."[71]

Crucially, however, diet kitchen managers, who often had upward of a thousand patients to feed three times a day, were appointed to oversee and coordinate the cooking rather than to stand at the stove themselves. Wittenmyer was at pains to point out that the women "were *not cooks; they superintended the work.*"[72] This explicitly set aside the diet kitchen managers from cooks and other hospital roles seen as less skilled, less genteel, and hence less desirable.[73] The role, that is, was classed as well as gendered. As the title implied, the manager's purview was supervisory. In most hospitals, once the cooperation of the surgeon in charge was secured, the diet kitchen manager was assigned a detail of between five and twenty men to follow her instructions and undertake the drudgery of cooking. A permanent detail of cooks was preferred to allow the women to teach the men the required skills, and so that the repetition of the work would make the men more efficient. How delighted these men, probably drawn from the invalid corps, were to undertake "women's" work under the supervision of women is unclear, but the system seems to have worked well in at least one hospital. E. W. Jones wrote enthusiastically to Wittenmyer: "We have very excellent men in our kitchen, seven white and three black. They are all delighted with the new order of things and say it seems very homelike. We all eat at the same table,—one or two taking turns to serve. The colored men at first positively declined, but now take their places as requested and we have a very pleasant, social table."[74] In Jones's account, this "homelike" diet kitchen was a domestic kitchen writ large. The quasi-familial setup, by positioning the lady manager in a maternal position of authority, effectively disguised the topsy-turvy hierarchy, which placed the male workers below the female, and saw an interracial group of coworkers eating together. William Boardman similarly transposed domestic roles and structures to the military hospital when he wrote to C. P. Lyford in praise of the diet kitchen system, claiming "it has the relative importance in the hospital that the mother and sister holds in the household when sickness has prostrated more or less of the family."[75]

However, while lady managers like Jones were able to draw on ideas about the domestic expertise of women to assert a certain amount of power and status within the confines of the kitchen space itself, beyond its walls, matters were more delicate. In carrying out traditionally female roles such as food preparation and nursing in a regulated, public space such as the Civil War hospital, diet kitchen managers were still obliged to operate within a male-dominated hierarchy and to seek the continuing approval of men.[76] This often required adopting what Elizabeth Leonard calls "male standards of professionalism" to legitimize their work.[77] Wittenmyer was all too aware of this. As the corresponding secretary of the Keokuk Ladies' Soldiers' Aid Society, she had faced accusations of wastefulness, inexperience, and even embezzlement and had introduced measures such as more detailed bookkeeping, salaried positions, and official positions to rebut these claims. Wittenmyer built such elements of professionalization into the diet kitchen system, too. Describing her workers as "lady managers" rather than "cooks" was significant, as Theresa McDevitt argues, "suggesting respectability and middle-class status but also the administrative nature of their work."[78] Moreover, not only were diet kitchen managers obliged to fill out large amounts of paperwork—including daily bills of fare for the surgeons in charge, and financial accounts/written reports submitted monthly to Wittenmyer herself—but they were also paid a monthly wage of twenty dollars.[79] This was where Wittenmyer departed from earlier advocates of domestic management. Wittenmyer has often been held up as the archetype of conservative female benevolence, able to participate in philanthropic activity due to her independent wealth and status as a widow. As the first president of the Women's Christian Temperance Union after the war, she frequently appears in scholarship as a foil to her more "radical" successor, Frances Willard.[80] As Lisa Guinn has recently demonstrated, however, Wittenmyer's story was rather more interesting: far from a comfortably off widow, she was a divorcée who did not always enjoy financial security.[81] Her precarious social status, as well as her hostile encounters with male authority figures while working for the KLSAS, drove her conviction that women's war work could not rely solely upon self-sacrifice and Christian virtue but must be systematized using language and schemas recognizable to, and respected by, men. Her insistence that her workers should receive a wage set her apart from Beecher and her acolytes, who balked at the idea that women's management of their own households might be financially compensated.[82]

While the use of professionalizing language and methods helped diet kitchen managers command authority, the smooth running of the work was still contingent upon the acquiescence of men. Ultimately, Wittenmyer acknowledged, the preparation of special diets remained "dependent upon the consent or requisition of the surgeon in charge," who told the women what dishes were required, and controlled the supplies issued by the hospital commissary.[83] Negotiation and compromise were therefore needed to ensure that the diet kitchens occupied a position within the delicate and hierarchical hospital ecosystem that was acceptable to all involved; as Leonard points out, the managers had to demonstrate "at least the impression of deference to ostensibly more official, typically male, institutions and styles in order to avoid as much friction as possible and to allow the work to continue."[84] Wittenmyer therefore advised—"so as to be above the shadow of reproach"—that managers defer to surgeons at all times, consult them in all matters, and at no point meddle in any sphere of hospital life that did not immediately pertain to the work for which they had been commissioned (advice that was also issued to male delegates working alongside chaplains, surgeons, and officers).[85] Wittenmyer stressed that managers should be impartial in their treatment of patients, and that "personal preferences and prejudices should be put away, and hearty, earnest cooperation be given to all who labor for the physical or spiritual welfare of the soldiers."[86]

Wittenmyer was at pains to stress that this deference often paid off. "Medical officers in charge of General Hospitals," she claimed, "receive this offer of assistance and cooperation with great favour, accepting the plan as *simple,* and *practical and in harmony with hospital arrangements and the interests of the sick.*"[87] She further claimed that "most of the Chaplains cooperated heartily in the diet kitchen work and were earnest in their efforts for the physical comfort and spiritual welfare of the patients for whom they were called upon to labor."[88] Sure enough, some medical practitioners responded favorably to the system, and were obliged to alter their views on female war work. In September 1864, Henry Burrit, the surgeon in charge at Holston General Hospital, Knoxville, Tennessee, wrote to Wittenmyer praising the "prudent, energetic, and discreet" efforts of Mrs. Athow, the diet kitchen manager under his jurisdiction. He expressed his gratitude and indebtedness for her work among the two hundred patients on special diets, as well as his concern for her health. However, he closed his letter by alluding to a recurring problem for female war workers. "I feel bound to make this acknowledgment," he wrote, "as my previous experience had not been favourable to the employment of female nurses or cooks in hospitals."[89]

But while Burrit's opinion was favorably altered by his experience of working alongside Athow, many other men encountered by the diet kitchen managers proved far more intransigent and hostile. Despite the efforts of the USCC and of Annie Wittenmyer and her disciples to create a system that slotted neatly into the hospital hierarchy and that worked efficiently as part of the army machine, the diet kitchens did not always function smoothly. While published USCC accounts of the system were largely positive, Wittenmyer herself did concede that there were "one or two exceptions" to the gratitude and respect with which diet kitchen workers were generally treated.[90] For example, a Miss Hardenbrook, working in Memphis, found herself at loggerheads with a cowardly and unsympathetic army chaplain who, despite Hardenbrook's entreaties, refused to listen to the pained, frightened ramblings of one dying man, leaving him "without a word of prayer or comfort."[91] In this case, the conflict occurred when the diet kitchen manager was perceived to have stepped outside the remit of her work and began to challenge the chaplain's ability to perform his duty. There was clearly a fine line between the proselytizing permitted for male chaplains and delegates and the more introspective comfort permitted for women. Traveling from Fortress Monroe to Norfolk, Virginia, with a group of lady managers, Mary Shelton met with a hostile reception from the USCC agent there instead of the assistance and respect she expected.[92] Clearly, although the Executive Committee had heartily approved Wittenmyer's plan, not all Christian Commission foot soldiers were as enthusiastic at the prospect of working alongside women.

This lukewarm response by a USCC delegate was not an isolated incident. Amanda Shelton, Mary's younger sister, developed a strong dislike of Mr. Russell, the agent in charge of the Christian Commission rooms at Louisville, where she was working in June 1864.[93] She found his treatment of her disrespectful while he, in turn, found her inexperienced and insubordinate, and complained about her to Wittenmyer. McDevitt concludes that Russell refused to accept the increasing involvement of women in civilian relief work, and that Shelton did not adequately conform to societal expectations of female modesty and passivity; in short, "the delegate and the lady manager were not able to navigate the shifting sea of gender expectations and so were unable to work harmoniously together."[94] To a great extent, these examples suggest, the success of the diet kitchens was measured in terms of male approval and cooperation, and conversely, failure was measured in terms of male disapproval or hindrance. Despite the self-congratulatory narratives constructed about the diet kitchens after the war, then, the reality of operating the system required women to react and adapt rapidly to unfamiliar, trying, and sometimes dangerous circumstances and to engage in work that was often strenuous and frustrating.

As the Ladies Christian Commissions and the diet kitchen system demonstrate, the roles carved out for women by the USCC were designed to apply the attributes expected of genteel women to the wartime situation. If the male delegates were manly soldiers for Christ, then women workers of the Christian Commission were, in theory, nurturing angels ready not only to contribute to the Union war effort but to uphold the reputation of the Christian Commission as a respectable and pious institution. Women were expected to use their skills as household managers, mothers, caregivers, and socially engaged philanthropists to endorse the patriotic, pious domesticity espoused by the Christian Commission. Their work was intended to exercise the moral authority believed innate to women over the men for whom they cared, whether remotely, through the packages and financial donations women made to the USCC, or in person, through the activities of the diet kitchen system.

CHAPTER THREE

Evangelization and the Printed Word

In seeking to convert every soldier in the Union Army to Christianity, the evangelicals of the USCC set themselves an ambitious target. Delegates and diet kitchen workers alike strove to alleviate misery, whether physical or spiritual. For some, these actions were individual acts of kindness that followed the loving example of Christ. For others, however, these acts of benevolence were freighted with deeper meaning. The cataclysm of the Civil War, surely a sign of divine retribution, made the reformation of America an urgent priority for evangelicals and made the army the epicenter of this reforming, converting drive. If society could be reformed, and if enough souls could be saved, would America finally prove itself worthy of God's blessing? The delegates of the USCC devised strategies to cleanse the army of vice and sin, lead souls to Christ, and prepare men to die happily and piously. Indeed, the drive to reform the morals of the army and win converts for Christ informed every aspect of the Commission's endeavors. This chapter, on the widespread distribution of religious literature, and the next, on preaching, prayer meetings, and hymn singing in the army camps, explain the methods developed and applied by delegates to minister directly to soldiers' souls. Crucially, by placing conversion and the fate of soldiers' souls at the heart of the USCC's mission, these methods reflected the Commission's faith that the army's salvation was the key to the fulfillment of America's destiny as God's redeemer nation. The methods employed by the Christian Commission to target the soldier's soul were devised with two aims in mind: first, to solve the problem of vice and sin in the Union armies and create a morally upstanding, godly army to fight the rebellion and, second, to convert soldiers to Christ.

These aims were related; in order to be receptive to the appeals of religion, men first had to reform their behavior and cast aside pastimes and thoughts that prevented them from receiving and understanding the word of God. How the Union Army lived and fought, according to the USCC, bore implications for the fate of the divinely ordained redeemer nation—America—and would either secure God's blessing or incur his wrath. As one delegate put it, "it is a solemn truth that under God we must save the army, or it will come back and destroy us; unless it is saved . . . it will prove a worse scourge to us than the enemy."[1] The delegates were not the only ones calling out for a reformation of behavior and morals. Officers, too, worried about the implications of immorality for discipline and control.[2] There were widespread concerns over the flourishing of vice, crime, and immorality within both Confederate and Union armies, concerns that were not entirely without foundation. Officers struggled to maintain control of a hastily trained fighting force made up almost entirely of citizen volunteers and draftees, unused both to army discipline and life away from home. In particular, soldiers frequently engaged in activities such as gambling, intemperance, possession of obscene material, profanity, and sexual promiscuity.[3] Such behavior did not necessarily have negative repercussions—Judith Giesberg's recent study of pornography in the Civil War, for instance, reveals that exchanging, viewing, and discussing erotic material could help men "to build fraternal bonds across rank and region."[4] Engaging communally in illicit behavior helped generate camaraderie and foster comradeship, and acted as a bulwark against fear and boredom. However, the military and religious authorities rarely subscribed to this way of thinking. In their view, "immoral" behavior could compromise the fighting fitness of the army. Gambling led to ill feeling and could motivate men to steal or cheat to make up for lost winnings. Intemperance led to violence against fellow soldiers or civilians, impaired judgment and reactions in battle, and rendered men insensible to the orders of superior officers. And visits to bawdy houses and sex workers resulted in high levels of venereal disease that incapacitated men, sometimes permanently.[5]

For the USCC, persistently immoral behavior was indicative of a godless attitude among these green recruits and of a rejection of the morality ideally inculcated in a man by his mother in the domestic safety of the home.[6] Recall that the USCC developed out of the antebellum Young Men's Christian Associations. These were organizations primarily preoccupied before the war with the spiritual well-being of country boys who had migrated to the cities in search of work. Used to the moral surveillance and close-knit kinship networks of rural communities, they now found themselves exposed (reformers feared) to the apparent temptation, vice, and immorality of urban life.[7] The sudden change in status from civilian to soldier experienced by thousands of new army recruits posed similar challenges to the transition from rural to urban life. Like migrants to the metropolis, soldiers experienced the abrupt removal of well-established familial and communal disciplinary structures, especially the idealized virtue and piety of female relatives.[8] The USCC, continuing the YMCA's intention to alleviate vicious temptation and act as a surrogate for familial moral surveillance, sought to establish a positive, restraining influence in the armies.

The delegates of the Christian Commission approached the behavior of the Union armies with a mixture of cautious optimism and resigned pessimism, sometimes perceiving changes in the overall behavior of the men and other times despairing of ever making an impact on camp morals. Many delegates were dismayed by the apparent intractability of the immorality they encountered. "I do regret exceedingly to say," E. Colton reported dejectedly after a six-week stint stationed at Martinsburg, West Virginia, "that Swearing, Intemperance, Lewdness, Stealing, Sabbath-violation, Card-playing, &c are very, *very* prevalent in this place."[9] Similarly disheartened, W. C. Strong described Tullahoma, Tennessee, as a "moral desert."[10] Much of the despair felt by delegates centered on the frustratingly temporary effects of their work. "If I rebuke profanity in a thousand men," George Hesser lamented, "they will do the same again! And while I have been talking against it in one tent foul oaths would be heard all around in other tents."[11] Nevertheless, some delegates chose to perceive permanent, positive changes in troop behavior. "Drunkenness is very rare indeed," A. D. Morton reported as he left service in the Army of the Cumberland. "Profanity is less than expected, and is rapidly declining."[12] William Winterbottom was similarly optimistic, believing the vice he encountered to be "no deeper than the surface."[13]

Christian Commission workers understood that a well-disciplined army was essential to expediting victory and restoring the Union. R. B. Godfrey, working at Camp Parole, Annapolis, highlighted the need for military efficiency, warning that a failure to reform the behavior of the Union armies could gift the Confederacy victory. "Unless there is a speedy & radical change for the better," he wrote, condemning the gambling and profanity he observed daily, and comparing the behavior of the Union armies unfavorably to that of Confederate soldiers, "we need to tremble exceedingly in view of the result."[14] He cautioned that only "right conduct as well as a righteous cause" would guarantee success. For Christian Commission delegates, immoral and ungodly behavior constituted a more pressing manifestation of evil than did the threat of the Confederate enemy.[15] Eliminating vice and encouraging moral behavior in the armies was thus vital to the successful execution of the war, not simply because it would make more focused and hence more lethal soldiers but because it would reflect the righteousness of the Northern cause and would ultimately secure the blessing of God, without which military and spiritual victory would be impossible. Yet military triumph alone was not enough. The Christian Commission believed eradicating immorality was also integral to its evangelizing mission and winning an eternal, spiritual victory through the conversion of the armies. The priority in tackling vice in the army was not only the outward comportment of the men, but also their inward morality and the state of their souls. Criminal and vicious behavior served as a visible indicator of internal moral and spiritual decay and was thus a gauge of the progress of the USCC in cleansing and converting the armies. Whether through the distribution of moral literature, preaching, prayer meetings, or personal conversation with soldiers, the work of Christian Commission delegates was channeled toward one ultimate aim: bringing souls to Christ.

Conversion was (and remains) crucial to evangelical Christians. Despite major doctrinal differences between nineteenth-century American evangelical denominations, four common features united evangelicals: a belief in the atoning death of Christ; a commitment to the spiritual truths laid out in scripture; the public, social expression and performance of the teachings of Christ; and an obligation to seek and convert other souls.[16] Evangelicals were defined above all else by their quest for a crisis-like conversion experience; that is, the transformation (and ultimately salvation) of the soul by the grace of the Holy Spirit. This conversion followed a period of "conviction" during which the penitent sinner underwent a personal struggle for faith, and ultimately resulted in the convert being "born again." The USCC's commitment to conversion was built upon the theological realignments of the previous several decades. The Calvinist orthodoxies that reminded congregants of the total depravity of man and the predestination of the soul were increasingly called into question in the late eighteenth century by a new generation of populist, radical preachers and theologians who placed a greater emphasis on the ability of human beings to influence their own spiritual fates. It is no coincidence that this transformation of American theology followed in the wake of the Revolution. As common people agitated for political representation on an even keel with elites, they also claimed greater autonomy over their spiritual lives, championing the ability of the individual to question the teachings of educated ministers and to forge a personal relationship with God.[17] This crisis of authority initiated a new wave of religious pluralism characterized by populist sects that catered to a newly democratized, enlightened congregation.[18] These denominations increasingly embraced the idea that humans were capable of choosing faith and accepting salvation. Come the 1820s, radical theologians like Nathaniel Taylor and Charles Grandison Finney pushed the envelope further, preaching the importance of free will, the perfectibility of the soul, and the responsibility of the already converted to educate and persuade the unregenerate to choose to accept salvation.[19] God was still central to the process and held ultimate power over the fate of the human soul, but, no longer burdened with innate depravity, humans could actively choose to reject sin and live morally, and thus make themselves and others candidates for salvation.[20] As Lincoln Mullen puts it, "religion shifted from being an identity that nineteenth-century Americans could inherit to being an identity they were obliged to choose for themselves."[21]

This theology was, at its heart, postmillennial. This eschatological position held that the prophesied Second Coming of Christ would be preceded by a thousand-year utopia on Earth, and that human beings were capable of bringing about this millennium of peace, justice, and Christian ethics.[22] Postmillennialism was inherently optimistic, especially in comparison to the premillennialist position, which argued that the Second Coming, a destructive and terrible act of cleansing and remorseless judgment initiated at an arbitrary time by God's will alone, would occur without the intervention of human action.[23] By contrast, the centrality of human action in the postmillennial interpretation meant that Christians had an urgent duty to reform and moralize the entire world in order to create the longed-for utopia. As James Moorhead and others have explored, American Protestantism flourished on the premise that America was "a new Israel, destined to build up the waste places of Zion in preparation for the latter-day glory."[24] It was this premise that fueled the evangelical reform enterprises of the antebellum period as evangelicals, believing that a millennial utopia would result from "the victory of the good in a war between cosmic powers for control over the spirit," attempted to rid the nation of the sins and vices that would impede America's progress toward apocalypse.[25] The advent of the Civil War intensified this postmillennial conviction in certain circles, contributing to a rhetoric of impending cataclysm stridently articulated by Protestant preachers. In their eyes, America had been tasked by God with a providential mission to perfect the world in preparation for the millennium.[26] Given that a necessary step in paving the way for the Second Coming of Christ was the conversion of the entire world, the Civil War not only suggested that American society was reaching some sort of boiling point but also appeared to provide a perfect opportunity for mass evangelism.[27]

Many of the most vocal and prominent members of the Christian Commission subscribed to this vision of America as a nation blessed by Providence and tasked with bringing about God's Kingdom on Earth, and concurred that the Civil War was the great battleground where this destiny would be fulfilled. Delegate E. E. Adams spoke excitedly of the progress he perceived in the armies and the brightness of America's future. "Our future as a people is to be pre-eminently glorious," he wrote. "I do not forget that we are still sinful; but we have drawn the sword for a good and holy purpose; multitudes in our land are bowing in heart to the great God."[28] At a public USCC celebration at the Philadelphia Academy of Music in 1864, the tide of the war already firmly turned in favor of the Union, W. J. R. Taylor, corresponding secretary of the American Bible Society, echoed this optimism. "A better day is coming," he promised the four thousand–strong audience. "I see the mountain tops already thick with gold, and down their shaggy sides roll the billows of glorious light. We stand to-day on Lookout mountain, and see nothing but liberty—on Lookout mountain fighting God's battle in the name of God."[29] The fate of the world, USCC evangelists believed, was tied to the conversion of the Union armies. Were enough soldiers converted, Commission Treasurer Joseph Patterson argued, a snowball effect would be initiated that would convert the whole country, an effect that would extend beyond the borders of America. Loudly proclaiming the role of America as God's redeemer nation, he wrote, "the best *interests of the world* demand that the power of religion be felt in our army. . . . The arbitrament of the world's destiny, the fate of the liberty of mankind, depends on the American army and navy."[30] Patterson believed that the USCC's work would lead to a global moral reformation, which would, in turn, catalyze the long-awaited utopian millennium. This postmillennial framework drove the Christian Commission to prioritize the evangelization of the Union Army and Navy and to devise and adapt methods deemed effective in converting souls, devoting millions of dollars to applying these methods in the field.

THE POWER OF PRINT

Perhaps the work for which the USCC became best known was its widespread distribution of religious literature among Union soldiers. This was an established and popular method of proselytization among antebellum evangelical reformers. Technological advances such as the cyclical steam press, cheaper paper production, bookbinding machines, and more efficient transportation fueled a boom in religious publishing before the Civil War.[31] Religion, according to Peter Wosh, "dominated the antebellum book market," with national reform societies such as the American Tract Society and the American Bible Society buying their own stereotype plates and presses to enable them to churn out millions of inexpensive books, pamphlets, and tracts.[32] By 1830, the American Bible Society was printing over a million Bibles a year, enough to supply over a third of households in the

United States.[33] The American Tract Society was producing five million tracts annually by 1828, weaving moral lessons into compelling narratives, often using sensationalist language to instruct through entertainment.[34] The scale of this investment illustrates how, at the apogee of antebellum moral reform, evangelicals "idealized the power of print" to educate, convert, and ultimately save American souls.[35] By attempting to flood the nation with religious literature, they sought to combat and overcome negative secular influences, transmit doctrine in a digestible format, reach new congregations of potential converts, strengthen doctrinal identities, and knit together scattered communities of believers.[36]

The work of the Christian Commission translated these endeavors to the Civil War battlefront. Delegates were tasked with supplying troops with vast quantities of Bibles, tracts, religious newspapers, prayer books, and other printed materials in the hope that engaging seriously with these texts would eventually lead these men to embrace Christ and achieve salvation.[37] This was no small undertaking. According to the USCC's *Annals,* the value of the literature distributed by the Commission amounted to an estimated $1,034,327.35 over the course of the war.[38] This included, according to official records, 1,466,748 Bibles and Testaments, 1,370,953 hymn and psalm books, 8,308,052 knapsack books, 767,861 magazines and pamphlets, 18,126,002 newspapers, and 39,104,243 tracts.[39] The Bible Society and the Tract Society, pioneers of the religious literature approach, collaborated with the USCC during the war, printing texts on their behalf and relying upon USCC delegates to distribute large volumes of reading matter. A closer look at the rationale behind this tactic reveals the importance of material items like books as tools of evangelization.

The USCC identified a clear and pressing want for this reading matter among the troops as men sought to distract themselves from the tedium and trauma of army life. "Everywhere men are ready and waiting," F. N. Pelobet reported; "the religious paper neglected at home is read here: the tract, scorned and wasted at home, is grasped eagerly here with a 'thank you.'"[40] From Fairfax Courthouse, P. S. Pratt reported "frequent + earnest calls for *hymn books*—also for Bibles."[41] This thirst for reading material was, by and large, indiscriminate, and the USCC was all too aware of this.[42] "I fear often if we had a supply of secular reading it would be greatly preferred," George Hesser mused in August 1864.[43] The Commission's expensive and carefully coordinated system of distribution was designed to flood the camps with moral literature, keeping the balance of available literature firmly skewed against secular texts, and thus eliminating the competition it posed for the attention of the men.[44] George Stuart identified three positive effects stemming from the distribution of literature and the establishment of

EVANGELIZATION AND THE PRINTED WORD 67

libraries in the army: "preventing gambling and other vices of idleness . . . cheering and invigorating the invalid, and . . . consoling and directing the troubled soul."[45] He and his colleagues hoped that literature, in an environment where over 90 percent of white soldiers were literate and printing and transportation innovations had made cheap, disposable reading material readily available, would be a spiritually nourishing distraction from the sinful temptations that stalked the army camp.[46] As delegate George Ainsworth concluded, "if not furnished with mental aliment in printed form, [the soldier] will resort to games and then to gambling, or to the rough and profane amusements so rife in camp."[47]

The Commission produced religious literature in various formats, mindful of the different circumstances in which men might be prevailed upon to read and the different approaches and attitudes they might bring to that reading. The USCC sought to shape how men engaged with religious literature to maximize its impact on their behavior and the state of their souls. In particular, several types of texts distributed lent themselves to what Rolf Engelsing calls an "intensive" mode of reverential, ritualized (re)reading.[48] While the mass production of cheap—and hence more disposable—texts ushered in more casual, desultory reading practices in the nineteenth century, religious texts were frequently afforded greater devotion. Readers memorized religious texts, reread them, and read them aloud to each other in an attempt to access the moral truths within.[49] The USCC encouraged similarly intensive engagement with the texts they produced and distributed, believing they had the ability to stimulate spiritual reflection and ultimately aid men in their struggle toward conversion.

This is well illustrated by Francis Boynton's account of reading a Silent Comforter (a plaque with a large-print Bible verse on it) hanging on the wall of his hospital ward while he lay recuperating from illness: "My eyes turned again + again from the blank walls to the [plaque]. I read it over + over again, although the words were perfectly familiar, + they made a deep impression upon my mind."[50] Another delegate also testified to the efficacy of intensive reading, reporting, "I have seen many a soldier's face grow sober and thoughtful as they have traced out the tract, and I have no doubt the woodcut in our rooms at Chattanooga has sent many a man to his tent seriously pondering."[51] Meanwhile, George Stuart wrote to a Tennessee soldier who had received several books from a delegate, and wanted to extract the greatest benefit from their texts. "Let me ask you earnestly, in reading these few books, to look upon them as God's Messengers," Stuart wrote. "Try to consider the words and the ideas as all meant *for you* and withal—keep looking up—and if anything may seem to you hard to understand—think on them all the more—do not reject this, and read the Bible for explanation of such passages also—for although men call it "mysterious" sometimes, yet I rather think that it is the key to all heart-mysteries—no matter how great. Above all pray—Prayer carries the wanderer to Jesus . . . Prayer is its own answer, my Brother."[52] Testaments, too, were designed to be read intensively.[53] Delegates reported that soldiers often read Testaments thoroughly, rereading the texts multiple times to better internalize the ideas within them so that the act of reading became comforting and almost ritualistic in its familiarity.[54] This, it was hoped, reinforced the messages of the Gospels and created a state of mind conducive to conviction and conversion.

The Bibles distributed by the USCC, bulkier and more expensive than the slimmer Testaments, were also intended for repeated, intensive reading and often formed the basis of communal reading experiences intended to bring men closer to God in the ways Stuart described. Bible classes were established in several regiments, both by religiously inclined soldiers and under the supervision of USCC delegates, providing a source of companionship and social interaction, intellectual stimulation, and, the USCC hoped, spiritual enlightenment. Guidelines issued by the YMCA to soldiers at Chickamauga emphasized the benefits of collaborative, focused reading, suggesting that students concentrate on one verse and ask questions of each other to push their understanding further. "Remember, this book was written for you personally," the guidelines read. "Give at least twenty minutes each day to the study. Memorise the verse you like best. Always ask God to help you understand it and then believe He will."[55] Soldiers often reported the positive effects of Bible classes; one man recalled that "the Holy Spirit seemed to open our understanding, as we talked together about the sweet truths of inspiration."[56] Testimonies like this reveal that it was not merely the form in which the word of God was packaged, but also the experience of reading that word, that helped men in their search for salvation. The USCC sought to shape that experience wherever possible.

Nevertheless, the exigencies and caprices of war meant that men did not always have the time or energy to dedicate themselves to intensive, reflective reading, and the Christian Commission was anxious to provide reading material that could be more quickly and easily digested while still making an impression on the soul. Some text forms tacitly acknowledged through their brevity and subject matter that reading was often a hurried activity sandwiched in pockets of time between drills, dress parades, and fighting—soldiers did not always have the luxury of time for Bible study and intensive personal reflection.[57] The USCC's widespread distribution of religious newspapers provided a different reading experience that also contributed to the dissemination of the Commission's central message. Newspapers, already a staple of American society before the war, became "an urgent necessity of life" when relatives were

EVANGELIZATION AND THE PRINTED WORD 69

parted, and the population clamored for war news.[58] Families frequently sent local newspapers to their sons and brothers to remind them of home, and the religious newspapers provided by the USCC supplemented these, also providing a vital link with the home front and subtly reinforcing and extending the moral influence of home and mother to the distant army camp.[59]

The demand for newspapers was high, and the USCC struggled to keep stock plentiful and up-to-date, even at the end of the war when they were circulating over one and a half million papers per month to the various armies.[60] As with many aspects of the Christian Commission's work, the Executive Committee adhered to its policy of interdenominationality by distributing titles published by all the major evangelical denominations and representing various interests within the Commission from the *Presbyterian Standard* and the *National Baptist* to the *New York Evangelist* and the *Christian Times*.[61] These newspapers, unlike extracts from scripture and religious tracts, were distributed more as an alternative to undesirable entertainments and camp pursuits than as instruments of conversion, but they were important in cultivating a regular national readership for a press that interpreted politics, society, and culture through a religious lens and in transmitting this interpretation to the armies.[62] Nor was their evangelical potential entirely lacking; newspapers, as the first annual report stressed, had the power to "present Gospel truths in articles terse and attractive, and illustrate their benign power by narratives of conversion, revivals, and hallowed Christian examples of holy living and happy dying."[63]

A format more explicitly designed to encourage reflection and conversion was the tract. Tracts were simple narratives, often only four or five pages long, containing a clear moral truth at their heart. This format developed in the antebellum period in response to the perceived threat from secular publishers churning out cheap, sensational fictional texts. Religious reformers, keenly aware of the potential power of the printing press but also convinced of the moral degradation caused by novels and adventure stories, developed the tract format as a means to "engage the enemy on his own ground, on his own terms, with his own weapons," by creating accessible, popular texts that were cheaply produced, easily distributed, and firmly aimed at a mass plebeian audience.[64] The Christian Commission made widespread use of this design during the Civil War, the versatile format allowing writers to vary the content and themes of the tracts. Many revolved around the "sinner's prayer," an oft-repeated formula of a wretch praying for salvation and receiving it, often instantaneously.[65] Some USCC tracts appealed directly to the experiences and preoccupations of soldiers, using scenes of army life or military metaphor as their basis (for instance, "The Little Captain"), while others, such as "Come to Jesus" and "The Blood of Jesus," were more general.[66]

"The Lamp and the Ticket," a tract widely distributed by the USCC, highlighted the ways in which tract writers blended ancient scriptural lessons with contemporary, quotidian scenarios to illustrate how Christians could apply the laws of the Bible to nineteenth-century life. Using the metaphor of a railroad conductor inspecting tickets as its central device, the tract concluded with a powerful combination of the ancient and the modern:

> The honest man, who holds in his hand a genuine ticket, shrinks not from the light, yea, he rather courts, and delights in its brilliance, inasmuch as, the brighter it is, the more fully and speedily it makes manifest his unquestionable title to be where he is. "For everyone that doeth evil hateth the light, neither cometh to the light, lest his deeds should be reproved. But he that doeth truth cometh to the light, that his deeds may be made manifest, that they are wrought in God" (John 3:20–21).[67]

The Christian Commission hoped that reading these simple tracts, whether hurriedly in a brief lull in routine or carefully and repeatedly while awaiting marching orders or convalescing in hospital, would lead men to consider the fate of their souls and to eschew immoral behavior in favor of spiritual contemplation and improvement.

With characteristic optimism, most delegates were anxious to emphasize the positive reception that greeted the distribution of religious literature. Instances of rejection were usually mentioned to demonstrate their rarity and to affirm that literature was almost universally well received. Josiah Zimmerman wrote to the Philadelphia office about the perpetual shortage of reading material at his station and the men's hunger for fresh books and papers, reporting that "one refused the word of God! Thank God only one!"[68] Most accounts did not mention such rejections. E. T. Quimby spoke warmly of the "unexpected readiness of the soldiers to receive religious reading and religious instruction," while L. W. Brinkwall, struggling to cope with the demand for literature at City Point, confidently reported that he had "reason to believe what was given to them was thoroughly read."[69] Frequent requests for supplementary deliveries of reading matter to sate demand in the camps prompted the USCC to escalate its distribution of literature as the war progressed and to diversify the ways in which troops were supplied to maximize the number of recipients, and thus the number of potential converts.

The Christian Commission's system of distribution was intended to reach every soldier and sailor fighting for the Union.[70] In conjunction with auxiliaries such as the American Bible Society and the American Tract Society, the USCC distributed religious literature in various translations—chiefly German, but also

French, Norwegian, Dutch, and other languages spoken by the sizable immigrant portion of the Union armies, with delegates reporting that troops were "very much pleased to get tracts in their own language."[71] Delegates also took unilateral steps to establish literacy programs and impromptu schools for Black troops, efforts that became somewhat more systematized by the end of the war.[72] The Commission began distributing the *Freedman* newspaper on behalf of the American Tract Society and eventually collaborated with the American Bible Society to source Bibles for Black troops and freed people.[73] But the USCC, spying a prime constituency of potential converts, realized that tracts and Bibles would be of little spiritual use to those who had been systematically denied access to literacy. "Something must be done to teach them," E. F. Williams declared.[74] There was a flurry of activity toward this end late in the war.[75] Delegates attached to the Twenty-Fifth Corps provided "tables, primers, spelling-books, writing-books, black-boards, slates, pens, and ink—in short everything that was needed to give to all an opportunity for mental improvement."[76] Black troops were put to work building log-cabin schoolrooms at stations along the James River, and in the closing months of the war the Commission began placing advertisements in religious newspapers calling for teachers to staff schools for newly emancipated people.[77] The delegates involved in these efforts were eager to testify to their popularity, ingenuity, and success.[78] The tone of these reports frequently echo the clumsy blend of pride, idealism, paternalism, and prejudice found in the writings of white officers such as Thomas Wentworth Higginson.[79] Delegates emphasized the naïveté and eagerness of their students—one recalled a young man working late into the night, studying by the light of a campfire to "decipher his letters."[80] "It is not an uncommon thing to see them go forth in the morning, to a twenty-four hours' picket duty, with a musket in one hand and a book in the other," another claimed.[81] Stationed outside Richmond in September 1864, J. W. Harding could not hide his surprise when he described teaching a "brawny cavalry six-footer," who was eventually able to "spell out the words which shall unseal for him the fountains of knowledge."[82] Nor could Z. R. Farrington, who marveled that the Black teamsters he was teaching "certainly learn to read as fast as the white do, and are very earnest in their efforts."[83]

The primary aim of the lessons was clear: to equip Black men with the tools they needed to read and absorb the word of God for themselves. The supposed rewards spoke for themselves. "Those taught in our schools were more obedient and respectful to their officers," Williams boasted. "Discipline was improved; habits of vice were checked, and in many cases genuine religious interest was excited."[84] "To be able to read the New Testament was to these new-made men a marvellous acquisition," Lemuel Moss claimed, "and to own the Book itself was to secure an incalculable prize."[85] Delegates, unable to break free of prevailing tropes about Black intelligence and mental capacity, frequently praised what they saw as the innate piety and simple faith of Black troops ("a child's faith, true to fact, whatever may be thought of its form," A. P. Johnson suggested).[86] To reach maturation, this faith needed only the careful direction and instruction provided by the Bible. Distribution of religious literature among Black troops—and the teacher recruitment drives and makeshift schools that accompanied this work—thus fit into the Commission's wider priorities of getting the most suitable reading matter into the hands of individuals in the context most conducive to its consumption.

Broadly speaking, the Commission attempted to make reading material available to soldiers wherever they might be; in USCC reading rooms in major cities, daily and weekly newspapers were regularly restocked, and libraries full of moral literature were provided for men passing through or recuperating from wounds, with placards placed around each reading room exhorting men to "sit down and read."[87] Even on Union gunboats, which, as Michael Bennett has explored, were often seen as strongholds of irreligion and immorality, the USCC set up a system of supply, hiring small boats to ferry between vessels delivering bimonthly packages of books and newspapers.[88] At sea for months at a time, in an environment that was cramped, dangerous, and even more exclusively male than the army camp, the sailor's separation from the moral influence of home was more complete than the soldier's, and therefore made him not only a more urgent target for the Christian Commission's evangelization but also a potentially more grateful recipient of religious guidance.[89]

The loan library system established in 1864 indicated the Commission's commitment to providing ready access to spiritually and intellectually stimulating material for all Union soldiers and sailors. Proposed by Joseph Thomas, chaplain of the Eighty-Eighth Illinois Volunteers, the libraries originated in the Western theater of war but soon expanded eastward, with over four hundred libraries in operation by 1865.[90] Made up of secondhand books donated by citizens and cut-price contributions from publishing houses friendly to the USCC, each library offered an extensive catalog of books "in good variety—religious, historical, scientific, and poetical—such a library as any soldier or officer who cares to read will be glad to have access to."[91] Each library was different, but the catalog for the library at Harpers Ferry illustrates the range of texts to which soldiers had access. From T. S. Arthur's popular temperance tract, *Ten Nights in a Bar Room* (1854), to volumes of Chambers's *Pocket Miscellany;* from Nehemiah Adams's discourses on *Christ a Friend* (1858) to George Quackenbos's *First Lessons in Composition* (1851), the loan libraries compiled both religious and secular

EVANGELIZATION AND THE PRINTED WORD

literature—so long as the secular literature was deemed sufficiently moral and educational for the purposes of the USCC.[92] The libraries performed a variety of functions that all ultimately contributed to the USCC's mission. One chaplain observed that the scheme "has a deep and abiding influence—intellectually, morally, and spiritually," and reports from delegates in the field supported this positive assessment.[93] Charles Wiener, in charge of library number 228 aboard the US flagship *New Hampshire,* spoke to the moral influence of the books, reporting that "the library is having a good effect. It is lessening profanity and intoxication," as did the delegate-supervisor of library number 11, who noted a "marked improvement in the social life and deportment of the patients and attendants of this hospital . . . since the introduction of the libraries."[94]

The above assessment of the behavior of the patients implied that a moral army and navy was also, by extension, a docile and obedient one. However, such sentiments were relatively rare: delegates paid greater attention to the signs of moral self-improvement and spiritual awakening among the troops than they did to their tractability. More typical, in the case of reports about libraries, were assessments of their contribution to conviction and conversion. Delegates in charge of libraries were obliged to fill in monthly reports detailing statistics, such as how many times each volume had been borrowed, and also to submit for the Executive Committee's consideration interesting incidents concerning the soldiers' use of the books.[95] One note attached to the Harpers Ferry ledger illustrated the conversionist priorities of the USCC. W. A. Kelton recounted in some detail his encounters with a French soldier, Jules Bernard of the Fifth New York Cavalry, who, when first approached, scornfully rejected Kelton's offer of a testament:

> He appeared to be intelligent and well informed. I asked if he would like to read a French book. He eagerly replied Yes, intimating at the same time that it must be something besides the Testament. I carried him *No. 87,* "Lucile, ou La Lecture de la Bible". I did not see him again for two or three days. When I saw him again he manifested great pleasure + began to tell me about the book. It had taken hold of him + now he asked for a *Bible—*a *French Bible.* On the fly leaf of the book he had written, "I like this book. I will read the Bible. Give me one . . . Please send me a French Bible." I sent to Baltimore today for a copy for him. May God bless it to his conversion.[96]

Kelton's account of his meetings with Bernard illustrates several elements of the USCC's method. It not only reveals the Commission's commitment to ministering to the immigrant elements in the armies but also demonstrates how delegates tailored their approach to different individuals, recognizing that one method of proselytizing would not necessarily touch all. The report also exemplifies how delegates relied on personal conversations to form connections with their charges and used these conversations to invite confidence and persuade previously stubborn soldiers to consider the USCC message. Finally, and most importantly, Kelton's closing prayer that Bernard's new Bible might bring about his conversion emphasizes the fundamental aim of the entire work of the USCC: to win converts for Christ.

TALISMANS AND TEARS

The USCC remained convinced of the power of literature as a vehicle of moral education and a stimulus for conversion throughout the war. Delegate reports and official publications were filled with stories that aimed to prove that handing out Bibles and tracts *worked*. The scenario most often presented as evidence that soldiers were receptive to reading matter distributed by the USCC and could be turned away from vice through it was that of the delegate persuading soldiers to exchange their playing cards or dice for reading matter. Most of these anecdotes implied that the troops' attachment to gambling and card playing was fickle and rooted solely in boredom and that, if given the opportunity, they would rather be reading. When William Winterbottom approached a group of cardplayers, proposing to trade their cards for Testaments, the men "seemed highly pleased and said they had got at the cards for the want of something better to do."[97] "We don't care for the cards," one gambler told J. A. Hough as he distributed religious newspapers at Fort Reynolds, "only we must have something to do."[98] Reports like this lent weight to the USCC's policy of flooding the camps with literature, so that troops' first instinct in moments of idleness would be to pick up a Bible or tract rather than to shuffle a deck of cards. While some delegates expressed concern that the effect of such exchanges would only be temporary, the recurrence of these exchange stories within delegate reports emphasized the USCC's belief in the power of religious literature to eradicate sinful behavior and create a morally upright army worthy of the righteous Union cause.[99]

Furthermore, the exchange of books for dice or cards suggests that the books themselves, as physical objects and bartering tools, were items powerful and holy enough to lead men from vice—even before the words within were consulted. The totemic power of books was hardly a novel concept in 1860s America. As various book historians have explored, books as objects could and did perform multiple nontextual functions—as gifts, as ornaments, as relics, as tools for divination, and as magical talismans, for instance.[100] Once status symbols

EVANGELIZATION AND THE PRINTED WORD

as indices of wealth, books did not automatically lose their symbolic power as objects with the advent of the print revolution. This was particularly true of religious texts—family Bibles, for instance, were frequently handed down and adorned with careful inscriptions, and books were rebound and repaired as repeated reading wore them out.[101] The reverential treatment of books also had a commercial edge; as Alice Fahs argues, the practice of owning and displaying books, whether religious or not, was indicative of a material culture that "celebrated the proliferation of objects."[102] The Christian Commission, however, was concerned more with the religious, often miraculous potential of these objects, than with their commercial value.

The best illustration of this concern was another trope that cropped up frequently in USCC workers' writings: the bullet-stopping Bible shielding its carrier from the physical dangers of war. William Schaeffer, for example, encountered a soldier who claimed to owe his life to his Testament. "A bullet struck the Testament and entered the Breast came out of his side of it penetrating just the edge of his left lung," the soldier told Schaeffer, declaring, "the Testament prevented the ball from going directly through the Breast."[103] In another attempt to prove that reading far supplanted gambling in the hearts of common soldiers, one delegate maintained "a soldier never goes into battle with [cards] on their person, but they frequently carry their Testaments."[104] This implied that soldiers would be ashamed to die with the trappings of vice on their persons, and that they placed greater trust in the word of God as a talisman on the battlefield than they did in cards and dice. The supposedly miraculous physical protection provided by Bibles and Testaments was interpreted as a sign of the blessings the Union Army would receive if it collectively reformed its behavior and converted to evangelical Christianity.

The dual function of religious books and pamphlets—as texts and as objects—was reflected in the ways delegates measured the impact of their work distributing literature. Frequently, delegates presented the work of distributing literature as a matter of life and death, maintaining that the work had the power to save men's lives—whether on Earth or in eternity. Religious literature did more than save life on the battlefield by providing physical protection. According to delegate reports, it also led to the salvation of men's souls for eternity through conversion, thus fulfilling the great aim of the Commission. B. Crist was inspired by the enthusiasm with which one tract he distributed was received and remained confident that it "proved the Power of God not only to awaken but to convert the Soldier to Christ."[105] J. A. Hough recounted one man's conversion experience brought about by a copy of Richard Baxter's phenomenally popular seventeenth-century Puritan devotional text *Call to the Unconverted* left in his barracks by

Hough and his colleagues. The man picked up the book because he could find nothing else to read and later told Hough, "for three days, I was almost constantly in tears, + then I began to think less of myself and *more about Jesus,* and soon his love came into my heart. Such sweet love!"[106] This particular conversion, as well as illustrating the swiftness with which a soul could be filled with grace, demonstrated the importance of making religious literature readily available and the impact the printed word alone could have on the souls of the unregenerate.

While some soldiers found salvation by reading texts distributed by the USCC alone and in private, delegates were instructed wherever possible to combine the distribution of literature with a more personal, active ministry, using the handing out of books and tracts as a prime opportunity to strike up conversation with soldiers, to help them understand the texts they had been given, and to ascertain their spiritual state. E. Colton described how delegates combined the circulation of reading material with personal ministry, reporting that, at the Martinsburg station where he worked, "we mainly give the reading with our own hands, see where it goes, drop a word where we can . . . and give all the *right influence* we can."[107] The combination of reading material—that could be consulted again and again and carried as a shield against moral and physical danger—and individual conversation was seen as effective in targeting souls and prompting men to consider their spiritual fates.

Religious literature distributed by the Christian Commission, therefore, was carefully designed in format, content, and availability to maximize the impact on the individual soul. The millions of books, newspapers, and pamphlets printed or ordered by the USCC, as well as the hours of delegate service dedicated to their distribution, illustrate the centrality of print to the Commission's conversionist mission. This branch of the USCC's work demonstrated the evangelical commitment to individual agency in the fate of one's soul, promoting independent, critical thought and revealing a fervent belief in the transformative power of the written word. The distribution of reading material served both to reform behavior by providing a virtuous distraction from vicious temptation and, more importantly, to regenerate the soul by encouraging not only the inculcation of moral lessons but deep, sustained reflection on one's spiritual state and the implications of an unconverted death.

CHAPTER FOUR

Preaching and Praying

The Christian Commission's attempts to convert the entire Union Army were not limited to the distribution of religious literature. The Commission also devised modes of ministry that sought to cultivate more sustained contact between the delegate and would-be converts, utilizing the spoken word to target men's souls and facilitate conversion. The principal vehicles for these spoken-word endeavors were sermons and prayer meetings. These methods of group proselytization were intended to promulgate the Commission's message effectively and immediately, making temporary congregations from groups of men banded together by the experience of war and catering to the peculiar nature of army camp life by capitalizing on men's boredom and anxiety. Christian Commission delegates used the spoken word to encourage spiritual reflection and aid conversion, expanding its audience by employing informal, populist styles of worship, transmitting simple theological messages through short sermons, and encouraging participation and a sense of community through inclusive prayer meetings. Delegates devised methods and spaces of worship that deliberately evoked memories of hometown religious instruction and ritual, reinforcing the legitimacy and morality of the USCC message and creating a powerful web of associations that bound God, home, and country together. These improvised acts of worship—collective and individual—constituted a sincere and responsive lived religion that was hostage to the receptivity of the intended congregants and the rhythms of the war but nonetheless vibrant, determined, and (at least for the delegates who created it) spiritually nourishing.

78   TABERNACLES IN THE WILDERNESS

The evangelicals of the Christian Commission were convinced of the efficacy of preaching in the army, not least because soldiers were considered a particularly receptive and, to an extent, captive audience. "No men in the world listen with deeper interest than our brave live volunteers, to living words of truth," George Stuart claimed, "none are moved more powerfully by generous and noble sentiments; none more hopeful for the power of the gospel."[1] One delegate, identified only as B. H., submitted a lengthy report on the work of the USCC to the Philadelphia office, endorsing Stuart's idea of the army regiment as the ideal congregation. He, too, believed that soldiers were, more than other groups, "willing to hear the truth."[2] Both Stuart and B. H. romanticized the soldiers' receptiveness to preaching, but B. H. also suggested practical reasons why the army might prove a particularly fruitful pulpit. Firstly, he argued that preachers addressing civilian congregations struggled to tailor their sermons to diverse audiences, whereas army preachers faced "but one style of audience"—young men with common concerns and preoccupations, many of them centered on the fragility of their own mortality and on the suffering they and their comrades endured daily. B. H. argued that separation from home and loved ones (which might also include fallen comrades) naturally turned soldiers' thoughts to spiritual matters and encouraged them to seek solace and "feel after God."[3] Furthermore, the daily routine of army life made sermons appealing to the men; in camp, the soldier's life was not "harassed by family cares" such as chores and breadwinning—secular concerns that distracted from the spiritual—but consisted instead of a constant stream of orders and disciplinary measures and, most importantly, of "so much wearisome monotony." This boredom, punctuated only by drills, inspections, mealtimes, and troop movement, meant any form of entertainment was a welcome distraction; this applied equally to sermons as to card games, impromptu dances, and baseball games. As B. H. wrote, "many who would not take the trouble to attend Church when at Home, would now gladly listen to anything or anybody," and, as they had tried to ensure that men had readier access to religious literature than secular, the delegates also took it upon themselves to ensure that men were regularly exposed to morally upright, spiritually comforting messages.[4]

Potential hurdles to establishing regular and effective preaching in the army—the interference of army routine, resistance from the troops, and conflict between delegates and chaplains, to name but a few—did little to diminish confidence in the mission. "If a man has a spark of fire in his soul," delegate Cyril Pearl wrote to G. S. Griffiths, president of the Baltimore branch, "he cannot spend six weeks with our soldiers in camp + hospital, and battle field, without having the spark intensely kindled. He cannot preach stale stereotyped sermons, nor waste words in commonplace conversations."[5] Many delegates reported positive results. At

Vermont Station, George Marc Smith found his sermons always well attended (particularly after the erection of a chapel tent), concluding "there are many educated men among our private soldiers."[6] E. P. Lewis, working in the Department of the Cumberland, was also impressed by the attentive and intelligent caliber of his congregations. "They will turn out en masse whenever they hear of preaching or religious service of any kind," he wrote. "They always listen to what you have to say with interest."[7] Like B. H., Lewis suggested that a soldier's heightened awareness of his own mortality was likely to drive him to spiritual contemplation, concluding that his services were well attended because soldiers "feel that they must decide the question of their soul's salvation now, knowing that now is the accepted time, now is the day of salvation."[8] Reports of overflowing chapel tents and captivated audiences seemed to prove the efficacy of preaching and its appeal to the men.

Delegates sometimes shared preaching duties with the regimental or hospital chaplain, but Christian Commission workers were often left alone to deliver sermons and organize worship for the troops. The Commission was thus anxious to recruit men who were well adapted to preaching, especially in unfamiliar situations and environments. "Ministers are wanted who can command audiences in the open air," one call for delegates read, acknowledging the ad hoc nature of many places of worship in the army camp, "men who have a knowledge of the world, experience in business, and ability in affairs, and those who are adapted to interest others in social meetings and personal intercourse."[9] The official commission (that is, the paper document) signed by each delegate at the start of his service, which contained details of his remit and obligations, also emphasized the worth of delegates "who can command audiences in the open air, of rank and file."[10] Delegates were bombarded with instructions and guidelines to shape their preaching: "addresses should always be brief, kind, patriotic, breathing of home, earnest and affectionate for the men, and fervent for Christ," one pamphlet advised.[11] Addresses to troops, whether individual or collective, should "encourage them in every right way, discourage every vice . . . explain the work of the Christian Commission in their behalf, cheer them to duty, and above all persuade them to become reconciled to God through the blood of His Son, if they have not already done so."[12] The advice given to delegates was thus designed to help them maximize the impact of their sermons on the souls of their listeners. While references to vice and duty suggest that the Commission was not unaware of its ability to influence the outward behavior of the troops or of the potential benefits of this control, the ultimate aim of the sermon was to bring about reflection and conversion among as many as possible.

IMPROVISING THE PULPIT

The USCC hoped that delivering sermons would occupy large periods of time in the delegate's daily routine, a fact reflected in the copious paperwork filled out by delegates at each stage of their service. The exit report obliged delegates to record the number of services they had attended (under the subheadings "Preaching," "Prayer," and "Funeral") and the total number of soldiers in attendance at these services.[13] The weekly reports demanded the same details, broken down by day and location, as did the daybooks kept at each station, and the monthly reports filled out by station chiefs.[14] Delegates often expressed regret that they had failed to keep accurate records of their activities, and were hence obliged to estimate these figures. A. Tobey, for example, claimed that his statistical report "does not by any means give the whole of what was done of the different sorts of labour indicated."[15] Regardless how approximate, these statistics do help to illustrate how strenuous and time-consuming preaching could be. Cyril Pearl, a minister from Freeport, Maine, and erstwhile agent of the American Tract Society, kept statistical records that reflected the variety of preaching duties a delegate might be expected to perform.[16] In his six weeks of service, Pearl preached forty sermons, most of them delivered on Sundays. In addition, he gave five patriotic addresses, three temperance lectures, led six prayer meetings, and officiated at eight funerals, three weddings, and seven baptisms.[17] Pearl's account also revealed the frequent traveling that shaped the delegate's working day—his field included various stations along a ten-mile stretch of the Potomac across Maryland and West Virginia (including Sandy Hook, Harpers Ferry, Weverton, and Knoxville), necessitating daily, time-consuming travel. It is likely that this grueling preaching schedule was not uncommon among USCC delegates.

With preaching constituting such a vital part of USCC ministry, delegates (most of whom were trained clergy or experienced lay preachers) adapted existing patterns and modes of preaching to the wartime situation to increase their sermons' impact on the souls of their listeners. Christian Commission preaching emerged from a distinct and dynamic American homiletic culture, characterized by extemporaneity, storytelling as a vehicle for simplified theological lessons, and a corpus of performative gestures and rhetorical motifs designed to captivate and move large audiences. It was not always so. In the eighteenth century, preachers explained complex doctrine through scholarly, rather than emotional, argument and employed conservative styles that took for granted the status of the preacher in the community as an unquestioned, distant figure separated from his congregation by his exegetical prowess and, physically, by the elevated pulpit.[18]

However, changes in religious and secular life from the turn of the century drastically altered this style. Disestablishment and a new populist, anticlerical attitude to worship described by Nathan Hatch as "a disdain for the wrangling of theologians, an assault on tradition, and an assertion that common people were more sensitive than elites to the ways of the divine," severely challenged the unquestioned authority and status of the preacher and led to the foundation of new,

Sample Delegate Exit Report, 1863. (Delegates' Statistical Reports, 1863–65, United States Christian Commission Records, 1861–66, Records of the Adjutant General's Office, Record Group 94, National Archives Building, Washington, DC)

independent theological seminaries that transformed religious education.[19] The flourishing of new, populist denominations that blurred the distinctions between the laity and the clergy—especially among the Methodists and Baptists—inspired innovation and experimentation in homiletic style as the scramble for converts gathered pace. The clergy competed not only with each other for the attention of Americans but with the rise of popular, secular literature that addressed the concerns and sentiments of everyday existence in a more entertaining and relatable manner than dry, esoteric sermons.[20] As a result, preachers began to employ techniques more common to secular writing, inserting anecdotes and personal stories into their sermons to make them more accessible and to prove the relevance of Christianity to daily life.[21] This also reflected the influence of frontier revivalists who specialized in emotional appeals and simplified, sentimentalized scriptural messages to reel in converts from all walks of life.[22] Preaching became more than an intellectual exercise: it became a performance.[23] The minister's tone of voice, physical appearance, use of gesture and silence, and ability to elicit an emotional response were all evidence of divine influence, and set the preacher apart as one "who seemed to see more clearly than ordinary mortals the divine realities of Christian faith and who spoke with eloquence, fervor, mental agility, and—so it seemed—inspiration."[24]

This was a different kind of separation from the aura of mystery and authority commanded by eighteenth-century preachers—the nineteenth-century preacher was humanized and encouraged to speak to his congregation as an equal, not a superior.[25] However, he was still set apart, not by his intellect, but by his *character*. As Roxanne Mountford has argued, the nineteenth-century clergy, galvanized by a "national anxiety over the status of white men as well as institutional anxiety within mainline Protestant denominations over the declining status of the minister," believed preachers should demonstrate their transcendent "manliness," not only in their sermons but in their everyday lives, through traits such as courage, sympathy with nature, earnestness, and benevolence.[26] Furthermore, evangelical preachers were prized for their magnetism and ability to captivate and move congregations. The camp revivals of the Second Great Awakening, for instance, saw charismatic firebrands like Lorenzo Dow employ colloquial, humorous, and often crude language alongside urgent and frightening calls for repentance, to whip large gatherings into emotional and physical frenzies, often moving people to call out or writhe on the ground in their search for salvation.[27] These measures were controversial and were often tempered and restrained in urban settings, but they left an indelible imprint on the face of American preaching.

Perhaps the most significant change in homiletic style by the middle of the century was the growing prestige attached to extemporaneity. The ability to preach from minimal notes not only gave the minister freedom to experiment with tone and gesture, creating a more engaging, exciting spectacle for the congregation. It also suggested divine inspiration and guidance and conveyed a sense of immediacy and urgency to the congregation, "allowing [the minister] to transmit the religious affections at the core of Christian belief and practice directly to his hearers," and proving the minister's piety and mental dexterity.[28] This made the sermon a collective, communal experience, binding the listeners to each other and to the minister in the act of receiving and interpreting the message. Given the nature of antebellum preaching described above, it is likely that many delegates, especially seasoned preachers accustomed to packed congregations and protracted meetings, did not preach from notes and instead extemporized their addresses. The fear that army business, such as roll call and maneuvers, could at any point interfere with worship meant short, off-the-cuff sermons were probably the norm.

Of course, this poses challenges for the historian seeking to examine how and what Christian Commission delegates preached. While several transcriptions of sermons delivered to congregations on the home front by returning delegates survive, very few texts of sermons preached in the field remain. Traces can be recovered from written transcripts and recollections, suggesting some common themes and messages employed by USCC preachers in their quest to captivate and convert the army. Delegates frequently noted, in their diaries and reports to the head office, the passages of scripture they used to frame their sermons. Their choices ran the gamut from Cain's murder of Abel (Genesis 4:5) to the baptism of Christ by John the Baptist (Matthew 3:14). Others focused less on compelling stories and more on questions of faith and of God's nature—one delegate stationed in Nashville was fond of Proverbs 23:26 ("my son, give me thine heart, and let thine eyes observe my ways").[29] Louis Miller Albright, stationed near Chattanooga in the final weeks of the war, diligently recorded the date, location, and scriptural reference for all twenty-nine of his sermons. He frequently recycled texts—perhaps for efficiency's sake, but perhaps also because the verses in question spoke to him and his congregations in profound ways. It is telling that his favorite verse, Jeremiah 8:22—"Is there no balm in Gilead; is there no physician there?"—which he used at least four times, reflected upon a civilization in strife and the prospect of God's power to punish or to heal.[30]

Robert Love, a delegate from Milwaukee stationed at City Point, enclosed a handwritten copy of his "Lay Sermon to the Soldiers" with one of his weekly reports to Philadelphia. His transcription supports the hypothesis that Christian Commission sermons, whether extemporized or not, were usually brief and simple. Love focused on what he saw as the three elements of Christian love:

God's love for humankind, humanity's love for God, and humans' love for one another. He peppered his address with scriptural evidence and exhorted his congregation to apply these messages to their present situation. "The want of this Love is the cause of the lamentation mourning and sadness that is around and among the people of the land," he told them. "This is the reason why you are here today, harnessed for the deadly strife on your way to the front." His concluding remarks emphasized the evangelism at the heart of the USCC's mission. Commanding his audience to consider the fate of their souls in the face of death, he asked them, "Why will you not give your hearts to Jesus Christ to day believe and be born again and Love God your Father and he will help you carry out the great Law of Love towards all men, will you do it?"[31] The themes and texts used by delegate preachers like Robert Love were diverse but were ultimately used to advance theologically simple messages designed to encourage moral behavior and spiritual reflection. The brevity and simplicity of the sermons, and their extemporized nature, catered to the rhythms and preoccupations of camp life around which delegates were obliged to work.

So, too, the spaces delegates adopted as their makeshift pulpits reflected the unpredictable and ad hoc nature of delegate service. Places of worship were often improvised by delegates, whether from hastily erected stockades, buildings temporarily requisitioned to act as chapels, or even church buildings that fell into Union hands.[32] As Benjamin Miller has recently noted, religious space was a fluid concept in the Civil War army camp, and these improvised spaces were rendered sacred by the rituals that bound worshippers together there.[33] The most common church was the open air, in a suitably large clearing in the army camp. While open-air chapels had their benefits—not least unlimited space and a sense of closeness with nature and God—they were also less than desirable for their poor acoustics and, more importantly, for their exposure to the frequently punishing elements. The weather was a constant nuisance for delegates attempting to hold services; H. H. White, stationed at Falmouth, Virginia, bemoaned that the inclement weather "for the most part rendered the holding of prayer meetings impracticable and preaching impossible" and obliged him to confine his work to making personal visits to the men huddled in their tents.[34] Delegates learned to make do with the resources available to them; Henry Safford, for instance, recalled that he "preached in various places, sometimes in regimental chapels . . . other times out of doors to wagon trains, ambulance trains, supply trains, + to regiments without chaplains."[35] Safford and his colleagues frequently preached in a multipurpose building nicknamed the "Camp Theater," relying, like many other delegates, on the grace of commanding officers when securing buildings and areas for communal worship.[36]

PREACHING AND PRAYING 85

Headquarters of the Christian Commission, Germantown, Virginia, 1863. (Library of Congress Prints and Photographs Division, Washington, DC; photograph by James Gardner)

USCC representatives were aghast at the difficulties soldiers faced in finding appropriate places for worship. That these places were frequently unsheltered and subject to disruption, they wrote to Secretary of War Simon Cameron at the beginning of the war, was "depriving the soldiers of the moral and religious influence so indispensable to elevation of character and efficiency in the public service."[37] To counteract the disadvantages of the makeshift chapels, not least the tendency of officers to commandeer worship spaces at a moment's notice, the USCC soon began purchasing canvas "flies" for use as chapel roofs, and swiftly graduated to funding portable, spacious chapel tents, which cost between $350 and $600. The dimensions of these large, sturdy tents varied according to design, but the standard, mentioned in several letters from the head office, measured thirty by forty feet.[38] To provide as many regiments as possible with a tent, the Executive Committee set aside $40,000 from its treasury in late 1864 to fund their manufacture.[39] In addition to these appropriated funds, newspaper appeals urged home front congregations to sponsor their own chapel tent.[40] "I cannot conceive of anything in which a benevolent Christian can make such a good investment for Christ, as in the presentation of a Chapel Tent to the Army," one read.[41] These appeals made much of the biblical antecedents to the chapel tent, suggesting that these "tabernacles in the wilderness" were descended from

86 TABERNACLES IN THE WILDERNESS

the portable structure built by the Israelites upon their escape from slavery and their journey to Canaan (Exodus 25–31, 35–40).[42]

This, then, was another way for civilians on the home front to pledge their allegiance to the Christian Commission; in addition to setting up a Ladies Christian Commission, church communities could collect donations to fund a chapel tent to further the proselytization of the Commission. An inscription on each sponsored tent, Lemuel Moss explained to one interested minister, highlighted the generosity and patriotism of the congregation in question.[43] The sponsored chapel tent linked the home front and the battlefield, acting as a surrogate extension of the stone or clapboard church building of a specific civilian community. Delegate W. W. Condit felt this association keenly when leading evening worship in the chapel tent at his station. "It was as refreshing to us as it was to the soldiers, thus to mingle with each other in the social prayer meeting," he wrote to the Philadelphia office. "It makes the army seem like home," he claimed of the atmosphere and space of the chapel tent.[44] Another delegate claimed that chapel tents provided "circumstances as homelike as possible."[45] Chapel tents, with their plain canvas and rustic benches, could replicate to a certain extent the spatial structure and sparse decor of evangelical church buildings, and were also reminiscent of the tent revivals of the antebellum period—more a feature of Southwestern frontier revivalism, but not unheard of in the North, and probably familiar to many rural recruits. Men even set about decorating the tents with branches of evergreen foliage and regimental insignia to make them more inviting.[46] The chapel tent, therefore, was intended to create a temporary, close-knit, homelike congregation deliberately separate from the secular discipline of the regimental camp. The USCC flag atop each tent acted as a crude steeple, positioning the tent as a nucleus, a rallying point within the camp. The second annual report urged soldiers to "go stand in the chapel tent, with its red, white, and blue flag afloat above it, inscribed 'U. S. Christian Commission Chapel,' crowded inside and around."[47]

Delegates were grateful for the shelter and semipermanence provided by the chapel tents, especially as they could double as storerooms, offices, reading rooms, post offices, and accommodation for delegates. The tents and other spaces set aside for Commission activities were used for more than preaching; in fact, the informal, nonliturgical format of evangelical worship meant that sermons frequently constituted just one part of a service, which might also include personal testimonies, singing, and prayer.[48] Edward Parmelee Smith recalled one service at a Commission chapel in Chattanooga that reflected the flexible structure of worship, writing that "the first half hour of the evening was given to prayer and relation of religious experience; then came the sermon by a Delegate or Chaplain, followed by a special service for those who desired to become Christians."[49] This variety involved different modes of participation from the makeshift congregation of soldiers: whereas sermons required careful listening and quiet reflection, other parts of the service gave troops the opportunity for more active, vocal involvement.

"SOULS SEEKING JESUS"

This was particularly true of prayer meetings, another important component of religious life in the armies. USCC delegates were instrumental in establishing regular prayer meetings throughout the Union armies and dedicated significant time and resources to leading and maintaining them, believing them to be a direct and effective way of reaching men's souls and bringing about the sought-after conversion crisis. The centrality of the prayer meeting to fieldwork was clear from material issued to Commission workers, which reminded delegates that a key part of their service was "encouraging special and stated meetings for prayer amongst the men in the field and in the hospital."[50] Delegates were urged to hold prayer meetings frequently, ideally daily, and where possible, to hold "two services a day, one social and the other preaching," so that through a combination of techniques requiring different modes of congregant participation—listening, praying, singing, and so on—the effect on the soul would be maximized.[51]

These meetings and the USCC's dedication to the format reflected the importance of prayer to Protestantism and especially to its nineteenth-century, evangelical, American offshoots. Protestantism, of course, was premised on the ability of the individual to communicate directly with God without an ordained intermediary. Evangelicalism emphasized this personal intercourse with the divine, placing the constant and evolving process of seeking salvation and grace at the heart of faith, a process furthered only through fervent and frequent prayer. The enduring centrality of petitionary prayer to American evangelicalism was evident in revivalistic worship methods such as the protracted meetings and anxious bench popularized in the 1820s and by the ways in which denominations across the evangelical spectrum adapted and customized such prayer-centric methods for their own uses.[52] For all the theological splinterings and methodological infighting that characterized the antebellum period, prayer held ecumenical appeal: as Rick Ostrander writes, "the efficacy of prayer was something that nineteenth-century Christians across the theological spectrum could agree on."[53]

An unshakable, universal commitment to the medium of prayer was reflected in Edward Norris Kirk's address at a meeting held in Philadelphia in May 1864 for

88   TABERNACLES IN THE WILDERNESS

the purpose of organizing a national network of Ladies Christian Commissions (discussed in chapter 2). Kirk urged the audience of female representatives to "pray for your country, the government, the army, and the navy," and expanded on this exhortation by launching into a lengthy discussion of the nature, purpose, and power of prayer.[54] "What is prayer?" he asked. "It is the heart, not the head, uttering itself to God. It is the soul pleading in the name of Christ, for great blessings which God alone can bestow. Wherein lies its power? In these elements, desire, humility, confidence, thankfulness. Specific and strong desiring is the essence of prayer; always consenting to be refused, always preferring God's will to its own."[55] Kirk's explanation placed the burden of communication with the divine on the human soul, justifying the USCC's sustained efforts to target the souls of soldiers. Furthermore, Kirk's definition of prayer reflected the Arminian tenet that human beings, although flawed and sinful and ultimately subject entirely to God's will, had the ability to influence their own salvation if their prayers were offered in a sufficiently meek and trusting manner.

Prayer was thus central to the conversion process, and prayer meetings were considered conducive to prayer and conversion because their communal format was designed to help converts encourage others to follow the same path to grace. The revivalists of the Second Great Awakening often encouraged sinners to talk about their experiences and their struggle for salvation before an audience, to "rise for prayer" by moving to the front of the gathering so that the whole congregation could focus their prayers on those in greatest spiritual anguish, and to cry out and respond vocally to prayers. These performative elements waxed and waned in popularity across the antebellum period, inflected heavily by concerns of class, region, race, and denomination, but the public, participatory nature of evangelical prayer meetings persisted into the postwar period (and, in fact, to the present day).

USCC delegates were keenly aware of the heritage of prayer meetings, which paved the way for camp worship, comparing their own work and experiences to earlier revivals that had informed and shaped their own religious maturation. B. H., in his lengthy report on the work of the Commission, alluded to the prominence of prayer in antebellum revivals and said proudly of prayer meetings he witnessed: "for sincerity + earnestness I can compare them only to the old Fulton St daily prayer meetings during the great Revival, + they must contribute to the benefit of the pastor as well as of the soldier."[56] While the relatively recent revival of 1857–58 provided the most obvious frame of reference for USCC delegates, many of whom had been involved in the YMCA's work publicizing and organizing prayer meetings in urban centers, some delegates were reminded of older experiences. Stephen Ives was enthusiastic about the conversions he witnessed from the outset of his labors at Broad Run Station, Virginia, and recalled that "after the first two days [the Spirit of God] came down with wonderful power, equal to any thing I ever saw in the great revivals of thirty years ago with which I was familiar."[57] Testimonies like this illustrated that prayer meetings were an established part of the fabric of evangelicalism long before the Civil War—it remained only to adapt the format to the highly structured but unpredictable environment of the army camp.

Certainly, the USCC believed the prayer meeting format to be ideal for its work in the field. Prayer meetings could gather any number of men with very little warning, and with no need for resources beyond a space large enough to accommodate the congregation. As with extemporized sermons, informal, impromptu prayer suited the contours of army life, which revolved around troop movements and army discipline. In more permanent locations and in periods of lull, regular meetings could be scheduled to cater to the demands of the troops, providing an alternative form of worship and religious instruction to sermons. Beyond these logistical considerations, however, prayer meetings were also seen as particularly effective in touching men's souls in an army setting. Delegates aimed to tap into the sense of brotherhood forged by the mutual experience of war and to foster companionship and solidarity by bringing men together in the intimate and personal but shared act of prayer.

The conversion process as conceived by nineteenth-century evangelicals was a complex continuum that began with inquiry, during which the sinner struggled through levels of doubt and fear before finally receiving grace. Would-be converts needed to constantly reaffirm their faith and to feed off encouragement and help from others during this often-lengthy process, for which a sense of community was vital. The army camp was the ideal environment to generate this community. Troops endured suffering, hardship, and boredom together. They confronted death together. "They sit . . . in their grave clothes," one delegate wrote of the prayer meetings, convinced that the meetings helped men to channel their thoughts to the state and destination of their souls.[58] In the view of the Christian Commission, the community of potential converts was further strengthened by shared memories of childhood religious instruction and maternal nurture. "The good seed sown in the Sunday-school, the church, the home, after long lying dormant," the Commission claimed, "is suddenly caused to germinate, grow, and ripen by the certainty of death near at hand. Then comes the delegate with his counsels, pointing the way of life."[59] Of the purpose of USCC prayer meetings, one pamphlet claimed, "we propose to encourage in them whatever is good, and keep fresh in their remembrance the instructions of earlier years."[60] The moral influence of childhood and home could be sustained and augmented by the extension of army prayer meetings to the home front; that is, by the construction of a national congregation through the collective power of prayer. As early as 1862, Commission literature began urging each town's Christian Commission branch to meet "if possible, every Sabbath evening, in the various churches, to pray for our country, for the conversion of our soldiers, and for the sick, the wounded, and the bereaved."[61] In sum, prayer meetings were considered a powerful medium that targeted souls by capitalizing on the bonds of solidarity between soldiers, their heightened sense of their own mortality, and their enduring loyalty and deference to the spiritual lessons ideally inculcated in them since childhood.

The reports and incidents collected by the USCC from delegates in the field were filled with positive accounts of prayer meetings that seemed to point to the format's success. At one of the hospitals at Nashville Station, A. B. Clough reported having "seen souls seeking Jesus," while his coworker R. A. Foster was cheered by the level of earnestness and enthusiasm demonstrated by his flock. "Much interest manifested by the congregations," he wrote of one prayer meeting in February 1865. "Some good impressions made a blessed day."[62] The ways in which delegates measured the success of the prayer meetings varied. The most obvious was by audience size; a well-attended prayer meeting satisfied delegates that an intense and sustained religious interest had gripped that particular camp or hospital, as in Chattanooga where, Edward Smith recalled, "a half hour before the time for service the chapel was often so crowded as to make it difficult to go through the aisle to the pulpit. Twenty, forty, and one night more than one hundred, asked for prayers."[63] Others used instances of interdenominational harmony as evidence of the power of prayer and its influence over the diverse armies. "In feeling and in action," Asa Farwell wrote of the congregation at one ecumenical prayer meeting at Bristoe Station, "they became *as one.*"[64]

Delegates were particularly encouraged when they felt they were making progress with the unconverted and reaching soldiers previously unreceptive to religion. Delegate A. S. Fuller was delighted to report significant progress among a previously unregenerate group. "Members who at first did not care to be seen in the meetings," he wrote, "would gather about the chapel + listen to the old familiar songs, + soon we found them inside the tent, + in some cases they were speedily brought to the foot of the cross, no longer ashamed of Jesus + his people."[65] Fuller believed invoking memories of home and childhood religious instruction could draw in the skeptical, and attributed much of the progress he witnessed to the associations reawakened by familiar religious melodies such as those sung in Sabbath schools, churches, and private homes. Some delegates needed no outward signs of success but relied instead upon faith when gauging the efficacy of prayer meetings. At Mount Pleasant Hospital, A. B. Chase was convinced that the prayer meetings he organized were divinely blessed: "felt that God has been with me in the noble work," he wrote. "In our public meetings in particular the Divine presence was evident."[66] Another delegate simply and confidently stated, "the Spirit of God has been with us."[67] Throughout the armies, therefore, delegates organized prayer meetings and reported great success—no matter how they measured it—back to the Executive Committee, convinced that the format was effective in reaching the souls of men otherwise exposed to vice and moral decay.

The precise format of prayer meetings, given their informal and often impromptu nature, varied widely, depending on the delegate, the size of his congregation, and the resources available to him. As with preaching services, delegates often had to improvise meeting places, sometimes squeezing as many men as possible into a tiny office or leading hundreds in prayer in the open air or on the deck of a gunboat.[68] One common feature of prayer meetings was the act of "rising for prayer"—a public display demonstrating that a congregant was actively seeking salvation, and prompted the rest of the audience to pray urgently for those searching for grace. This action owed much to the "'anxious seat'" popularized by Charles Grandison Finney during the Second Great Awakening, as men seeking prayer would move to the front of the gathering and crowd together. The delegate or chaplain then urged men to focus their prayers in the direction of the penitent, creating an intense atmosphere that disposed men to reflect on the state of their own souls. Delegates frequently measured the success of the prayer meetings by the number of men who rose for prayer and recorded these figures diligently, often commenting also on the progress of the most interesting cases. "One evening nine soldiers came forward for prayers in the Soldier's Rest and ten the following evening," George Marc Smith wrote in May 1864. "Two days after at Forest Hill Prison for deserters, among the most hardened men, five soldiers came forward for prayers and showed great penitence."[69] Delegates were swift to report positive statistics such as these as they seemed to indicate that quantifiable progress was being made in the overall goal of converting the whole army.

Although rising for prayer or otherwise demonstrating a wish to be saved featured in most meetings, the controversies over revivalist techniques that plagued certain denominations in the antebellum period spilled over into the Civil War, despite the USCC's constant assertions of its ecumenism. Finney's "new measures" had come under fire for their exuberance and perceived loss of control, and although his vibrant, enthusiastic brand of revivalism persisted along the frontier, it remained the dominant style only among Methodists, with the 1857–58 Revival ushering in a more sedate, introspective tone that eschewed passionate outbursts and uncontrolled bodily movements.[70] There was, therefore, no real consensus within American evangelicalism over *how* one should pray, as Asa Farwell's cutting dismissal of the perceived disorder of the new measures demonstrates. "Some of the Christian elements found there had been educated to noisy demonstrations, + to what might be easily turned from the 'order' divined in the gospel," he wrote of the congregation at Bristoe Station, Virginia.[71] He was, however, optimistic that such unseemly behavior had been effectively checked and brought in line with the decorum preferred by his own Congregationalism, claiming, "overt acts were restrained + a delightful harmony prevailed, not only in feeling but in the forms of worship."[72] Farwell was deeply concerned with worshiping in a manner congruent with his interpretation of the Bible, a manner he believed was the only true way to communicate with the divine. Thus, the delegates' own attitudes and beliefs about the best ways of accessing men's souls also impacted on the nature of prayer meetings and shaped the ways in which the men prayed.

To gauge the success of these techniques, and the Commission's overall progress in its ultimate mission to bring about the Kingdom of God on Earth, delegates made great efforts to ascertain and quantify the impact of prayer meetings and sermons on the souls of the unregenerate. This was frequently a frustrating and imprecise process; H. H. White, for instance, despaired in his exit report that he had "no opportunity for ascertaining the effect my visits had on the minds and hearts of the Soldiers."[73] Despite the difficulty of measuring the impact of prayer meetings, delegates demonstrated optimism and confidence in identifying certain visible and quantifiable signs that indicated a rise in religious interest, a deepening of convictions, or, in the most successful cases, a conversion experience.[74] "I cannot say with certainty that during these few weeks of labor any soul has been converted," Thomas Lewis wrote from Murfreesboro, "yet the faith of Christianity has been quickened—good seed sown, and a nucleus formed or strengthened in each battalion for the further success of religious effort and for greater growth in grace."[75] As evidence for this "quickening," Lewis pointed to the thriving Christian Associations he set up in three separate regiments. Many delegates were similarly encouraged by the dedication soldiers showed in setting up and maintaining their own prayer groups. Asa Farwell reported that 135 men had formed an interdenominational union in April 1864 "so that the ordinances of the gospel might be enjoyed *in full*," while S. S. Cummings observed a similar process at Camp Barry: "A fraternity has been formed consisting of about thirty Christian men banded together to sustain the meetings," he reported.[76] S. D. Holman also witnessed men setting up their own associations, noting that "backsliders resumed their professing duties, Christians were quickened and advanced, and a marked change came over the whole number of the attendants."[77]

Beyond a general escalation of religious interest, Christian Commission delegates sought to identify seismic changes in the lives of individuals that might indicate conversion. In particular, delegates looked for physical signs of spiritual anguish and introspection to measure the influence of the prayer meetings. Crying was a surefire sign of successful or impending conversion. "The tears ran down his cheeks while he was talking of his home and his home in heaven," Charles Tarbell recalled of one recent convert.[78] Several men with whom Louis Albright prayed "came to me take me by the hand and promise to meet me in heaven. They wept freely," he wrote in his diary, admitting that he himself had been moved to tears by this sign of conviction.[79] "Their countenances and the falling tears indicated that the Spirit was present with his convicting power," James Cooper wrote of one prayer meeting congregation.[80] That tears—a physical reaction—could signify the transformation of the soul—an abstract process that transcended the body—emphasized the power of God's grace over both body and soul, and thus the importance of the link between the two for the work of the USCC.[81] Cooper was particularly concerned with outward, bodily manifestations of spiritual wrestling; of one particular soldier's distress, he wrote, "he could not return to his quarters until he had found relief; and after he left the tent where special prayer had been offered on his behalf, he withdrew to the silent woods with two of his comrades and there 'cold mountains and the midnight air/witnessed the fervor of his prayer.'"[82] Restlessness of body, in this case, reflected a similar restlessness of spirit that could only be quelled through penitent prayer. Embodiments of spiritual struggle were not always consistent; stillness, conversely, could also be a sign of soul-searching. One delegate at Brandy Station was encouraged by the attentiveness of his audience: "they do not sleep, they do not sit in a listless, careless manner. I have yet to see the first indication of levity or disorder of any kind in a meeting I have attended."[83]

USCC prayer meetings frequently occupied a central role in these narratives of converting/converted behavior, thus vindicating their usefulness for the USCC. For example, one unregenerate and apparently sinful soldier encountered by A. B. Dascomb in Nashville demonstrated the transformative impact that prayer meetings—with their power to awaken memories of home and family—could have on behavior, and, by extension, on the state of one's soul. "He was drawn into the daily prayer meeting," Dascomb wrote:

> The words which he heard brought back into vivid relief the thoughts he had had
> on the battlefield after he was wounded, his sister's and his parents' lessons and

love, his child-brother's little prayers. He had neglected so many early advantages that he was very ignorant, but he knew that there was a Deliverer; he cried mightily for His presence. The Lord heard the poor man's prayer . . . the change in his life was immediate and manifest. He attended the prayer meetings regularly, and became a kind of volunteer Delegate among his fellow-soldiers.[84]

Despite the problems encountered in maintaining regular audiences for prayer meetings or finding suitable venues for preaching, the Christian Commission persevered in using sermons and prayer meetings to evangelize to the armies. Building on antebellum modes of prayer and preaching, the delegates used the spoken word to convey the urgency of their spiritual message and to create an informal and inclusive atmosphere conducive to deep reflection. In contrast to the largely solitary act of reading, participation in prayer meetings or attendance at sermons drew soldiers into communal, congregative contemplation of the importance of turning to Christ, intensifying the pressure on penitent souls, and extending the reach of the USCC's message.

Combined, the methods discussed in the previous two chapters—religious literature, sermons, and prayer meetings—sought to cater to the realities of life in the army, bringing souls to Christ through a range of approaches, from private, silent reflection to public declaration. These actions were central to the work of the Christian Commission, and illustrate the importance of conversion to the mission. The leaders and delegates of the Christian Commission displayed not only deep concern for troops exposed daily to vice and sin but also an unshakable conviction that the Union Army was the most fertile field of endeavor American Christians committed to spreading the Gospel could hope to encounter. The organization expended huge amounts of time and money applying these conversion methods throughout the army and badgered its workers constantly for their observations and assessments of their efficacy. It was clear that taking the idea of conversion and making it real, urgent, and possible for the targets of the Commission's efforts took hard work. No matter their individual doctrinal idiosyncrasies or the particular local challenges delegates encountered, a picture emerges of earnest, committed young men trudging miles, stacks of pamphlets spilling from their haversacks, their sermons drowned out by the wind and rain, their subjects sometimes hostile or indifferent: all to save another soul for Christ.

CHAPTER FIVE

Clothing the Union Soldier's Body

Seven weeks after the Battle of Gettysburg, delegate Charles Torrey arrived at Seminary Ridge, where the buildings of the Lutheran Theological Seminary had been transformed into a military hospital.[1] Torrey, an old college friend of William Boardman, Commission secretary, arrived in Pennsylvania to find hundreds of wounded soldiers still in need of care, and soon got to work, forging a good working relationship with his fellow delegate, Isaac Sloan. Torrey and Sloan set about distributing supplies, caring for the wounded, and praying with those close to death or in spiritual distress. They quickly found themselves at loggerheads with the surgeon in charge, whom Torrey considered hostile to the aims of the Christian Commission and miserly with the supplies at his disposal. One episode struck Torrey as particularly cruel. "My heart was sad + even indignant," he wrote to his old friend Boardman, "when some twenty five wounded men, all having lost a leg, were sent off to Phila[delphia] on a cool morning with insufficient clothing, in some cases with only drawers—without blankets."[2] Torrey, aghast at their plight, plundered the Christian Commission stores for "what I could lay hold of"—mainly slippers, blankets, and underclothes—and distributed spare clothing to as many men as he could before they departed. Although pleased by the gratitude shown by the men, he regretted that he had not been able to do more, and that the men were forced to "ride all day in open cars, on rough hard seats + with half healed stumps + lips blue with cold."[3]

Torrey's preoccupation with the physical discomfort and ragged condition of the convalescent troops was indicative of the multifarious work USCC delegates undertook during the Civil War. As we have seen, delegates were, in the first instance, tasked with converting men to evangelical Christianity, whether by organizing prayer meetings, preaching sermons, handing out tracts, or engaging in private conversation about the fate of a man's soul. This was by no means the entirety of the work, however. The Christian Commission also devoted large amounts of energy and resource to alleviating the bodily suffering of Union troops, handing out food, clothing, medicine, and other supplies where they encountered and perceived want. Despite what some earlier scholars of the USCC have suggested, this bodily ministration was not a digression from the Commission's evangelizing mission.[4] Rather, the Commission and its workers believed that by alleviating physical suffering and caring for broken bodies, they would gain better access to men's souls and hence hasten and heighten receptivity to the grace of God. Furthermore, just as the spiritual ministry performed in the chapel tents and through Testaments and tracts wrote the souls of individual soldiers into a national narrative that anticipated the perfection of the world and the Second Coming of Christ, the Commission's bodily ministry was invested with symbolic significance. The bodies of Union soldiers, fed, comforted, healed, and clothed by Commission hands, became metaphors for the national body and presaged the physical and moral regeneration of America.

"There is a good deal of religion," George Stuart, Commission president, was fond of saying, "in a warm shirt and a good beefsteak."[5] In his eyes, the Commission's work alleviating the physical suffering of Union soldiers not only exemplified a laudable and righteous spirit of Christian charity but also transformed these warm shirts and beefsteaks into instruments of evangelization just as potent as the Bibles and prayer books delegates carried in their haversacks. According to the Commission, the distribution of food and clothing embodied the Christian compassion preached by Christ and was thus a godly and worthy act. While nineteenth-century evangelical doctrine held that conversion was the only true guarantor of salvation (that is, that good works alone were insufficient), evangelicals were nonetheless committed to living according to scriptural teaching and thus proclaiming the presence of the Spirit in their lives publicly. From the second commandment (Mark 12:29–31) to the parable of the Good Samaritan (Luke 10:25–38), the Bible contained ample encouragement to Christians to exhibit charitable and loving behavior neither encumbered by hidden motive nor tempered by prejudice.[6] The Commission drew upon these precedents as it charged its delegates with following the example set by Christ's healing and ministry. Delegates encountered these instructions on the report forms they were entreated to complete weekly for submission to the Philadelphia headquarters: "Our adored Elder Brother, the Lord Jesus Christ, was the Good Samaritan worker. How to deal with physical suffering, how to open blind eyes

CLOTHING THE UNION SOLDIER'S BODY   97

and unstop deaf ears, cure leprous hands, and cast out devils, his great infinite heart completely understood. The Christian Commission work, in all sanitary distribution and effort, should feel that it is for Christ, remembering that a cup of cold water given in his name, is not forgotten."[7]

This was not the only motivation for distributing material aid, however. The items of food and clothing handed out by USCC delegates could in themselves act as tools to convert the armies, predisposing recipients to listen to the Commission's message and even having a regenerative effect on the recipient's mind and soul. USCC workers were aware that, at first glance, handing out pairs of socks and dispensing beef tea might seem to replicate work performed by the overtly secular Sanitary Commission. Indeed, some scholarly interpretations of the USCC's work have suggested that the bodily ministrations performed by delegates were simply a result of the rivalry between the Christian and Sanitary Commissions and were primarily a means of appealing to donors whose main priority was the physical, rather than spiritual, welfare of their sons and brothers.[8] Christian Commission delegates, however, were at pains to stress the spiritual ramifications of these transactions. As one delegate explained, "[the Sanitary Commission] distinctly disavows any attempt to do, for our soldiers, that which, as Christians, we deem of most vital importance. It takes to the wounded and dying soldier relief for the body, but none for the soul. It takes him the soothing cordials, the cup of water, the careful nursing, the medical care which he needs, but it withholds the bedside prayer, the gospel message, the tender Christian consolation which he also needs."[9] The Christian Commission, its delegates believed, served both the body *and* the soul through its work.

Delegate reports often echoed Stuart's suggestion that bodily aid was an effective conduit to the soul, believing that it encouraged men grateful for the Commission's attention to listen to the delegates' evangelical message. Henry Lee claimed that his attempts to "supply physical wants" were frequently a "door to spiritual things."[10] W. J. Park echoed Lee's conclusion. "The sympathy manifested, for his temporal welfare, gains the respect and confidence of the soldier," Park argued, emphasizing the importance of bodily relief work. "The stout brave heart of the soldier seems melted and every avenue to it opened before you. Evil influences are driven away, and the soldier seems but a child of larger growth."[11] Park's suggestion that the soldier was rendered childlike by bodily ministration implied a return to innocence and uncorrupted morality. He predicted that the soldier's mind and emotions would become more malleable and impressionable, and thus more liable to listen to the Christian Commission's gospel. B. F. Woolston was convinced of the efficacy of this method: "I find you can reach souls much more readily by doing something for the body," he wrote.[12] This combination of ministry for the body and for the soul, delegates agreed, was intended to shape an army of Christian soldiers who lived morally, died courageously, and ultimately placed their faith in God.

"MEN IN TATTERS"

A large part of the Christian Commission's bodily ministry involved the distribution of clothing, bandages, blankets, and other items designed to alleviate physical discomfort. The USCC devoted energy and resources to this work not only because it provided material comfort to the men who gratefully received the donated clothing but because it represented a wider commitment to the symbolic restoration and salvation of an imagined national body. At their loftiest, through public pronouncements and circulars, Commission leaders suggested that clothing men—repairing and restoring uniforms to wholeness—helped to reassert a model of disciplined, moral masculinity and signaled the righteousness of the United States. For the delegates on the ground, meanwhile, clothing was another method of evangelizing: making the body whole and alleviating physical distress and discomfort opened the soul to receive spiritual ministration. A report produced by the Minnesota YMCA close to the end of the war stated this relationship explicitly: "You know that men in tatters will listen to those that clothe them, and receive the Gospel message into their hearts."[13]

USCC delegates dispensed mountains of clothing over the course of the war. Accounts of the stores forwarded from the Pittsburgh branch alone between April 1863 and November 1864 demonstrate the scale of this branch of the USCC's work.[14] In this period, Pittsburgh delegates were tasked with handing out an estimated seventeen thousand shirts (flannel or muslin), over eleven thousand pairs of drawers, eleven thousand pairs of socks, as well as countless handkerchiefs, pairs of mittens, dressing gowns, and mosquito nets. In addition to clothing, the Pittsburgh branch also sent bed linen (including blankets, pillows, pillowcases, and sheets) and hospital materials (including rolls of bandages, lint, arm slings, and gauze pads). The USCC was concerned with clothing the soldier's body, not only on the march but in camp and in the hospital, especially when that body was injured. Warehouse manifests anticipated that stations would have on hand a diverse range of items for speedy distribution wherever they were needed, including (in addition to the items mentioned above) caps, pants, sturdy shoes, quilts, haversacks, suspenders, and towels.[15]

The USCC collected clothing for distribution from two main sources: discounted factory orders placed by members with industry contacts and purchased

CLOTHING THE UNION SOLDIER'S BODY 99

using Commission funds, and, more usually, private donations from the home front, often coordinated by the Ladies Christian Commissions. As we have already seen in chapter 2, this sort of war work fit into the USCC's narrow definition of respectably feminine labor, and male leaders enthusiastically encouraged the women of the satellite associations to keep up the pace. Advising the citizens of Bethlehem of the best ways of contributing to the Commission, local USCC chairman Sylvester Wolle instructed them to send "cotton or flannel shirts and drawers, slippers, sheets, pillows, housewives, handkerchiefs, washrags, old linen, &c."[16] Advice like this was sent to congregations and LCCs throughout the North, acknowledging that female congregants, often veterans of antebellum sewing circles, were well equipped for the manufacture of clothing and bed linen. Much of this advice, designed to ensure that all civilian skills and energies were properly and efficiently employed, was specific in nature. Lemuel Moss, for instance, requested that one auxiliary divert their efforts from the manufacture of "hospital garments" to that of "Housewives and Comfort Bags."[17] Similarly, George Stuart instructed E. W. Rogers of the Paterson, New Jersey, LCC to make bandages out of old muslin, and sent along several bolts of flannel to be made up into pairs of drawers, enclosing a pattern to aid manufacture.[18] To maintain enthusiasm and a steady stream of supplies, Executive Committee members constantly wrote to LCCs and individuals, praising them for their efforts and urging them to keep up the good work. "We are most like our blessed Saviour when we show sympathy + love to others," Moss wrote to an elderly lady who had sent a sizable donation of hand-sewn and knitted garments. "You will never know, until in eternity, how much comfort you have given to men suffering + away from home."[19]

Once the clothing, bandages, and bedlinen had been delivered to the field agents at each station, the delegates swiftly distributed it, often ascertaining the wants of specific patients and soldiers when passing through hospital wards and barracks and engaging in personal conversation. Some stations also set up store tents where soldiers could come with specific requests. At Susquehanna, E. Clark Cline reported that he and his fellow delegates "tried to do what the delegates of the Christian Commission always do wherever they go: supply the soldiers with clothing (of which they were in the very greatest need) . . . and other articles that tended to their comfort and happiness."[20] The need was similarly great at Gettysburg, according to A. M. Palmer, who described the men there as "lamentably destitute of clothing." Once the USCC had taken delivery of a load of spare clothing (long before any other relief agency in the area, he was at pains to point out), he reported, "thousands of garments were distributed and the comfort and appearance of the men very much improved."[21] Delegates also distributed items that were more obscure or difficult to obtain while in the theater of war, such as spectacles.[22] N. R. Peck, the president of the Sacramento USCC, provided a particularly vivid description of the USCC's work in this department:

> The work begins while the battle rages. The delegate, under direction of the surgeon . . . assists in gathering the wounded from the field, even under the guns of the enemy if need be, and at the hospital assists the surgeon at the amputating table, or strips off the bloody garments from the mangled men, washes them, and puts clean clothes upon them. . . . This Ohio boy asks for needles and some thread. Good thread can scarcely be procured here, and needles soon become rusty, carried in the pocket as they must be. A poor fellow in hospital is without a change in under-clothing, and has been for weeks. He has lost his knapsack, with all he had in it; or his descriptive list, and cannot draw clothing. These, and numberless other wants, great and small, when brought to us by the men, or their friends, it is the work of the office or store to supply.[23]

Christian Commission delegates identified something of a sartorial crisis among Federal troops, and it was this that led them to devote large amounts of time and energy to procuring and distributing clothing. "Thousands," Lemuel Moss claimed after the war, "saw their garments falling by piecemeal from around them, till scarce a shred remained to cover their nakedness. They made long marches without shoes, staining the frozen ground with blood from their feet. They fought, or marched, or worked on intrenchments all day, and laid them down at night with but one blanket to three men. And thus in rags, without shoes, often without bread, they fought battles and won campaigns."[24] This description, although couched in Moss's default hyperbole, was not entirely inaccurate. Although the Confederate armies were often in a far sorrier state than their counterparts, Union soldiers also frequently contended with uniform shortages, finding themselves ill equipped to deal with weather conditions, arduous marches, and long hospital stays. From the outbreak of war, clothing the troops was a ramshackle, improvised venture. Many regiments relied on their families and on the efforts of the first ladies' aid societies to outfit them, leaving their towns and villages among great pageantry and fanfare, their packs overflowing with whatever knickknacks and superfluous items their friends and well-wishers pressed on them.[25] Some regiments donned the old militia uniforms of the antebellum period, ranging from the brightly colorful (famously, the highly conspicuous and impractical fezzes and bloomers of the Zouaves) to the drably gray. James Robertson points out that, far from the standardized navy blue that pervades popular representations of the conflict, many Northern militias adopted gray uniforms because cloth in that color was more abundantly available.[26] Although the Civil War occurred as the ready-made clothing industry was emerging, enabling some degree of mass production, standardized sizing, and machine cutting, federal attempts to standardize uniform stumbled as "unscrupulous contractors and corrupt officials" took advantage of the situation to trade clothing of inferior quality for exorbitant prices, and the limited range of sizes meant men struggled to find uniforms that fit properly.[27] Federal troops in the early stages of the war were clad in every shade, cut, and fabric imaginable, and these makeshift uniforms were rarely suited to the conditions of war. Footwear was scarce and frequently substandard.[28] Most soldiers were reduced at some point in their service to "some stages of raggedness," especially during the most drawn-out campaign seasons when the appearance of the army was not a high priority, and natural wear and tear took its greatest toll.[29]

THE SYMBOLIC POWER OF UNION UNIFORMS

Keeping soldiers properly clothed, therefore, was a perennial problem. Incomplete or subpar uniforms could and did compound soldiers' discomfort and compromise their physical health. In addition, however, these problems threatened the intended power of uniforms as signifiers of nation, military masculinity, and citizenship. According to the French cultural historian Daniel Roche, a key function of military uniform is control; that is, the control exerted by an established and legitimated hierarchy over both the bodies and minds of its soldiers.[30] This control aims not only to condition the wearer physically for mortal combat but to instill within the soldier's mind a set of values and beliefs that motivate and draw together those wearing the same uniform. Thus, uniform aims not only "to separate, in order to inculcate the military ethos and instil a sense of hierarchy," but also "to unite, so as to demonstrate a common adherence, encourage *esprit de corps,* and promote harmony."[31] Standardized uniform can embody ideas of national unity and power, while the etiquette and rituals surrounding uniform can engender pride and feelings of belonging in those who perform these rituals.[32] Uniforms are symbols of the control exercised over the bodies beneath, and over the character, behavior, and gender identity of the wearers.[33]

The meaning of uniform was particularly pointed in a conflict fought largely by citizen soldiers.[34] Federal uniforms were supposed to transfigure the farm boys and office workers of the North into disciplined fighting men who were ready to violently uphold a shared set of political beliefs and to embody an idealized masculinity comprised of courage, self-belief, self-control, and morality. Endless regiments of Union troops clad in clean, whole, identical uniforms would signal to the enemy, to the rest of the world, and to the troops themselves that America was (in theory, if not in reality) a powerful, united, modern nation with the ability to wage increasingly technologically advanced warfare to defend a shared political, social, and cultural identity.

However, the symbolic power of Union uniforms was troubled by their variety and, more importantly, by the ways in which they were damaged, sullied, or otherwise rendered incomplete.[35] Ripped, soiled, bloodstained, or missing pieces of uniform compromised their power as signifiers of national, masculine identity; furthermore, such damaged uniforms frequently exposed the wounds and evidence of trauma on the body beneath. Showing a willful disregard for uniform regulations, Lorien Foote has shown, could be a subtle but powerful means of protesting incompetent command.[36] Therefore, the integrity and viability of the national body could be called into question by the torn and tattered uniform that clothed the damaged individual body.[37] Prior to the Civil War, the Commission claimed, "few Americans had ever known what it was to suffer for want of clothing."[38] This was a dubious claim, to say the least, but it illustrated the power of clothing to communicate and construct national identity. To be a true American, that is, was to be properly clothed. By contrast, when Rev. John Hussey visited the notorious Castle Thunder prisoner of war camp in Richmond, he was appalled that the inmates were "treated almost like dogs" and denied adequate clothing or bedding.[39] A soldier's masculinity—even his very humanity—was tied to the integrity of his clothing. The project of providing men with clean, new clothing, as a result, served to remake and regenerate both the individual and the national body. New clothing, in a similar way to prosthetic limbs issued to amputees, could "re-member" the body even as it sought to forget the trauma inflicted upon it, erasing the tears and stains caused by battle and concealing the wounds beneath. If a soldier's masculinity had been compromised—by damage to the body that rendered him incapable of performing his duty as a soldier, or by damage to the uniform that symbolized his loyalty to that duty—then replacing and repairing his clothing was vital to its restoration.[40]

Soldiers were not the only ones who wore uniforms. Christian Commission leaders were acutely aware of the legitimacy and authority that uniform could convey, as well as the control it could exercise over the behavior of an organization's members. Consequently, they set out clear guidelines for clothing and equipping the delegates themselves. "The Commission furnishes a woollen and a rubber blanket, haversack, canteen, badge, [and] flannel shirt, if desired," one circular read. "Delegates should take a respectable suit of clothes, an old one is quite as good as any; a few shirts, collars, and socks, thick boots, flannel shirts, such as soldiers wear; and only such baggage as they can carry in a light bag or valise."[41] "Strong plain clothing, strong easy shoes or boots, with a cap or soft hat, make the best personal outfit," another pamphlet advised.[42] This rough uniform was designed not only to be practical but to demonstrate the inner morality and humility of its wearer. One journalist praised the frugal, modest appearance of the delegates he encountered. "They did not look like ministers," he reported. "I did not see a white neck-tie or a nice, black broadcloth coat, or kid gloves. They were more like a party of stevedores than men from the pulpit." They were dressed, he implied, for hard work.[43] At the same time, certain elements were quasi-militaristic, such as the shirts and boots that deliberately echoed army clothing; the small pin-badge with which delegates were routinely issued also mimicked military insignia and was often recognized by men as a symbol of authority and influence.[44]

As they did with all elements of their work, the delegates of the Christian Commission interpreted the distribution of clothing through an evangelical lens. As we have seen, many evangelical Christians in the North saw the preservation of the Union and the salvation of the republican experiment as essential to the execution of America's providential destiny as God's redeemer nation. Creating a Christian fighting force was, they believed, necessary to bringing about a national spiritual renewal and, ultimately, saving the Union. That is to say, to fight for the Union, in the eyes of the USCC, was to fight for Christ, and thus the uniform worn by Union soldiers was symbolic not only of a nationalist, masculine ideal, but of a pious ideal, too. Therefore, the aim of distributing clothing was always more than providing temporal comfort; clothing could also serve evangelical ends. The covering and healing of the body was an action closely linked, in the philosophy of the Christian Commission, with the moral reformation of the army and the salvation of the soul.

Simply put, if the body could be restored to wholeness—through medicine, nourishing food, or, in this case, by using clean, new clothing to obscure evidence of trauma and suffering and to shield the body from further destruction—then the soul within might also be regenerated. Providing soldiers with new, or at least intact, items of clothing was a task laden with religious significance, and delegates drew upon their biblical knowledge to justify and support it. The symbolic and spiritual meaning of clothing in the Bible is most closely associated with the role of nudity in the Fall: upon eating the fruit of the Tree of Knowledge, Adam and Eve become immediately aware and ashamed of their nudity (Genesis 3:7). The human practice of clothing the body was thus a constant reminder of the original sin and innate depravity in every human soul. But the absence of clothing could also indicate a lack of moral integrity or spiritual wholeness. Traveling in Gadarenes, Jesus and his disciples encounter a man possessed by demons.

The man, Luke records, "ware no clothes, neither abode in any house, but in the tombs" (Luke 8:27). Once Jesus commands the demons to leave the man's body, the people of the community witness that the man is once more "clothed, and in his right mind" (Luke 8:35). Thus, nudity could symbolize not only insanity but an unregenerate and immoral state, which could be rectified through the process of conviction and conversion.[45]

In justifying their work distributing clothing to Union troops, the Christian Commission frequently drew upon Psalm 147, which proclaims the greatness of God and his ability to heal bodies and souls ("The Lord doth build up Jerusalem: he gathereth together the outcasts of Israel; He healeth the broken in heart, and bindeth up their wounds" Psalm 147:2–3).[46] The verse suggested that God's healing power (expressed and channeled on Earth by pious people like the Christian Commission delegates) could restore not only individuals but entire nations. When applied to an American context, the verse's focus on the chosen people of Israel and their covenant with God took on new meaning. By repeatedly describing the distribution of clothing as literally and figuratively "binding up the wounds," USCC delegates fed—deliberately or otherwise—a vision of America as the "New Israel" charged with leading the world to millennium.[47] The act of clothing and bandaging soldiers' broken bodies, it followed, would contribute to the preservation of a nation and a Union blessed by God.[48]

HOUSEWIVES

It was not only ready-made clothing, footwear, and bed linen that delegates distributed. By some distance, the most popular item provided by USCC delegates was the housewife, otherwise known as the comfort bag. A simple roll of fabric (sometimes lined with protective leather or oilcloth) with several pockets, the housewife contained basic sewing implements and materials that enabled soldiers to carry out makeshift repairs on their clothing and kit. This basic item, according to the USCC, had "more joy in it oftentimes to a soldier in the trenches, than the most splendid mansion would have to a man rolling in wealth at home."[49] The housewife was not a Civil War–era invention; as Steven LaBarre has shown, the item was long a staple of the American soldier's pack, and throughout the eighteenth and nineteenth centuries, and into the twentieth, "not only accomplished the necessary and practical task of keeping oneself clothed, but furthermore proved to be a means of exerting one's individuality, ingenuity, and creativity."[50] Housewives were indispensable during the Civil War due to the shortage and poor quality of uniforms, the difficulty of replacing items of clothing from the strictly monitored quartermaster's department, and the wear and tear inflicted on uniforms by long marches, inclement weather, and grueling battles.

Far from emasculating soldiers by providing them with the tools of feminine domesticity (encased in an item with an explicitly gendered name), the house-wives upheld the owner's independence and resourcefulness and contributed to a long tradition of male sewing often overshadowed and ignored by the persistent association of femininity and needlework in both the contemporary imagination and subsequent historiography. In contrast to the rigid segregation of antebellum gender roles proposed by, among others, Carroll Smith-Rosenberg and Nancy Cott, male sewing in a variety of settings indicated that the domestic sphere was permeable and that household roles, far from being fixed, were frequently flexible and negotiable.[51] In addition to the all-male enclaves in which men sewed (such as Gold Rush mining camps, naval vessels, and tailors' workshops), men were also present in the sweating and factory systems of the emerging urban garment industry, and, in a domestic setting, often repaired their own clothes and mended farming equipment.[52] Sewing undertaken by Civil War soldiers, then, not only fit squarely within the experience of many civilian recruits accustomed to wielding a needle and thread but was also an age-old military tradition.

Mending uniforms (along with a raft of other hygienic rituals, such as washing and polishing) was an inescapable part of army life, as it had been for centuries. Roche suggests that, in addition to prolonging the life span of expensive cloth-ing and maintaining the image and prestige of the army, mending was designed to preserve the masculine ethos of the military by dispensing with the need for female seamstresses and washerwomen.[53] More than this, responsibility for the upkeep of uniforms, coupled with frequent inspections and parades, inculcated habits of cleanliness and discipline that "served to strengthen motivations and pride in bearing" and, in theory, transformed the recruit into a model soldier.[54] Thus, the housewife was an important tool for the development of good hygiene and uniform upkeep—a tool that could help the soldier reform his behavior and character.

Of course, the Commission was anxious that the housewife cater as well as possible to the practical requirements of its owner, describing the ideal contents of each pouch as: "quite a number of strong needles, with one darning needle; a lot of pins; an abundance of strong black thread, particularly black linen thread; a small ball of woollen yarn; lots of buttons (mostly strong horn or bone)."[55] Yet encouraging good disciplinary habits was not the only priority of delegates in distributing thousands of the small pouches; rather, the Commission saw the housewife as a channel for evangelism—another means by which the soldier might be converted. The USCC's preoccupation with the distribution of housewives demonstrates the consanguinity of their temporal and spiritual work and the elevation of bodily ministry above disinterested Good Samaritanism. To maximize the evangelical potential of the housewife, donors and makers on the home front were advised to include a short letter with each kit. Isaac Smyth, chairman of the St. Louis branch, called for donations from the Mississippi Valley, urging donors to write "notes of inquiry, sympathy or encouragement" to their unknown recipients.[56] Another circular directed, "Let each little girl write and put in a letter to the soldier who shall use her Housewife, just such a letter as her warm heart shall dictate; subscribe it with her name and address, so that the soldier may acknowledge it, if he wishes."[57]

These letters were intended to raise morale and remind men of home and the affection and moral guidance associated with family. George Stuart emphasized this function, advising one young boy that "while they read your little letters their thoughts will be carried back to home again—and they will be better able to meet the enemies of their country—because they know that loved ones behind them have not forgotten them."[58] Beyond this, however, it was often claimed that the letters contained in housewives could be the instrument by which men were led to conversion. "Not a few dated their Christian life from the simple earnest entreaty of some Sunday-school child," Lemuel Moss wrote after the war, "who through these little gifts assured them that they were daily remembered in prayer."[59] The USCC urged children and LCCs putting housewives together to write letters with a spiritual theme, promising to pray for the soldiers, or asking soldiers whether they read the Bible, and thus encouraging them to consider their own mortality and the fate of their souls even while they stitched buttons and seams. Donors might also insert small tracts or passages from scripture in addition to their letter and mending supplies to further encourage spiritual reflection.

Several delegates reported instances where the housewives and their contents were "blessed to the conversion of noble men."[60] For example, W. J. Park, stationed in Nashville, recounted that, on one occasion, "a letter from a little girl in Nashua, New Hampshire, contained in one of the little reticules was the chief instrument in leading a soldier to give himself to Jesus."[61] The USCC also actively encouraged civilians to send in replies from grateful soldiers, and published these in newspapers and circulars as evidence of the power of housewives to raise spirits and turn thoughts to God. Seven-year-old Clara Lizzie Edwards from Hamilton, Massachusetts, received a letter from Samuel Griffin of the 92nd New York Volunteers, in which Griffin expressed his gratitude for the housewife and its contents and spoke of the emotional and spiritual comfort it provided: "The pen cannot describe, nor words portray to you how thankful we soldiers are to receive such little notions from even strangers, especially the young ladies. We are happy to know that we are not forgotten by the young ladies. I thank you for the tracts. I promise you they will all be read by myself, and given to my brother soldier for the same purpose . . . I shall think of you when I am drinking a good cup of tea, some night when I am fatigued by the hardships of a soldier's life."[62] In addition to this letter, Edwards received two letters from Griffin's comrades and commanding officer, informing her that Griffin had been killed the day after he received the housewife, and reassuring her that it had brought him much comfort in his final hours.

The letters sent by E. A. Taylor, a Missouri soldier encamped near Warrensburg, were yet more explicit in illustrating the direct spiritual impact receiving a housewife and a letter could have. Expressing gratitude to the St. Louis Sabbath school pupils who had donated a batch of housewives, Taylor urged the children to pray for him and his comrades in the same way that they prayed for their own relatives and friends. "We are surrounded by every temptation that the evil one can beset us with," he wrote, "and unless we are assisted from on high, through the instrumentality of the prayers of God's people at home, I fear many of us will be forever lost."[63] He wrote at length of God's generous and merciful nature and stated his conviction that God would answer the prayers of pious children. Taylor also emphasized that these prayers, if they saved men from vice and sin and set them on the path to righteousness, would make the men not only "good and faithful soldiers," but also, once the war ended and they returned to civilian life, "ornaments to society, and a delight to all who delight in good."[64]

It was little wonder that this letter was published as an advertisement of the benefits of the housewives, as it spoke directly to the reforming and evangelizing mission of the Christian Commission, as did another letter written by Taylor, this time to the child who had made his particular housewife. In answer to the child's inquiry as to whether he read the Bible, Taylor reassured his correspondent that he did and that it provided him with greater comfort than ever before because it helped him to ignore the temptations and dangers of army life. "The darker the hour the brighter does the Word of Truth shine forth," he wrote. "The more numerous temptations become, and the more frightful they appear, in the same proportion do the people of God cling more closely to the cross of Christ, and the more they make the Word of God the Man their counsel." Asking the child to pray for him and his comrades, he ended his letter expressing a fervent hope that all soldiers who received housewives would be as touched by the communication contained within as he had been and as eager as he to discuss spiritual matters.[65]

The letters from Griffin and Taylor powerfully illustrate the emotional and spiritual benefit soldiers could reap from the housewives. These letters were carefully selected for publication by Charles Demond and Isaac Smyth, presidents of the Boston and St. Louis USCC branches, respectively, to emphasize the USCC's popularity and success. As a result, the degree to which the letters represented the responses of all soldiers to the housewives is open to question. However, the publication of these letters shows the USCC's deep interest in the converting and reforming potential of the items, as well as the physical comfort they might provide. The purpose of the housewife was thus multifarious. Although it would be a stretch to claim that they performed the same magical protective function as the Bibles and Testaments that soldiers often carried on their persons (as seen in chapter 3), the housewives themselves could become powerful talismans, symbolic of the affection, concern, and support of its manufacturer and, by extrapolation, of the home front at large. W. J. Park, who was constantly running out of supplies of comfort bags, reported that many soldiers promised to carry and keep their housewives "till they get home, or as long as they live."[66] If not quite supernatural shields from bullets, housewives could still act as a comfort and a remembrance of home in times of suffering and peril.[67]

It was not only the soldiers who reaped benefits from housewives; the manufacturers, too, could have their spirits raised and their dedication to the Union cause strengthened by their participation in this supply line. Significantly, many of the appeals for housewives issued by the USCC specifically targeted children. Executive Committee members wrote to Sabbath schools urging children to dedicate themselves to making the little kits, providing simple patterns and instructions so that even the very young could join the endeavor.[68] These appeals were targeted at boys and girls alike. "Can you not get all the little boys and girls of your acquaintance to make comfort bags and housewives . . . to send to our noble soldiers?" George Stuart wrote to one boy. "How much they will need during the cold cold winter!"[69] A circular from the Cleveland branch also highlighted the role of children in the production of housewives, and predicted that "all our young patriots who have not yet aided in this good work, will be glad to know, we are sure, that there is something for them to do which will greatly assist and comfort our brave and self-sacrificing defenders."[70] By making housewives, children—the Christian soldiers of the future—could demonstrate their patriotism and political engagement, no matter the level of their understanding of the issues behind the war. The Cleveland circular was overt in its political aims; the writer encouraged children to keep and treasure any replies they received from soldiers because "in coming years they will be valued reminiscences of the aid you were able to give in this great war for liberty and truth."[71]

Understandably, the testimonies of the soldiers who received housewives sometimes suggested that it was the item's practical and financial benefits, rather than the religious or emotional impact of using it, that they valued most highly. Lemuel Moss concluded that housewives saved soldiers "from $5 to $15 each" in prolonging the life span of clothing otherwise difficult and costly to replace, while a returning veteran reported that with a housewife to hand, he could "sew up a rip, put on a button or a patch," claiming that "they are as good as new clothes."[72] But the USCC was not overly concerned that not all soldiers were spiritually influenced by the housewives, for whether using the supplies or reading the letters within—whether deriving religious comfort, emotional support, or practical/financial aid from them—soldiers became involved in a network of patriotic supply that extended the political and moral influence of the home front into the army camps. As Charles Demond wrote, housewives "help bind the army and the people at the North together."[73] This was a reciprocal process, too, for the civilian population was brought closer to the trauma and gallant suffering of the troops by their written responses to the housewives, which were often published in local newspapers and read out at Christian Commission meetings. It was hoped that their resolve and dedication to war work (in the shape, ideally, of donations to the USCC coffers) would be strengthened by these compelling narratives.

The humble housewife became a vehicle for conveying the good wishes and prayers of civilians to the battlefront, a tangible and portable memento of those prayers, and a tool for repairing a uniform symbolic of the integrity of the soldier, the righteousness of the Union cause, and of the apocalyptic hope invested in that cause by the USCC. It was thus a repository of powerful associations and meanings that neatly illustrated the ways in which the Christian Commission used its ministry to knit the fates of the body and soul together. The distribution of clothing was a crucial element of the USCC's spiritual-temporal approach to the Union soldier, one designed not only to alleviate bodily suffering but also to bind the home and battle fronts together, shore up morale and reform the character of the individual, connect the individual soldier to a national fate, and, ultimately, lead his soul to God. One Commission writer neatly summed up how clothing could perform both temporal and spiritual functions in the context of the war, writing simply, "a clean shirt, to one suffering for it, has in it a world of comfort, and not a little gospel, if given by a disciple in the name of Jesus."[74]

CHAPTER SIX

The Gospel of the Loaf

"Hundreds + thousands are hungering and thirsting for the bread of life," delegate W. P. Tritsworth reported from Brandy Station.[1] He was not alone in his preoccupation. Working with the Army of the Cumberland in late July 1863, E. P. Lewis claimed the men he encountered were "starving for the bread of life."[2] Time and again, delegates employed this well-worn biblical metaphor to emphasize the urgency and necessity of their evangelization. In doing so, they rejected a doctrinally narrow Eucharistic interpretation of the phrase; instead, they used it to encompass the totality of their ministry, whether distributing tracts, or praying with dying men, or preaching the Gospel, or (as we saw in the previous chapter) dispensing housewives filled with comforting messages. Sometimes, however, the meaning was more literal: frequently, dispensing the "bread of life" meant actually handing out bread. Food was a crucial component of the Commission's work. The distribution of food and drink to soldiers in hospitals and camps, much like the distribution of clothing, combined temporal and spiritual ministry to further the Commission's evangelical mission. Delegates spent considerable time each day handing out crackers, lugging vats of coffee up and down hospital wards, unpacking boxes of preserved fruits and vegetables, and spooning beef jelly into the mouths of weak patients. This work was intended to provide nourishment not only for the body but for the soul as well. It drew upon Christian teaching on the regenerative power of food and drink, as well as nineteenth-century theories about the effect of diet on internal morality. Delegate Joshua Cowpland called it the "gospel of the loaf": the saving of souls through the restoration of the body.[3] As well as the physical benefits of

THE GOSPEL OF THE LOAF 111

a healthier, more plentiful diet—strength, energy, greater resistance to or swifter recuperation from disease and infection—the Commission hoped that the food and drink they distributed would render the consumer more receptive to the message of the Gospel, and more capable of digesting this message. As C. G. Coffin wrote, "farina, oranges, lemons, onions, pickles . . . given and distributed in the name of Jesus Christ, though designed for the body, are so transmuted that they give health to the souls of men."[4]

The idea that food and drink could affect one's spiritual state long predated the Civil War. During the antebellum period, certain individuals and groups theorized that what one ate was intrinsically linked not only to bodily health but to moral and spiritual well-being. Most obvious among these were temperance reformers whose increasing militancy had motivated the passage, in the 1850s, of various state laws prohibiting the sale of alcoholic beverages.[5] Debates about the moral power of food and drink went beyond the evils of strong liquor, however. Ethical, spiritual, sanitary, and scientific impulses informed a raft of dietetic theories that sought to control what and how people ate and vested food with considerable power to improve and perfect society. Perhaps most well known among prewar dietary reformers was Sylvester Graham, a Connecticut minister concerned by the rapid changes convulsing Jacksonian society, whose theory that "we should eat what Adam and Eve ate before the Fall" clearly identified the link between soul and body that would inform all of the Christian Commission's work.[6] Believing that participation in the emerging capitalist marketplace (an arena he considered bedevilled by faster transportation, widespread corruption, and mass production) led to physical stresses and excitements that polluted and irritated the body, Graham sought to solve the perceived ills of his age by championing a return to wholesome, homemade food unadulterated by the quest for profit.[7] He advocated eschewing rich food, especially meat, tobacco, alcohol, and spices, all of which, he argued, led to overstimulation and made the body less capable of fighting off irritation and illness, and adhering to a strict regimen of bland food, small portions, and teetotalism.[8]

More than the bodily effects of a certain diet, Graham was deeply concerned with the spiritual ramifications of what one ate. Stephen Nissenbaum concludes that at the heart of Graham's thought was a desire to "purge the souls of his generation by cleansing their debauched bodies."[9] This desire informed other antebellum movements concerning food and drink. For instance, vegetarianism, another concern of Graham's, attracted a small but committed band of adherents in the antebellum period.[10] Inspired to a great extent by William Metcalfe's 1821 essay *Abstinence from the Flesh of Animals,* which advanced what Colin Spencer calls a code of "moral dietetics," as well as by other famous vegetarians like

Percy Bysshe Shelley, American advocates of vegetarianism, such as Graham and Bronson Alcott, often focused on the corrupting, barbarizing effects of meat eating.[11] The movement, although fragmented, saw abstinence from meat eating as "a catalyst for total social reform" on a similar plane to abolitionism and women's suffrage, promoting individual action as the key to realizing a communal utopia.[12] These antebellum dietary theories and their reforming aims helped shape aspects of the Christian Commission's bodily ministry.[13]

More immediately, the distribution of food and drink by USCC workers represented a practical response to specific and acute need in the armies as Union soldiers faced considerable hardship and shortage when it came to nutrition.[14] While the daily rations apportioned to each man—which included one pound and four ounces of beef or twelve ounces of pork or bacon, as well as one pound of hardtack—may have been generous compared to Confederate rations, they were not always fairly or regularly distributed, and the staple items—bread, meat, and coffee—were hardly sufficient to maintain health and strength among the fighting troops.[15] A chronic lack of fresh fruit and vegetables—attributable both to the problems of transporting these items, and to ignorance of their importance—was a key contributor to sick rates among Civil War soldiers, slowing recovery times, ensuring that scurvy was a constant specter, and increasing mortality.[16] Hindered by supply problems, especially at the beginning of the war, and particularly when the armies were on the move and struggling to find effective ways of preserving large quantities of important foodstuffs, soldiers were often forced to rely on unreliable food sources such as packages from home, massively overpriced items procured from local vendors and army sutlers, and goods pillaged (or "foraged") from civilian settlements.[17] Consequently, the Civil War soldier's diet, on both sides of the fight, was overwhelmingly characterized, as William Davis writes, by "monotony, insufficiency, and improvisation."[18]

Families on the Northern home front were, as a result, anxious about the physical well-being and nutrition of their sons and brothers in the armies and looked to relief organizations such as the Christian Commission to channel donations and supplies to those in need. As well as sewing uniforms and havelocks and scraping lint, aid societies set up within days of the start of the war also dedicated themselves to collecting, packaging, and sending edible supplies to the armies.[19] To begin with, concerned relatives and communities dispatched boxes of supplies directly to their kin, but this meant that some regiments were better supplied than others and led to postal bottlenecks and widespread wastage. As a result, as Lemuel Moss explained, "the sending of private packages was to a great extent abandoned; local associations became tributary to national societies; and distribution was made impartially to the men from all sections, as necessity or opportunity might determine."[20] The Christian Commission was heavily involved in this process of controlling and channeling female benevolence so as to maintain, as they saw it, efficiency and abundance throughout the theaters of war for as long as the conflict might last.

To ensure this, the Commission issued detailed advice to Ladies' Christian Commissions and local congregations on purchasing and packing foodstuffs, which was printed in newspapers, distributed in monthly pamphlets, or posted through individual doors.[21] "Pack only in good strong boxes or barrels, well secured," one such pamphlet read. "Pack eatables by themselves. Never pack perishable articles such as oranges, lemons, bread, cakes, nor jars of jellies and jams with other goods. Tin cans should be soldered."[22] "We will thankfully accept any of the products of your fields or gardens and workshops," another circular read. "We can make use of grain, flour, butter, eggs, dried fruits, pickles, jellies, syrup, tea, chocolate, wine &c."[23] While some civilians resisted these attempts to centralize and standardize the donation and distribution of food, preferring to keep sending their packages directly to individual soldiers, as chapter 2 revealed, sufficient numbers of aid societies acquiesced and kept up a steady stream of food donations (and cash donations to fund further purchases) so that USCC depots were rarely empty throughout the war. According to the records of the Commission, delegates distributed a vast range of foodstuffs and beverages to soldiers, from staples like flour, sugar, rice, and dried beef, to luxury items such as dried fruits, canned oysters, bottles of condiments, cocoa, jellies, and lemons.[24] The restorative potential, both physical and spiritual, of food from home was vast. George Ainsworth, a delegate from Williamstown, Vermont, for instance, estimated that thousands of men had been "revived, strengthened and put on the way to recovery" by "delicacies prepared at far northern homes, by willing hands, and sent forward with sympathising prayers."[25]

CARGOS OF REFRESHMENT

The reports of Christian Commission delegates reveal that distributing food and drink was a major part of their routine, often occupying hours of their day. Distribution had to fit around other delegate duties, including preaching and praying and arduous administrative work. Charles Lorry, juggling preaching, stocktaking, and distribution at the sprawling Harewood tent hospital in Washington, reported that he spent three days each week "supplying the wants of the men in the Hospitals with coffee and crackers."[26] John Rhodes, whose poor spelling was unusual for a Christian Commission delegate, was also stationed at a hospital, where one week he "distributed blackberry wine to the diarier [diarrhea] patience, many are receiving great benifit from it, some got well + gone home."[27] Not all delegates distributed in hospitals, although the Commission conceded that its primary work was among the sick and wounded, as "those who were well and in active service could more comfortably subsist upon the ordinary rations."[28] Those in active service might still be weakened by their experience in battle and on the march, and the Commission attempted to supplement their diet where possible. For instance, when the Sixth Corps passed through Fairfax Courthouse en route to Washington, many of the weakest stragglers called at the rooms rented by the Christian Commission. "I prepared large kettles of coffee, + opened two barrels of soft crackers + a barrel of pickles," Isaac Jacobus recalled, explaining how he administered Jamaica ginger to men suffering from diarrhea. "How many were thus served I do not know," he wrote, "but the number was large."[29]

The Commission sought to provide men with staples such as crackers and coffee, and with luxuries to which they would not otherwise have access. Fresh fruits, nigh on impossible to acquire in the field due to problems of transportation and preservation, were a welcome break from the monotony and blandness of the army diet and were reminiscent of luxuries the soldiers might have enjoyed before their enlistment. In October 1864, W. A. Lawrence took delivery of fifty boxes of grapes, which he and his coworkers distributed to grateful hospital patients. He later recalled the "thanks, smiles, and sometimes tears of the soldiers, the light step and full hearts of the distributors, and the grateful look of the surgeon and ward officials," heartily blessing the donors.[30] J. H. Bomberger described a bag of peaches he distributed as "like the cup of cold water given in the name of the Master."[31] Similarly, W. P. Weyman took it upon himself to organize treats of watermelon for soldiers stationed in Nashville during one hot August: "The markets were ransacked," one account of the distribution read. "Carryall and gunboat wagons were loaded until enough were gathered for all, and a liberal portion given to every man of the thousands for whom the surgeons judged it to be safe."[32] This was no small undertaking, logistically or financially, for watermelons were selling for as much as $40 apiece by 1863.[33] Even the president of the Commission, George Stuart, was personally involved in similar fundraising ventures. While chairing a meeting in Saratoga Springs in July 1863, Stuart received a telegram from a delegate stationed with the navy besieging Charleston, urgently requesting a delivery of ice for the dehydrated sailors. Stuart stood on a chair in the dining hall of the Congress Hall Hotel and read out the telegram, appealing for donations to fund such a delivery. He did the same at the Union and the United States, both prominent hotels patronized by the wealthy of "that fashionable watering place," and met with considerable success, including a donation of $500 from a New York merchant.[34] Within a day he had raised enough to charter a vessel and fill it with ice and lemons, and soon, as Stuart himself later recalled, the ship was speeding toward Charleston "with her cargo of refreshment for our suffering men."[35]

The amount of energy and resource expended securing luxuries like ice and watermelon indicate that the Commission's concern with food extended beyond simply getting nutrients into bodies. They recognized the emotional and ritual power of food: what men ate mattered, and so did the contexts in which they ate it. In particular, they looked to holidays and festivals that frequently revolved around communal meals, in which Americans broke bread together to celebrate or commemorate a shared idea. By funding and facilitating feasts to celebrate these public festivals, the USCC bought into the patriotic solemnity and civil religious constructions of holidays like Thanksgiving and Christmas.[36] Both Abraham Lincoln and Jefferson Davis declared days of thanksgiving intermittently during the early years of the war, inviting their respective citizens to offer prayers and praise to God for his hand in military victories and his presumed blessing on each cause. Lincoln's proclamation of a Thanksgiving Day on the last Thursday of November 1863 set a precedent for the holiday as we know it today, and the text of this proclamation demonstrated the political roots of the festival, encouraging citizens to "fervently implore the interposition of the Almighty hand to heal the wounds of the nation, and to restore it, as soon may be consistent with the Divine purposes, to the full enjoyment of peace, harmony, tranquillity, and union."[37] The involvement of the Christian Commission in the celebration of this consciously political, patriotic festival illustrated the USCC's commitment to the national ideals represented by the Union, and their belief in the importance of Christianity to this national creed.

Union soldiers were adept at saving up money for luxuries such as oysters, turkeys, and oranges, finding decorations and entertainment to celebrate holidays, and even in times of great deprivation, at improvising makeshift feasts from whatever meager rations they had to hand, reveling in the "comfort of companionship" as much as in the religious or political significance of the festival.[38] The USCC (and other relief organizations) supplemented these efforts by providing supplies for Thanksgiving and Christmas celebrations across the armies so that all might feel part of the festivities. Sharing in the preparation and consumption of meals, whether lavish or simple, provided an important boost to morale, heralding a welcome break in the usual routine and forging camaraderie and community in the camps and hospitals. John Scott recalled one grand dinner put on by the Christian Commission for the patients of the

116 TABERNACLES IN THE WILDERNESS

hospital where he worked, the menu consisting of "roast + boiled beef hay ois-
ters chicken + vegetables," all of which "loaded down the tables."[39] The meal
was accompanied by hymn singing and various other amusements, including
"climbing a slippy pole running races round the tents + gaudy Dress . . . in the
evening was a concert + a band of music."[40] Kay Burnell and his colleagues in
Memphis held a Thanksgiving dinner at the USCC's rooms, where "the long
table was beautifully decorated with flowers, and an abundance of little 'red
white and blues,'" and at which the attendees sang songs pledging allegiance
to the flag and to Christ, emphasizing the potential for these events to become
expressions of both piety and nationalism.[41]

Meals like this were funded by special appeals issued by the Christian Commission: one Thanksgiving appeal, published in several local newspapers, solic-
ited funds and anticipated that "the most liberal contributions will be made to
an institution which is accomplishing the greatest amount of good at the lowest
cost."[42] The Pittsburgh branch issued a circular titled "Christmas Dinner for
the Soldiers," promising to provide a hearty meal for soldiers in and around
Pittsburgh and Nashville, and asking for donations of cash or items such as
apples, fruits in cans, fowls of all kinds, oysters, butter, eggs, and cakes.[43] Appeals like this drew both civilian donor and military recipient into a network
of concurrent celebrations, strengthening the ties between the home and battle
fronts, and investing the symbolism and rhetoric of national feast days with
increasing sentimental clout. The response to such appeals was often generous,
as the Commission's advertisements underlined not only the soldiers' hunger
but their homesickness and the difficulty of being away from home, in peril, at
a time traditionally dedicated to family.

THE ALCOHOL QUESTION

While the civilian population generally approved of endeavors such as Christmas dinners, other elements of the work were considerably more controversial.
Alcohol was not an official component of the Union soldier's daily ration (although sailors were issued a grog ration while at sea), but nominally restricted
access did not prevent men from devising multiple strategies to procure it.[44]
These included pilfering liquor, fermenting their own, buying illicitly from sutlers and peddlers, or feigning illness in the hope of being prescribed an alcoholic tonic. Soldiers' ingenuity, along with the disinclination of officers to waste
time and resources punishing intoxication unless it spilled over into violence
and destruction, contributed to widespread intemperance in the Union Army.[45]

THE GOSPEL OF THE LOAF   117

Authority figures' attitudes to alcohol consumption were far from consistent—some officers, medical practitioners, and politicians embraced alcohol as "a therapeutic agent, a reward, a soporific to harden the hard edge of war," while others reviled it as "the source of all evil behaviour and moral decline."[46] The delegates of the Christian Commission, many of whom had been involved in the busy temperance campaigns of the antebellum years, were primarily in the latter camp, interpreting consumption of alcohol as an outward manifestation of a weak and corrupt soul. Nevertheless, they were forced to admit its occasional medicinal usefulness; as David Raney argues, the exigencies of war led delegates to follow the teachings found in Proverbs: "give strong drink unto him that is ready to perish" (Proverbs 31:6).[47]

Following this scriptural precedent, the Christian Commission included alcohol in widely distributed lists of suggested donations; for instance, in October 1863, it published a list of suitable stores, including, under the telling heading "Stimulants," "Good Brandy, Madeira wine, Port wine, Cordials, Domestic wines," also attaching packing directions to ensure bottles and jars did not break or spill.[48] Annie Wittenmyer, despite her later career as the first president of the Women's Christian Temperance Union, included several recipes containing alcohol in her diet kitchen recipe book, including one for mulled wine, a milk punch containing brandy, a wine jelly, and a rice pudding flavored with wine.[49] Wittenmyer may have accepted that, given the wartime situation, launching a full-blown crusade against intemperance was unfeasible, reverting back to older medicinal uses of wine and spirits for purely pragmatic reasons.[50] Nevertheless, the diet kitchen recipe book did acknowledge the teetotal lifestyle that many managers (and their patients) followed; the recipe for eggnog, which in its original form contained "a little nutmeg and wine or rum," advised that "if the liquor is objectionable, substitute rich milk."[51]

Delegates and USCC leaders alike struggled to reconcile their moral revulsion of alcohol (and that of their donors) with its application as a remedy. Executive Committee members agonized constantly about the effect even this occasional use of liquor was having, not only on the soldiers imbibing it but on the reputation of the Commission as a moral institution. "We intend to curtail greatly our purchases of stimulants, as the Executive Committee are of the opinion that perhaps we have purchased too freely of them," George Stuart declared in August 1864. "They must be distributed with great discrimination."[52] The Commission was even potentially willing to compromise the physical health of the soldiers if the integrity of the USCC was at stake. "We cannot well be too stringent in our restrictions upon the distribution of liquors," Bernice Ames wrote to one delegate. "Far better that individuals should suffer inconvenience for the want of them, than that the Commission should be scandalized by their improper use."[53] Clearly, in the eyes of the Commission, the physical benefits of medicinal alcohol were outweighed by the spiritual benefits of temperance.

This attitude was influenced by ideas promulgated by the nationwide temperance movement, notably, that pollution of the body could lead to pollution of the soul. Drunkenness, perceived by early antebellum temperance reformers as indicative of sociopolitical collapse, was increasingly interpreted as a sign of immorality by mid-century.[54] Intemperance was understood to have an eternal impact; it was a barrier to the salvation of one's soul because, as Ian Tyrrell writes, "intemperance blotted out man's moral sense and his rational perception of spiritual problems and thus made him indifferent to the appeals of religion."[55] In other words, despite its medicinal benefits, alcohol was not only an impediment to discipline and fighting fitness but a potential obstacle to the conversionist goal of the Christian Commission because it clouded the mind and prevented the drinker from repenting and accepting Christ.

It is, therefore, unsurprising that many delegates were involved in setting up temperance societies in the ranks. While James Robertson argues that, almost without exception, such movements were "short-lived undertakings that ended in failure," the testimony of USCC delegates demonstrated that there was no small amount of enthusiasm for the ventures. W. H. Hayward reported that much of his time was taken up delivering temperance addresses to regimental "abstinence faculties."[56] He emphasized the determination of temperance advocates to stamp out intemperance entirely and was optimistic about the mission, observing that "soldiers who will not attend a preaching meeting readily come out to hear the temperance address." At Camp Barry, William Jewell also met with some success: "We have organized a temperance union and chosen Maj. Hall President," he wrote, reporting that the corresponding secretary of the American Bible Society, W. J. R. Taylor, had delivered a "most interesting address" at the inaugural meeting.[57] Henry Safford was pleased to report that, among the Fifth New York Cavalry, men joined the chaplain's temperance society with "zeal [and] enthusiasm," and that they were "not backward in signing anti-liquor pledges."[58] Of course, these reports did not indicate the longevity or impact of these associations, and for most delegates, it seems, antebellum temperance work was relegated in importance for the duration of the war. That there was no overall consensus on the distribution or prohibition of alcohol among Christian Commission delegates demonstrates the difficulties the USCC faced in avoiding controversy while making sure bodily ministry and spiritual ministry were always directed to the same goal.

FEEDING THE ENEMY

Alcohol was not the only element of food distribution that caused controversy; USCC delegates also agonized over whether to distribute resources donated or funded by Union citizens to Confederate soldiers and civilians. Delegates encountered thousands of Confederates during their service, whether as patients, prisoners, refugees, or wounded on the battlefield, and thus constantly wrestled to reconcile loyalty to the Union cause with loyalty to the tenets of Christianity. As we saw in the previous chapter, the bodily ministrations of the delegates bore nationalist implications, with the remaking of Union bodies symbolizing the renewal and reparation of the nation and the Christian values it embodied. However, the internecine nature of the war called into question how to define that nation. The Union refused to recognize the Confederacy as a separate nation and considered the seceded states and their citizens still part of America. However, with the South in open, armed rebellion and its people loudly condemning the Federal government and its supporters, it was unclear whether clothing and feeding those opposed to the idea of the American Union—an entity blessed, according to evangelicals, by divine Providence—would contribute to the moral regeneration of the redeemer nation in quite the same way as would clothing and feeding those loyal to the Union. The Christian Commission thus faced a dilemma in its ministry—extending this ministry to Confederate soldiers would symbolize a political, as well as moral restoration of the Union, but would tacitly endorse the principles and values of the Confederacy, many of which—not least slavery—chafed against the tenets of Northern evangelicalism. The dilemma posed by Confederate soldiers also concerned the limits of Christian compassion—ministering to the wounded bodies of enemies would demonstrate the benevolence and mercy preached by Christ but also risked accusations of treason being leveled against the USCC. As I have addressed at greater length elsewhere, the bond between piety and patriotism forged by so much of the Christian Commission's ministry was stretched to breaking point when delegates encountered Confederate troops.[59]

Despite these dilemmas, the delegates of the Christian Commission did not ignore the Confederate soldiers they encountered, and the *Incidents* compiled by Edward Smith after the war recorded many examples of workers ministering to Confederates and treating them kindly. Field Agent E. F. Williams, for example, working at Fairfax Courthouse, Virginia, took time from his work among Union wounded to take refreshments to a group of Rebels. When he distributed a cup of coffee to an enemy colonel, the man expressed surprise, saying, "Well, this beats me. We don't treat our prisoners so." Williams replied, "we make no distinctions."[60] Another delegate, encountering a South Carolinian prisoner who "seemed very fearful of retaliation," recalled how he and his coworkers "gave him refreshing drink, laid him in cool shade, giving him good counsel," using bodily ministration as an opportunity for spiritual conversation just as delegates did among Union soldiers.[61]

Despite the numerous examples of ministry to Confederates, the potential for controversy was not lost on the Christian Commission's workers. This was evident from the stirrings of trouble surrounding the USCC's work in Richmond late in the war. The USCC was swift to establish a presence in the fallen Confederate capital in April 1865, setting up depots for distributing food to stranded and impoverished civilians and manning aid stations for Union and Confederate soldiers awaiting demobilization. The Commission established a system whereby local clergymen alerted delegates of families in direst need, who were then issued with special tickets guaranteeing them rations of staples (such as flour, peas, and concentrated soup) from the USCC stores. Delegates also carried out home visits, distributing rations to devastated neighborhoods. "It is wonderful how those poor starving women + hungry little children instinctively come to the Christian Commission for help," Robert Patterson wrote to a colleague a week into the work, reporting that the men, giving out nearly two thousand ration packs daily, had swiftly exhausted the stores on hand, and had sent for five hundred barrels of flour.[62]

While the work in Richmond was well organized and apparently appreciated by civilian recipients, it was not without its critics. Shortly after the work began, Lemuel Moss became aware of reports in the *Chicago Tribune* accusing the USCC of spending funds intended for Union soldiers on feeding Rebels. Moss was anxious to refute these accusations and to clarify the Commission's stance on ministering to Confederates (whether civilians or soldiers). "What was done by us did not intrench either upon our proper work or upon the funds contributed for it," he protested to Robert Patterson. "We did not feed influential or unrepentant rebels, but the starving citizens of a desolate and conquered city . . . as speedily as possible this whole work was assumed by the governmental authorities."[63] The distribution of food, drink, and clothing, therefore, could endanger the reputation of the USCC in the eyes of the Northern public, even when dealing with noncombatants such as the women and children of Richmond.

To combat allegations of treason throughout the war, the Christian Commission needed to devise an ironclad justification for their work with Confederates, especially soldiers committed to secession. In doing so, the delegates turned to the Bible for inspiration, particularly Romans 12, where Paul, quoting Proverbs, tells his audience, "if thine enemy hunger, feed him; if he thirst, give him drink." This verse was echoed constantly in the recollections of delegates. At Gettysburg, George Duffield, a Presbyterian minister from Adrian, Michigan, came across a group of wounded Confederates lying on the bare ground in a barn. He took it upon himself to share food and drink with the men and recalled, "the distribution of the bread was in solemn silence, reminding me strangely enough of distributing on a communion-day the emblems of Christ's body and blood, as well as of the command, 'If thine enemy hunger, feed him; if he thirst, give him drink.'"[64] Similarly, another delegate, working at an ambulance depot overseeing hospital transports, related the following conversation with a wagon driver appalled at the suggestion that he offer some comfort to a Southerner:

> "Have you any wounded in this wagon, driver?"
>
> "Yes, two; one a Reb, and one of ours." "Well, give each of them a cup of that punch." "What! Give punch to Rebs?"
>
> "Why not? If the man is fainting, it won't hurt him."
>
> "That is new doctrine," Said an officer, standing by. "That is the Christian Commission doctrine. If thine enemy hunger, feed him. If he thirst, give him drink."
>
> "Well," said he, after a moment's reflection, "I go in for that Commission."[65]

Paul's advice, unlike the parable of the Good Samaritan or the commandment to "love thy neighbour as thyself" (Matthew 22:39), explicitly set aside the recipient of aid as an enemy rather than merely a neighbor or a stranger; thus, the frequent invocation of this verse by USCC delegates helped them to rationalize their distribution policy, maintaining their political allegiance and preserving their patriotism intact by condemning Confederate subjects as enemies, even as they ministered to their bodily needs. The justification for such controversial ministry lay in the second half of Romans 12:20, which in its entirety reads: "If thine enemy hunger, feed him; if he thirst, give him drink, *for in so doing thou shalt heap coals of fire on his head*" (emphasis my own). According to Paul, therefore, aid rendered to an enemy would constitute a purifying fire cleansing the recipient's conscience and eliciting remorse and shame for his crimes.

Consequently, for the USCC, what appeared to be acts of kindness and compassion were also intended to undermine the subject's misguided loyalty to the Confederacy and to encourage repentance for his disobedience. Several delegates endorsed this interpretation of Romans in their recollections. For instance, P. B. Thayer, working with the wounded at Martinsburg, recalled a rough, violent Confederate moved to tears by the kindness of the Commission. "I am no coward," the man said; "I can face the enemy and not wink; but this kindness kills me, it breaks me all to pieces."[66] Thayer thus implied that the resolve and loyalty of Confederate soldiers could be undermined and compromised, not by increasing their suffering, but by alleviating it, and by demonstrating the compassion and Christianity of the North. A South Carolinian taken prisoner at Gettysburg was overcome by the kindness of a delegate who offered him a handkerchief steeped in cologne, saying, "I can't understand you Yankees; you fight us like devils, and then you treat us like angels. I am sorry I entered this war."[67] Humanizing the Union and debunking myths that all Northerners were cruel, mercenary, and godless was thus an important method of diluting Confederate adherence to their cause. The words of a prisoner from Tennessee, reported in the Boston *Congregationalist*, emphasized the power of Christian compassion to erode dedication to the cause of secession: "how kind you Northern people are! . . . I used to have a prejudice against you, but since I have been in the army, and have seen what you do for the soldiers, I think you are a wonderful people."[68] The second annual report concluded that the Commission was "acting an important part in showing the South the groundlessness of its hatred to the North."[69]

Just as the Christian Commission aimed to convert Union soldiers to Christ, they set about where possible to convert Confederate soldiers to the Union. This was a necessary step to salvation; according to USCC logic, Confederate soldiers must repent of their sins, and in particular renounce the blasphemy of rebellion, before their souls could receive grace. The Commission was convinced that "in many instances kindness to [Confederates] has opened their hearts, and induced free expression of penitence as well as gratitude."[70] One seventeen-year-old Mississippi private received a comfort bag from a delegate, which contained a letter from a little girl from Massachusetts. The soldier wrote to her, thanking her for the token: "I hope you will not be disappointed by this, coming as it does from a Rebel." He closed the letter by expressing hope that "God may in mercy reunite us all again as brothers and sisters."[71] Small victories for the Commission like this—convincing a soldier to hope for the restoration of the Union— were materially meaningless in the wider picture of the war. The Confederates to whom the Commission ministered were, for the most part, prisoners unlikely to be exchanged once the cartels collapsed in early 1863 or invalids who would not be able to boost the lethality of the Confederate Army in any noticeable way. But these examples, isolated though they were, were symbolically essential to the narrative constructed by the Christian Commission and were a crucial part of the justification for ministering to Confederates.

The bulk of food distribution, however, was undertaken among Union soldiers, and the benefits of this distribution were measured in a variety of ways. The most basic was the bodily comfort derived from the temporal ministry of the Commission; delegates frequently recorded the physical improvements they observed among their patients. "Great relief and aid has been given to the suffering as the result of cordials that have been distributed," A. L. Pratt reported one Christmas.[72] He was not alone in observing the positive effect of cordials; William Robinson, going around the wards of the field hospitals around Petersburg, regularly distributed blackberry cordial—believed to be particularly effective in alleviating diarrhea—to grateful soldiers. As he passed through the wards, men asked for a serving, or shouted their thanks, blessing the Christian Commission as they did so. "I am fully persuaded that this branch of the work is of great value to the men," Robinson concluded.[73] William Learned encountered an old German soldier sick with fever, whose face he bathed with cold water. As Learned worked, the old man murmured, "das ist goot," and, Learned reported, "scarcely anything affected your delegate more with happiness" than that simple expression of gratitude.[74] George Stuart was particularly proud of the steam-powered coffee wagons operated by the Commission in each corps—each machine, according to his calculations, could prepare coffee, tea, or hot chocolate for twelve hundred men per hour, and could travel at eight miles per hour, winding up and down the rows of tents and stretchers. "How many lives of men wet, muddy, battle-worn, lying down on the ground, without shelter or fire, have been saved by the hot draught of coffee thus administered to them?" he asked.[75] C. H. Richards, a delegate from Philadelphia, was similarly enamored of the newfangled machine. His account of soldiers' curiosity and joy upon encountering the mysterious, noisy, fragrant coffee wagon extolled its restorative power:

> Up the hospital avenue it rumbled and rolled, past the long rows of white tents, stopping at this cluster and that, giving to all from its generous supply. You should have seen the wondering look of the men as it passed by. They rolled themselves over to get a glimpse of it. They stretched their necks for a sight of it. The wounded heads forgot to ache, and the wounded limbs almost forgot to cry for nursing in that moment of eager curiosity. Was it a new sort of ambulance? It didn't look like one. What did those three black pipes mean, and those three glowing fires? Is it a steam fire-engine, and are they going to give us a shower-bath? But the savory odor that saluted their nostrils, and the delicious beverage the engine poured into their little cups, soon put the matter beyond all doubt. They soon found that there was no necromancy about it, for it had a substantial blessing for each one of them, and they gave it their blessings in return.[76]

More important than the bodily comfort derived from food and drink, however, was the spiritual comfort these items could provide. Distributing food and

"The Coffee Wagon," in Lemuel Moss, *Annals of the United States Christian Commission* (Philadelphia: J. B. Lippincott & Co., 1868), 445. (Illustrator unknown)

drink contributed to the USCC's evangelical mission by demonstrating kindness and Christian love in action, and by providing opportunities for delegates to converse with recipients of aid about spiritual matters.[77] N. S. Burton, helping ambulances full of wounded soldiers arriving at City Point in July 1864, reported that his daily work of distributing food and drink and cleaning wounds presented him with "frequent opportunities to speak a few words of religious comfort and instruction."[78] "The men come to me all day long for the things the Comm. offers," J. P. Stryker reported after a particularly busy week's distribution, "giving me the opportunity to talk with them."[79] H. G. Thomas also combined bodily aid with spiritual conversation, demonstrating the power of Christian compassion through his ministry; "our duty at first," he wrote, "was mainly to distribute clothing and some delicacies and to speak words of kindness and cheer to our wounded soldiers, and likewise to our enemies." He concluded that he and his colleagues had witnessed "several converts to the faith of Christ who experienced the kind and soothing hand to relieve their want and then in their deep distress their hearts were open to hear the love of Christ."[80] Delegates soon found that the weak and injured—a somewhat captive audience—were better disposed to listen to religious ministry than the fit and able, especially if patients were provided with bodily care at the same time. "The heart that would not quail before the cannon's mouth," W. W. Condit believed, "would be melted to tears by religious instruction mingled with kindness."[81]

The combination of bodily aid and spiritual conversation was also evident in the work of the diet kitchen system described in chapter 2. The diet kitchens, by providing light, easily digested food designed to remind men of home and maternal care, sought to alleviate not only physical suffering but mental, emotional, and spiritual distress. The female diet kitchen manager's role was far more complex and multifaceted than simply overseeing the preparation and distribution of food, and incorporated elements of emotional and spiritual care in addition to the provision of physical nourishment. There is no evidence that diet kitchen managers were provided with pamphlets, Bibles, and newspapers to distribute among the men, as male Christian Commission delegates were, nor that they were permitted to preach or set up prayer meetings (unlikely, given the conservative attitudes of the Commission toward female preachers). However, diet kitchen managers were actively encouraged, when time allowed, to visit the wards and speak to the men about Christianity, using their suppos-edly innate compassion and kindness to access even the most stubborn of sub-jects. Annie Wittenmyer, the founder of the diet kitchen system, believed this secondary work, although conducted on a less formal basis, was as successful as the work preparing and distributing food, and that "their kind words, Christian sympathy and solicitude so much needed and so gratefully received, were the means of bringing hundreds to Christ and the knowledge of the truth to the saving of their souls."[82]

The diet kitchen recipe book distributed to managers contained a long list of "Suggestions," which covered such themes as dress, comportment, activities, and cooperation and, crucially, addressed how women might go about ward visit-ing.[83] Many of these instructions drew on assumptions of innate female piety and exhorted women to draw on their domestic experiences as mothers and moral guardians, roles that included concern for the destiny of a charge's immortal soul. For instance, the volume advised that when entering the wards, "the step should be light, the manner cheerful and dignified, the words kind and encouraging, the offers of assistance generous and hearty, and all the deportment show that the visitor has been with Jesus, and learned of Him, who is meek and lowly in heart"—the ideal combination of motherly and pious behavior. Wittenmyer con-tended that ward visiting could help to bring soldiers closer to the dual "homes" of mother and Christ; "such sympathy," she claimed, "is all the more grateful to the sick, as it comes to them when they are far away from home and friends, and at a time of bodily suffering and mental anxiety, when they most need the sus-taining influence of Christian counsel." Finally, the "Suggestions" concluded that to be fit for diet kitchen service, women "should be impelled by the highest and holiest motives—should be influenced wholly by love to God and humanity."[84]

It seems that women managers took to this ward-visiting role with great enthusiasm—whether because of their religious zeal, their wish for personal contact with the soldiers, or their enjoyment of the variety provided by this break in routine. Theresa McDevitt, in her detailed study of the diaries of Mary and Amanda Shelton, who were involved in the diet kitchen system from its inception, notes that "their spiritual work in the wards with the soldiers received the most attention in their diaries."[85] Similarly, in a letter to Wittenmyer, Mrs. E. H. Jones, a reverend's wife based at Point of Rocks, Virginia, promised that "I mean to find time, if my health don't fail, to feed the soul as well as the body."[86] Ward visiting explicitly linked the work for the body and the work for the soul, demonstrating the importance of both to the USCC's evangelism. Edward Parmelee Smith praised the dual function of the diet kitchen, describing the lady managers as "at once the agents through which all our choice hospital stores could be conveyed directly to the most needy men, and also laborers for the Master, touching a soldier's heart more readily and deeply than men can do."[87]

The body was a conduit to the soul: bodies restored to full health and vigor by the Commission's beef tea and watermelons were, they believed, vessels ready for spiritual restoration. In extolling this view of the spiritual benefits derived from the distribution of food and drink, Commission workers turned to biblical teaching. "The loving Father provides the Christian delegate with a healing cordial for the fainting and grievously wounded spirit," the Minnesota YMCA proclaimed, entrusting delegates with the task of "pouring in oil and wine" to soothe, restore, and save the soldier's soul through bodily ministration.[88] This combination of oil and wine frequently recurs in the Bible. In the parable of the Good Samaritan (Luke 10:25–37) they are tangible manifestations of Christian brotherly love and charity. In Psalms, they appear as measures of God's endless bounty: "He causeth the grass to grow for the cattle, and herb for the service of man: that he may bring forth food out of the earth; And wine that maketh glad the heart of man, and oil to make his face to shine, and bread which strengtheneth man's heart" (Psalm 104:14–15). For the Christian Commission, the "oil and wine" manufactured and donated by its home front auxiliaries were gifts from God, gifts that would not only nourish and heal the body but that would "make glad the heart of man"—that is, would transform and quicken the soul.

Delegate A. S. Fuller also drew upon scripture when he reflected on the bodily ministrations he performed as part of his delegate service. Recalling the long hours he spent dragging a refreshment wagon through Camp Stoneman, District of Columbia, he described his work as "literally carrying the water of life to thirsty, dying men."[89] Fuller's use of the phrase "water of life" deliberately evoked a raft of biblical imagery, from the symbolic cleansing and purification experienced in baptism to the "pure river of water of life, clear as crystal, proceeding out of the throne of God and of the Lamb" shown to John in the book of Revelation, and which awaits the righteous after the Day of Judgment (Revelation 21:6, 22:1–21). Christ explains the concept of "water of life" in John's Gospel when talking to a Samaritan woman by a well in the town of Sychar: he promises her that "whosoever drinketh of the water that I shall give him shall never thirst; but the water that I shall give him shall be in him a well of water springing up into everlasting life" (John 4:14). By consciously equating the distribution of food and drink with Christ's saving grace, Fuller emphasized that such bodily ministrations were as central to the evangelization of the army as were sermons and prayer meetings, and that Christian kindness had the power to lead the soul to God. This principle shaped the Commission's distribution of food and drink throughout the Civil War, combining Christian charity with urgent evangelicalism and, as with the distribution of clothing, trusting that the restoration of bodily health and wholeness would lead to internal, spiritual restoration.

CHAPTER SEVEN

Death, Salvation, and the Christian Commission

The Civil War killed over 750,000 people, according to recent estimates.[1] Such a death toll—roughly 2 percent of the population—could not fail to change the ways in which people thought about death and dying. Antebellum Americans were intimately and inescapably familiar with death—high infant mortality rates, industrial and transportation disasters, and frequent epidemics made sure of that.[2] The Civil War, however, forced the nation to confront the violent, often instantaneous death of the relatively young on a mass scale, bringing the "suddenness, disorderliness, extent, variety, and appearance" of death in wartime to the attention, not only of the soldiers who directly witnessed the gore and chaos of the battlefield but, through letters, stories, and most notably photographs, of the civilian population.[3]

Among those who confronted and attempted to make sense of the carnage were the workers of the Christian Commission. Encounters with the dead and dying saw delegates take on numerous roles. They comforted dying men in moments of distress, pain, and confusion; they helped to convey to distant loved ones vital information about the manner of men's deaths, their last messages, the likely destination of their souls, and the location of their remains; and they prepared and buried dead bodies with accompanying ritual. The Christian Commission's work with the dead and dying was, in many ways, the apotheosis of its mission. Delegate encounters with the dying served not only to provide solace and comfort but also tied Union deaths into a national narrative of righteous, Christian martyrdom by framing the political project of the Union in explicitly evangelical terms. The dying bodies of Union soldiers presented USCC delegates with one last chance to secure another convert to Christianity, while the physical actions and verbal declarations of the dying provided vital clues as to the state of the departing soul and, thus, a way of gauging progress in the task of converting the army. Ultimately, dead bodies and the graves in which they were interred became powerful symbols of the sacrifice and bloodshed that would cleanse America of sin.

Civil War thanatology is a growing field. Scholars continue to explore the ways Americans died, and how they thought about and came to terms with death during and after the war.[4] Drew Gilpin Faust and others have contended that before the war, a sentimental culture of death pervaded that used familial structures to help people normalize and accept the constant presence of death. This culture enshrined the ideal of the Good Death, whereby the dying passed away peacefully and lucidly at a ripe old age, surrounded by their nearest relatives, to whom they imparted spiritual and moral wisdom before the end.[5] Whether or not this bore any resemblance to the ways Americans died before the conflict, the Civil War rendered this antebellum Good Death impossible for most of the soldiers who perished during its course. Soldiers died in violent, sudden, lonely, delirious ways that violated and perverted the Good Death, and denied family members that sought-after deathbed vigil. The Christian Commission, in its work with the dead and dying, demonstrated a desire to alleviate this problem, acting as a proxy to observe and convey messages and descriptions from the deathbed to the distant family and to reassure them that the deaths of loved ones were ordained by divine Providence and were thus part of a larger plan. "It aimed to reach and link together," Rev. Herrick Johnson testified after the war, "the heart of the soldier, the parent's heart, and the heart of God."[6]

This impulse prompted the establishment of the Christian Commission Individual Relief Department (IRD) in 1864.[7] Its mission statement claimed that it provided "a sure and effective medium of communication between the wounded or sick soldier—whether in the Camp or in Field or General Hospitals—and his home friends," writing letters on behalf of the incapacitated, and using the influence of the USCC to make inquiries about the fates of soldiers with whom relatives had lost contact.[8] In reality, however, the IRD functioned more often to inform families of their sons' deaths and burial places than to reunite the living. This was reflected in the advice given to those investigating IRD requests, which was printed on the forms filled out by delegates and subsequently submitted to the central office:

> In cases of extreme sickness or death, use great care to get last messages and mementoes, the soldier's testament, diary or hymn book, or a leaf from the tree

130   TABERNACLES IN THE WILDERNESS

over his grave, and give full particulars of his last hours and place of burial. This department has special value in time of battle, and when the wounded come to hospitals. The *first* mail after the fight should carry your home message respecting the wounded or dead you have found. Remember hearts are breaking; let their first relief come in a Commission envelope.[9]

The ledgers recording the contents of letters sent by delegates on behalf of the IRD further illustrate that the department dealt more with death than with life; while some letters reassured families that their sons were safe and recovering, many others implored them to visit as swiftly as possible, if the soldier in question was not expected to live, to inform family members of the manner of a man's death and of the details of his burial place, or to pass on the effects of the deceased—"precious beyond estimate"—such as hair, jewelry, or books.[10] The IRD was thus instrumental in reinforcing the links between the home and battlefronts and bringing comfort to bereaved relatives, often through material objects.

Providing comfort to families who had lost loved ones was important in maintaining home front support for the war, but the rationale behind the Commission's provision of this comfort remained resolutely evangelical. In describing a dying soldier's last moments, the delegates—both those who worked for the IRD and those engaged in general service in hospitals and camps—hoped to convey to the absent family the destination of their relative's soul and ideally provide reassurance that he had found salvation and achieved eternal life. Delegates were tasked with recording deathbed scenes in the absence of relatives and providing comfort and spiritual guidance in the final hours, acting as "evangelist as well as surrogate kin and record keeper."[11] Deathbed narratives were frequently sentimental and sanitized, rarely focusing on the pain and gore of wartime deaths but on triumphant declarations and professions of faith. As Frances Clarke has argued, we must resist the urge to dismiss the idealistic, sentimental language and structure of narratives like this as meaningless. Their authors, she writes, "were not mouthing simplistic platitudes. They were engaged in an effort to take control of wartime carnage, invest it with meaning, and turn it to individual, political, and cultural advantage."[12] We can see this in the meanings USCC delegates extrapolated from deathbed encounters. Recording their conversations with dying men, delegates were obliged to assess the religious state of their patients and record their observations in IRD ledgers. The phrases used illustrated the lengthy struggle that preceded the conversion crisis, as they described men as, variously, "penitent," "believing in Christ," and "professing faith in Christ," for example.[13] The brief descriptions also indicated that, while delegates made progress with some patients, some remained im-

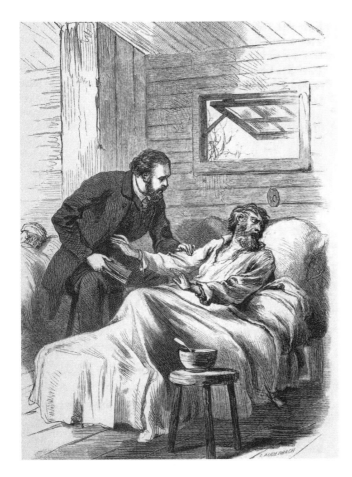

"I Cannot Come Now—I Will Not," in Edward Parmelee Smith, *Incidents of the United States Christian Commission* (Philadelphia: J. B. Lippincott & Co., 1869), 463. (Engraved by James W. Louderbach)

mune to the ministry of the Commission, and were dismissed as "backsliders" and "not professors."[14]

Furthermore, delegates were sometimes prevented from accurately assessing a man's religious state if he died before someone could speak with him or became too delirious to make conversation. Such instances were distressing to delegates anxious to prevent men from dying in an unconverted state. James B. Whitten reported with some regret that William Kenney of the Twenty-First Pennsylvania was "too low ... to ascertain the state of his mind" when Whitten visited him.[15] John Davidson was similarly distraught that he had not been able to converse with John Smith of the Forty-Fourth New York. "Dead, religious condition not known," Davidson wrote in the IRD ledger, lamenting that he had been called to speak to the dying man and "reached him to feel the last pulse beat."[16] These rather more pessimistic assessments were confined to the private ledgers of the Christian Commission, however, as delegates wrote lengthy letters to anxious relatives reassuring them that their sons and brothers died bravely and piously. Delegates also recorded particularly touching or encouraging scenes in their diaries and discharge reports, collecting evidence that their evangelizing work had not been in vain. Descriptions of triumphant, spiritually encouraging deaths that conformed to the USCC's wartime version of the Good Death were widely published in religious newspapers, circulated in the monthly "Information for Army Meetings" pamphlets, which were distributed on the home and battlefronts, and ultimately collated by Edward Parmelee Smith, secretary, in the postwar volume *Incidents in Hospital and Camp* (1869). The publication of these positive narratives indicates that the Christian Commission sought to do much more than comfort bereaved families through their efforts with the dead and dying. In fact, the USCC used the observations collected by its delegates to advance its evangelical mission to convert America.

In particular, the many victorious scenes collected by the USCC were presented as evidence that faith in Christ had been affirmed, a conversion experience had taken place, eternal life had been secured, and that the now dead soldier had contributed to the Christian Commission's target of "burning over" the army and, ultimately, the nation. Many of these narratives provided detailed personal information about the man they described, including his name and hometown, religious history, the cause of his death, and his final words. While these details went some way toward rescuing individual soldiers from the anonymity threatened by the sheer scale of the slaughter, the language used by the Christian Commission to frame these narratives and the common themes that recurred in the dying words of Union soldiers also subsumed each fallen man into a collective, national deathbed narrative. This shared rhetoric was central to the combination of piety and patriotism espoused by the USCC and to the concept that the deaths of Union soldiers were simultaneously martyrdoms for Christ and America.

THE "SENTIMENTAL TRINITY"

In the deathbed narratives parsed by USCC delegates we catch glimpses of the ideas and values that helped them make sense of their impending deaths. Gary Laderman suggests persuasively that a "sentimental trinity" of symbols—God, home, and country—appeared repeatedly in their reports of soldiers' dying words and framed how USCC delegates made sense of these deaths.[17] But these were not discrete entities with stable, distinct definitions. Some men did reference them separately—the last words of a man dying at a hospital in St. Louis, for instance, were reported to have been "my God—my country—my mother!"[18] Others conflated them. "Home" was a particularly slippery concept. Christian Commission delegates witnessed dying men long for the people, traditions, and physical landscapes of their native town or village; just as often, however, men used the language of "home" to anticipate a future, more permanent reward. E. Clarke Cline, stationed at Susquehanna, sat with a young boy bleeding to death from a severed artery and was touched to hear the boy tell him, "Jesus has a *home* in heaven for *me*."[19] The dying solider projected the happiness and peace he associated with the domestic sphere onto the celestial realm.

The deathbed rhetoric widely employed by dying soldiers and their witnesses during the Civil War often broke down distinctions between heaven and home, reimagining eternity as a homecoming.[20] This interpretation of heaven was not new; the increasing valorization of the family and the home as a haven of morality and virtue during the antebellum period also inflected changing conceptions of the beyond, imagining heaven as an idealized replica of the Victorian home, a pastoral oasis of security and peace away from the sin, pain, and commercialism of the world, a place of "love, union, peace, and harmony," where familial reunions would be joyful and eternal.[21] Furthermore, the decline of Calvinist predestination as the predominant theological tenet during the antebellum period granted the individual some agency in securing salvation, and made this domestic heaven theoretically accessible to all.[22] Although this domestic imagination of heaven was not precipitated by the bloodshed of the Civil War, the disruptions the war caused to burial and mourning traditions lent it increasing weight. When soldiers were parted from their families for long periods, and when families were denied the comfort of surrounding the deathbed and preparing the body for burial in a hometown plot, it was comforting to reimagine heaven as "an eternal family reunion" where the separation and suffering of war were entirely and eternally absent.[23] The dying words of one soldier whose death Samuel Wright witnessed endorsed this imagery. The man repeatedly said, "I'm going home," "I'm going home to Jesus," and "on Jordan's stormy banks I stand."[24] Another delegate watched a mortally wounded man die "amidst the outward signs of extreme bodily anguish." Despite the pain, the man was able to answer the delegate when he asked him where he was going: "I am going home," the man replied. "Yes, I am going home to be with Jesus."[25]

Antebellum interpretations of heaven focused not only on the materiality and domesticity of heaven but on its proximity to the mortal world. Inspired by the work of theologians like Emmanuel Swedenborg, the father of Spiritualism, increasing numbers of Americans saw the boundary between heaven and Earth as "blurred, flexible, and likely to be pierced at any time."[26] This permeable boundary meant that glimpses of heaven might filter through to the still living, especially in their dying moments when the soul was preparing to depart; this prompted deathbed observers to scrutinize the countenances and utterances of the dying for clues as to the nature and properties of heaven, both as reassurance of the deceased's spiritual destination, and to provide hope for their own future in eternity. Christian Commission delegates, often acting as proxies for absent relatives and friends, engaged in this scrutiny as they watched over the deathbeds of countless soldiers. They recorded many instances where the dying seemed to catch sight of heaven and where heaven seemed to be close to Earth. At Perryville, a delegate overheard a surgeon tell a wounded man that he had moments to live. "This is the best moment of my life," the man replied. "It grows brighter and brighter." Drawing on the pastoral, sunny celestial archetype that pervaded nineteenth-century pictorial depictions of heaven, the delegate then reported, "he went away into the country where light dwells."[27] Light suffused these brief, deathbed glimpses of heaven. Another man, in his dying moments, implored those gathered around his hospital bed not to weep for him. "I am not afraid to die," he told them. "I don't know how the valley will be when I get to it, but it is all bright now."[28]

Thus filled with light, heaven was a place of beauty, purity, and majesty, recognizable to Earth's inhabitants, but more perfect, more holy than their mortal abode. The contrast between the perfection of heaven and the base suffering of Earth was accentuated by the places where Civil War soldiers died. Hospitals— when soldiers survived long enough to reach them—were rarely bright, airy, comfortable places. Just as often, soldiers died outside, in makeshift field hospitals, or where they fell on the battlefield, surrounded by squalor and gore.[29] A delegate recounting the death of a prisoner of war in the notorious Confederate prison at Andersonville, Georgia, described how the man died "peacefully, even gladly," instructing the reader to "imagine the contrast between Andersonville and heaven."[30] Emphasizing the beauty and perfection of heaven in contrast to the earthly privation and pain endured by Union soldiers cast ascension into heaven as a just reward for that endurance and identified service for the Union (and, especially, dying in the course of that service) as a godly pursuit that fitted men for heaven.

Despite this, USCC personnel did not abandon their commitment to evangelical theology. They stressed that although faith and prayer might be helpful, salvation was gained through grace alone; that is to say, they did not express the heretical notion mooted by some that dying for the Union was sufficient to guarantee salvation.[31] Rather, the Commission remained convinced that "if [soldiers] have died in the Christian's faith, they are not lost. Though suddenly cut off, they have only given up this short, weary, changing life, for a bright, peaceful immortality!"[32] This evangelical ethos meant delegates were deeply concerned with whether the dying men they encountered had undergone conversion and were thus confident in their hope of eternal life. As we have seen, the work of Christian Commission delegates—whether explicitly, through methods such as preaching and religious literature, or more implicitly, through physical ministrations—was designed to target souls and bring about conversion. Encounters with the dying constituted, in many ways, the culmination of these efforts and a final chance to gauge the progress and success of the USCC's work.

Delegates supposed that hope of salvation would be manifested in the manner of a converted man's death, allowing him to die without fear or reluctance. As Lewis Saum writes, "death could be a powerful lesson and reassurance for the living, and . . . a final outward sign of an inward grace evidenced by the departing."[33] The search for evidence of conversion was a common theme in deathbed narratives. William Schaeffer, for instance, encountered a dying soldier at Harrisburg whose newfound faith in the resurrection allowed him to die happily. "I have every reason to believe when he died . . . he was a Christian," Schaeffer wrote. "He said he felt that he was a new creation he felt his sins were forgiven he had an interest in that Lamb of God that taketh away the sins of this world he died happy praising God with his last breath."[34] The confidence and happiness that accompanied conversion were evident in the death scene of James Davis of the Thirty-First Maine, who died in November 1864 of typhoid fever, typically a painful and protracted death characterized by delirium, abscesses, dehydration, and intestinal hemorrhage. Despite this, the delegate assigned to his ward, Charles Hyde, recorded that Davis died "happily with trust in God."[35] Davis's death illustrates another important point: like a high proportion of soldiers on both sides, he died of disease, not of wounds sustained while engaging the enemy in battle. Although Davis's death did not bear the hallmarks of heroism and patriotism commonly associated with combat deaths, he was not denied the prospect of eternal life because of his trust in God and his apparent conversion. Battle deaths may have been more useful to the Christian Commission's construction of a powerful narrative of patriotic martyrdom and blood atonement, but—because grace alone secured salvation—there is no indication that delegates perceived death in battle to be a greater guarantee of eternal life than other causes of death.

Unsurprisingly, the suffering endured by the Civil War dying often made religion look a more enticing prospect than it might otherwise have been.[36] Some delegate accounts implied that soldiers were more favorably disposed to the

136 TABERNACLES IN THE WILDERNESS

word of God at the hour of their death. Jack Smock, working in Indianapolis, lamented that many remained unrepentant on their deathbed but was encouraged "to meet so many that seemed to feel their need of the Saviour as they passed through the dark valley, and so attentive to, and eager for, counsel and prayer."[37] J. M. Rookwood's conversations with Charles King succinctly captured the power of impending death to turn one's mind to Christ; at first, Rookwood wrote, King hoped he would recover from the destruction caused by the minié ball that ripped through his abdomen and was "unwilling to entertain religious thoughts." When it became clear that he would not recover, however, King "manifested a tender spirit and a desire that Christians sh'd pray for him."[38]

Thus, the deathbed rhetoric employed by dying Union soldiers and the USCC delegates who bore witness to their deaths was based heavily on ideas of "home" and "God"—ideas that frequently bled into each other as men strove to articulate what drove them to fight for the Union and their hopes for the afterlife. The third element of Laderman's "sentimental trinity," that is, "country," was equally important to this rhetoric and equally difficult to separate neatly from the other two. Dying men repeatedly made vague, apolitical references to their country as a primary motivation both for their service and their pride in dying in the course of that service. In the deathbed narratives edited and published by the USCC, however, this love of country was almost always twinned with an equivalent expression of love for God. In one case, a dying man had lost most of his kit and possessions on the battlefield but clutched tightly to the United States flag he had been carrying during the fight. As he died, the delegates asked him whether his Savior was with him. They reported, "He whispered, 'Do you think He would pass by and not take me? I go, I go.' And wrapped in stars he went up among the stars."[39] This scene drew direct parallels between the stars on the flag and the stars symbolizing heaven and the hope of finding eternal life there. Another deathbed scene was even more explicit in equating the cause of God and the cause of country and rendering ambiguous the precise cause for which the soldier died. The dying words of the man in question were reportedly, "I have a good many friends, schoolmates, and companions. . . . You can let them know that I am gone, and that I die content. And, Chaplain . . . my brother in the navy—write to him and tell him to *stand by the flag and cling to the cross of Christ!*"[40] The symmetry of this last entreaty linked and equated the two causes.

The combination of piety and patriotism forged by such rhetoric also fueled the Christian Commission's interpretation of the Civil War as a holy crusade that would cleanse America. Many delegates believed that converts who died in the name of a divinely sanctioned Union were akin to martyrs. In the eyes of these delegates, it was not only by converting to evangelicalism that

Union soldiers could help to bring about America's long-held destiny: the courageous deaths of these converted men would also further God's Kingdom.[41] Christian Commission personnel contributed heavily to an emerging vocabulary of blood sacrifice and atoning death that attempted to explain and justify the horrific death toll of the war, and that emphasized America's role as God's "redeemer nation." At their most extreme, Northern religious commentators increasingly cast the war in terms of good and evil, of justice and revenge, interpreting Union victories as signs of God's blessing and defeats as signs that God was "purifying His people through the fires of adversity so that they would come to depend only on Him."[42] These moral absolutes demanded similarly absolute warfare and absolute bloodshed and provided a lens through which the slaughterhouses of Cold Harbor and Chancellorsville became comprehensible, even acceptable: the blood of the fallen soldiers would atone for the sins, not only of slavery and Northern complicity in the institution, but also of Northern materialism, greed, and secularism.

Many of the leaders and ministers of the Christian Commission fed the image of the war as a bloody but necessary rebirth. Redemption gained through bloodshed was, for example, a recurrent theme in the hymns commonly sung at USCC prayer meetings and services. The Commission printed hymn books for distribution among the troops, with hymns and songs grouped into categories such as "Praise," "Prayer," "Saviour," "Warnings and Invitations," "Death," and "Heaven."[43] Two of the most popular hymns, written in the mid-eighteenth century but closely associated with nineteenth-century revivalism, were steeped in the imagery of cleansing sacrifice. William Cowper's famous 1779 hymn begins, "There is a fountain filled with blood drawn from Emmanuel's veins / And sinners plunged beneath that flood lose all their guilty stains," a refrain often echoed by delegates seeking to comfort men at their hour of death. Similarly, "Come, Thou Fount of Every Blessing," also popular at camp revival meetings, emphasized the centrality of Christ's blood to atonement. The third stanza begins, "Jesus sought me when a stranger, / Wandering from the fold of God; / He, to rescue me from danger, / Interposed his precious blood." In both these cases, the blood involved was that of Christ; however, this gory symbolism took on a new significance amid the bloodshed of the war, as the sacrifice of Christ crucified was increasingly equated with that of the Union soldier dying on the battlefield. Thus the cleansing blood of Christ was substituted with the blood of Union soldiers staining the fields of Virginia—as J. B. Roberts said at one San Francisco meeting, "[the Union soldier] sacrifices himself for the nation as Christ sacrificed himself for our redemption."[44] Nowhere are the martyrdoms of Christ and the soldier more explicitly linked and compared than in Julia

138 TABERNACLES IN THE WILDERNESS

Ward Howe's "Battle Hymn of the Republic," another favorite of the Christian Commission, commonly sung at anniversary meetings and thanksgiving celebrations: "as He died to make men holy, let us die to make men free."[45]

Just as humanity was washed clean of sin by Jesus's blood, so the Union was being cleansed by the blood of young martyrs falling in their thousands, prostrating themselves on the altar of the nation.[46] The soldiers themselves began to endorse this connection; at one nighttime prayer meeting, a delegate recalled, "there was an allusion, by one who prayed, to the garden scene of Gethsemane, the blood of the son of God, in connection to the blood shed for our country."[47] The men had gathered outside to pray the night before the battle, just as Jesus and his disciples gathered in the garden the night he was betrayed, and, just as Christ prepared himself for death, so, too, the praying soldiers were readying themselves for the fight and, by extension, for death. Field Agent E. P. Smith, who would go on to compile the *Incidents* after the war, also emphasized the simultaneously pious and patriotic symbolism of spilled blood. "The man who dies for us! Can the claims of any other be compared with his?" Smith asked. "Passing in a moment away, shedding his blood for us, are we not solemnly bound, if we can, to make it sure that, for the soldier, the precious blood of Jesus shall avail in the last solemn day?"[48] Worshiping Christ became an intensely patriotic act. Vice versa, fighting for the Union became an act of religious service. To all intents and purposes, not only were piety and patriotism mutually reinforcing in the eyes of Commission leaders—even one and the same—but were crucial components of the successful regeneration and eventual salvation of America. "Love for the country and the Savior," according to one report, "gives the tongue of fire to those who speak, the soul of bounty to those who give, the apostolic spirit to those who serve without pay, the tireless energy to those who work; . . . and over all throws the halo of the millennial dawn, harbinger of the long-awaited day."[49]

BURYING BODIES

Saving souls on the brink of departing was not enough. The Christian Commission was deeply concerned not only with the state of the Union soldier's soul but with his body, too, both as a conduit to spiritual regeneration and—as we saw earlier—as a visible indicator of religious conviction and conversion. This concern with the body did not cease at the moment of death; the delegates of the Christian Commission very much endorsed the antebellum belief that the countenance and pose of the dead body could provide evidence of the spiritual state of the deceased. This was particularly important during the Civil War, when men often died suddenly or alone, without anyone to observe their dying moments or record their final words. During the battle of Nashville in December 1864, one man was shot in the head, dying instantly. B. F. Jacobs, the station agent there, was anxious to give the man a Christian burial and looked for clues in the man's body to testify to his religious state. "He was a magnificent-looking soldier," Jacobs wrote, emphasizing the man's athletic masculinity and heroic form; "his whole appearance and physique were of the finest. There was no change upon his face as his comrades bore him back; the smile of rest even was undisturbed."[50]

Dying with a smile on one's face was often interpreted as a sign that the man had died happy, accepting and even embracing his death, both in the knowledge that his demise represented heroic and patriotic sacrifice and in the hope of eternity achieved. The delegates at Nashville encountered another corpse that seemed to embody this combination of piety and patriotism in its final, frozen expression: "in the morning we found a smile in the eye and on the lips of the dead patriot, which seemed to be still repeating—'Dear Jesus, You love me and You know I love You.'"[51] Sometimes the body's posture and facial expression alone did not betray any evidence of the man's spiritual state, prompting the delegates to look elsewhere for clues. Unloading dead and wounded soldiers from the *City of Memphis* at Mound City, Kay Burnell found one corpse covered in a blanket, the limbs already straightened out by the man's comrades. While moving the body, Burnell noticed the man's pocket Testament tucked under one arm. "It was open," Burnell wrote. "I looked into it as it lay, and my eye caught these words of eternal consolation to the Christian: 'let not your heart be troubled.'"[52] Burnell conceded that he could not conclusively prove that these were the last words the man had read but suggested the mere presence of the Testament was indicative of the man's devotion.

In addition to scrutinizing the bodies of the dead for evidence of salvation, the delegates of the Christian Commission were frequently involved in the burial of those bodies. The practical problems of identifying and burying the dead in their thousands after major battles, the often insufficient methods improvised by the authorities to tackle these problems, and the horror expressed by soldiers and civilians alike at the prospect of an anonymous, shared resting place unconsecrated by ritual, have been widely documented.[53] Mass burials, often without coffins or individual grave markers, were commonplace, and bodies were often left to lie unclaimed on the battlefield for days or even months, allowing birds and animals, unscrupulous looters, the elements, and the steady march of decomposition to strip the bodies of their individuality and humanity. With the Union and Confederate governments struggling to deal with the problem, civilian agencies often took matters into their own hands. While the

140   TABERNACLES IN THE WILDERNESS

Sanitary Commission's efforts to oversee burials, manage hospital graveyards, ship remains back to the home front, and keep death registers, were more extensive and better funded than those of the Christian Commission, the USCC still demonstrated a desire to give as many men as possible what they deemed a decent, Christian burial.[54] Delegates routinely oversaw funeral services in the absence of a regimental or hospital chaplain. For example, K. Atkinson at Camp Convalescent reported conducting an average of five funerals a week; this seems to have been an unusually high figure by Christian Commission standards, but even those who performed funeral services only sporadically, such as William Jewell at Camp Barry, placed great importance on the duty, and looked back on the funerals they conducted as "solemn and interesting" occasions.[55]

One of the USCC's most dedicated delegates, George Bringhurst (whom we met in chapter 1), demonstrated the importance of burial to the Commission's evangelical mission in a sermon preached at All Saints Episcopal Church, Philadelphia, upon his return from a term of service on the front. "We allow no soldier to be buried without a religious service," he claimed—an easier promise to fulfill when stationed at a hospital where deaths might be staggered than on a battlefield, where deaths were both more numerous and tightly clustered, swiftly outstripping the capacity of both military and civilian attempts to secure individual burial for all.[56] Bringhurst and his colleagues considered a decent funeral incomplete without the religious rituals familiar to civilian life, rituals that during the Civil War sanctified the ground in which the men were buried and publicly validated their sacrifice.[57] At the hospital where he was stationed, Bringhurst and five fellow delegates led a procession of convalescing patients to the small cemetery a short distance away. Carrying the bodies of the dead on stretchers, they sang hopeful hymns that spoke of eternal life and the importance of the soul in securing it: "when I am called to die / sing words of holy ecstacy / to waft my soul on high!" After holding a brief religious service, Bringhurst led the men in a final hymn, which employed the language of home and heaven discussed above to emphasize the glorious rewards awaiting the Union dead: "in the Christian's home of glory / there remains a land of rest!"

On another occasion, Bringhurst encountered a detail of men burying two fallen comrades. In a move that suggests the importance of religious rituals to the enlisted men as well as to the evangelicals seeking to minister to them, one man approached him and asked him to preach over the graves. Bringhurst agreed readily and recounted to his Philadelphia congregation how "just as that Sabbath morning's sun burst forth in glory, I committed the remains of these heroic boys to the grave, with a sweet trust in the Sun of Righteousness, the resurrection and the life!"[58] Bringhurst's recollections of this impromptu funeral service demonstrate how the Christian Commission frequently and explicitly linked the earthly heroism of Union soldiers who died in the service of their country to the attainment of eternal life. As noted above, the USCC did not claim that death in battle alone would secure salvation and remained devoted to the notion that acceptance of God's grace was the only route to heaven. However, it is notable that Bringhurst, in this anecdote, did not inquire after the spiritual states of the men over whose graves he preached. Instead, he was willing to assume that their souls were bound heavenward.

A final excerpt from Bringhurst's sermon clearly illustrates how the Christian Commission conceived of the Union dead as martyrs for a holy cause. "We smoothed the dying pillow of those heroic boys of ours," Bringhurst recalled: "We wrapped them in their blankets and strewed their forms with flowers. We caught the loving accents meant for loved ones, fond and dear. We bore them to their lowly graves, and shed a sacred tear. May those sacred ashes rest in peace! May the God of heaven watch over those lonely, though holy graves! And may the memory of those heroes ever be fresh. God bless their sacred dust! We shed over their memory a silent tear, and leave them with their God."[59] Again, Bringhurst linked heroism to sacredness, implying that death in the service of the Union contributed to the sanctification of the deceased's memory. Yet further than this, he suggested that the sacred memory of that heroism was preserved indelibly in the material evidence left behind—the "holy graves" and the "sacred dust" interred within. The soldier's body, therefore, did not cease to function as a symbol of piety and patriotism once the soul departed; once buried, the body continued to serve as a reminder of the heroism—a quality the Christian Commission often elevated to martyrdom—of its owner. The graves in which Christian Commission delegates helped to bury the Union dead, therefore, symbolized the mixture of evangelicalism and nationalism the Commission espoused in its work.

Susan-Mary Grant's work on the national cemeteries established during and shortly after the Civil War reveals the role of these formal, permanent spaces as sites of memory, symbols of the sacrifice that permitted the rebirth and consecration of America.[60] The plain, identical headstones of Gettysburg and Arlington, and the nationalist rituals of commemoration that swiftly developed surrounding these sites, were deliberately designed to sublimate individual deaths into the larger American project, and contributed to the emergence of a postbellum civil religion, which drew heavily on the themes of blood sacrifice and redemption so central to the memory of the Civil War.[61] These permanent, carefully designed cemeteries were important shrines to the memory that postwar America (more specifically, the Northern leaders who dictated the shape of postwar commemoration) wished to preserve and promote. But what about the

142 TABERNACLES IN THE WILDERNESS

hastily arranged, undistinguished resting places where the Civil War dead were initially interred, such as the impromptu graves over which USCC delegates often found themselves preaching?[62] Despite the lack of monument or fanfare, the Christian Commission conceived of these rudimentary graves as vital symbols of sacrifice and redemption, and of the hope of heaven, especially in the case of those whose families could not afford to have their sons' remains reinterred.

The importance of these makeshift resting places in the eyes of the Christian Commission was evident in the care they took to adorn and mark them.[63] In the same way that the physical appearance of a corpse yielded clues as to the heroism and piety of its owner, the appearance of a grave could broadcast the sacred sacrifice of the man entombed within. Thus, delegates frequently displayed a concern for the beauty of the graves over which they presided. One delegate expressed a dedication to ensuring "that the beautiful life might end in a beautiful grave," while another wrote to a bereaved family reassuring them that their son "would be buried in a beautiful cemetery."[64] E. Clark Cline, presiding over a burial at Hagerstown, Maryland, recalled how he and some local women and children joined together in "trimming the body with flowers"—in this instance, the dead man was fortunate enough to have been granted a coffin.[65] Efforts to beautify the graves of the Union dead in the midst of war emphasized the status of the cemetery, no matter how basic or temporary, as "a liminal ground—between death and eternal life," the crude decorations and markers anticipating the eternal holy beauty of heaven.[66]

The Christian Commission was, however, keenly aware that individual, ritualized burial was all too often impossible to secure, and innovated methods for identifying and reinterring remains through the distribution of small identifier tags, a rudimentary precursor to metal dog tags.[67] These flimsy card tags left space for the name, regiment, and rank of the soldier, and on the reverse, a forwarding address where family could be contacted and to which effects could be sent.[68] These tags illustrated several facets of the USCC's work in relation to death. They displayed the Commission's interest in promoting the ordinary soldier from an anonymous cog in the Union Army machine to a mortal individual and complemented the work of the IRD in attempting to contact bereaved families with news of the fates of their sons. Most importantly, however, the tags suggested a controversial and powerful association: the equation of the soldier's death with the death of Christ. On the reverse of the card tags, a famous Bible verse was printed: "For God so loved the world, that he gave his only begotten Son, that whosoever believeth in him should not perish, but have everlasting life" (John 3:16). This verse held a dual significance; not only was it a reminder of the promise of salvation and life after death and comfort to the soldier advancing

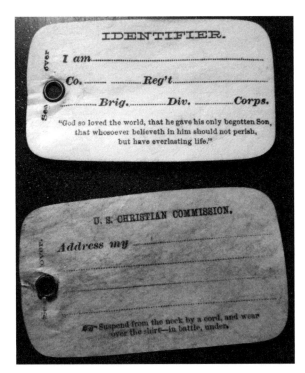

Identification Tag, n.d. (Scrapbooks 1861–65, United States Christian Commission Records, 1861–66, Records of the Adjutant General's Office, Record Group 94, National Archives Building, Washington, DC)

into battle and imminent destruction, but its inscription on an item explicitly designed to contend with violent death implied that the willing sacrifice of the bearer in battle was on a par with Christ's own violent death. In the same way that Christ crucified symbolized the absolution of the human race from sin, the corpses of the Union dead symbolized for the Christian Commission the cleansing and regeneration, not only of the Union but of the world.

Delegates' efforts to secure and confirm the conversion of the souls of dying Union soldiers, as well as the meanings they ascribed to dead and dying bodies and to the graves in which they were interred, thus encapsulated the philosophy of the Christian Commission. The Commission combined bodily and spiritual ministry—even at the last—in an urgent evangelizing mission that delegates often invested with national significance. In addition to the benevolent work of comforting bereaved civilians and facilitating the identification and repatriation of remains, the delegates used the final utterances and physical appearances of dead soldiers to gauge the overall progress of this mission. They tied individual deaths—and graves—into the fulfillment of a national destiny, developing a compelling rhetoric of blood sacrifice that, theoretically, vindicated the carnage of the war, anticipated the moral cleansing of America, and secured a central role for the Christian Commission in bringing it about.

EPILOGUE

"See What the Lord Hath Wrought"

The Christian Commission concluded its work with a final gala festival in February 1866. Held in the Hall of the US House of Representatives and chaired by Speaker of the House Schuyler Colfax, the event perfectly encapsulated the USCC's persistent and powerful blend of piety and patriotism. Along with the Executive Committee and prominent members of the USCC, "All the leading public men in military, naval, political, and civil life now in Washington" were there, among them Ulysses S. Grant, Chief Justice Salmon P. Chase, prominent Methodist Bishop Matthew Simpson, and Maj. Gen. Christopher Augur.[1]

The event was a sellout. "All the seats on the floor and in the galleries were filled at an early hour, and many persons were unable to obtain admittance," the *Baltimore Daily Commercial* reported.[2] "Such a packed house I never saw," Charles Henry Howard wrote to his sister. "I stood up for over three hours—but the exercise were intensely interesting & I felt fully repaid."[3] Not all attendees were quite so effusive. Julia Wilbur, an antislavery activist from Rochester, was forced to perch on a step throughout the evening. "Hot & tiresome," she wrote tetchily. "Speaking of ordinary character. Crowd came to see the notables rather than to hear."[4] Others were scandalized that such an "impious" gathering should have gone ahead at all given its scheduling on the Sabbath day. Far from healing the wounds of the war, the leaders of the Reformed Presbytery feared that the self-congratulatory gathering would bring "more wrath upon Israel."[5]

Despite the naysayers and grumblers, the evening was a success much lauded in the evangelical press. The proceedings were punctuated by hymn singing and musical performances. The thronged crowds joined together in singing Christian

"Closing Exercises of the Christian Commission," in John W. Hutchinson, *Story of the Hutchinsons (Tribe of Jesse)* (Boston: Lee and Shepard, 1896), 431. (Illustrator unknown)

Commission favorites, including "We Are Rising as a People" and "Jesus Shall Reign Where'er the Sun."[6] The famous Hutchinson Family Singers, on tour in the District and Maryland, performed "I Live for Those Who Love Me" and "The Good Time Coming," new hymns of hope that called on Christians to have faith in the future coming gladness.[7] Most newspaper reports of the meeting focused on the performance of Philip Phillips, a well-respected tenor with a "wonderfully sweet voice" from Jamestown, New York, who had already forged a name for himself arranging and composing popular hymns.[8] Phillips was no stranger to huge fundraising gatherings like the one held in the House of Representatives in February 1866. Indeed, at the third Christian Commission anniversary the previous year he had performed Ellen H. Gates's popular "Your Mission" to rapturous applause.[9] According to several reports, during the performance, Abraham Lincoln, who was present, had passed a scrap of paper to George Stuart asking that Phillips repeat the song. "Don't say I called for it," the note said.[10]

Almost exactly a year later, Lincoln—now nine months dead—haunted the Commission's celebration. A memorial to the slain president, at which dignitaries led by the historian George Bancroft would eulogize Lincoln, was scheduled to take place in the hall the next day; the room was already draped in black crêpe in anticipation, lending the USCC's celebration a patina of gloom. Many attendees could not help but think back to Lincoln's presence at the third anniversary event the previous year.[11] George Stuart recalled with fondness his private meeting with Lincoln, praising the "genial smile" and "characteristic light" that animated Lincoln's face.[12] Lincoln's support for the USCC during his life was hardly zealous, yet the Commission's supporters were all too keen, especially after his death, to identify signs of his approval and blessing in his words and aspect. The *New York Herald* remembered Lincoln's "care-furrowed face and his nobly throbbing heart" at the 1865 meeting.[13] Many speakers expressed confidence that Lincoln was now present in spirit, blessing the gathering. "Our martyred one looks lovingly upon the scene," Bishop Matthew Simpson promised.[14]

Political supporters, including Sen. James Doolittle of Wisconsin (as well as the presiding Speaker Colfax), and clergymen, including Benjamin Chidlaw, an Ohio-based Presbyterian originally from North Wales, and Herrick Johnson, an enthusiastic graduate of Auburn Theological Seminary in New York, addressed the gathering at length. The lengthy orations praised the Commission's "victories over suffering, victories over disease, victories over death itself."[15] It was not only Lincoln who looked down approvingly from heaven: the speakers repeatedly invoked the memory of those "whose souls have been marching on since they fought their last battle, who were made soldiers of Christ through the agency of the Christian Commission, before they met and conquered their last foe."[16] Letters from various dignitaries read aloud to the throng further heaped on the adulation. Admittedly, it must have rankled that famous correspondents like General Grant and General Meade carelessly lumped the Christian and Sanitary Commissions together in a general narrative of philanthropic do-gooding. Some testimonies, too, were rather more grudging than others—the USCC's old nemesis General Sherman conceded, "at times I may have displayed an impatience when the agents manifested an excess of zeal, in pushing forward their person and stores," but protested "I have always given them credit for good and pure motive."[17]

The vast majority of letter writers, however, were filled with praise and optimism for the future. Major General Patrick prayed "that the good seed it has so freely sown by all waters may continue to spring up and bear fruit abundantly, to the glory of Him whose light failed us never, even in the days of our deepest darkness."[18] Salmon P. Chase, a devout Episcopalian, simply said of the Commission's work: "it reached beyond time."[19] The writers and speakers echoed the Christian Commission's own framing of its delegates as soldiers for Jesus—in his opening address, Speaker Colfax detailed how delegates, "clad in the armor of the nation . . . went forth to win the glorious victories they so gloriously achieved—victories over suffering, victories over disease, victories over death itself."[20] The delegates' self-sacrifice and hard work were persistent themes throughout the evening; Charles Demond, too, reminded the audience: "they labored hard; they lived upon camp fare; they slept often upon the ground." Their penury and suffering, he suggested, echoed the example of Christ, "who left the glories of heaven to seek and save the lost."[21]

The supporters of the Christian Commission maintained that the organization's effect on the moral character of the nation was profound and lasting, even eternal. Some praised specific elements of the USCC's work: aid for refugees, teaching work with freed people, providing comfort to the dying and deathbed testimonies to the bereaved. Benjamin Butler suggested that the USCC had helped soldiers reintegrate into civilian life by maintaining links to the home front. RA Charles Davis agreed: by keeping the "moral influence" and "restraints of society" alive on the battlefront, the USCC had ensured that men returned to their families "not hardened and corrupted, but strengthened."[22]

The audience left the auditorium cheered. There was work left to be done, and the future was bright. The work of evangelization would continue and would save the world. Herrick Johnson believed that the Commission, while ceasing to exist as an organized entity, would become "an unseen, subtle power entering into the moral forces that are henceforth to do their part in God's great evangelism. It is not dead," he reassured his listeners. "It will never die."[23]James

Doolittle believed that America had come through the trial of war stronger and more godly, and that the Christian Commission's continued influence was proof that "he is with us, leading us upward, and heavenward, in order that we as a people may realise upon earth a higher, a better, a diviner life."[24] Charles Demond, the chair of the Boston USCC branch, was confident that the Commission's work was simply the beginning of the road to millennium: "May we not hope that this army work, so strange, so unique in the world's history, may be the beginning of the day when all the branches of the host who love the Lord Jesus, like the different corps of a great army, shall march together under one leader; striving only in this, that each shall do its part in hastening on the time when the kingdoms of this earth 'shall become the kingdom of our Lord and of his Christ'?"[25] The speakers tasked the departing crowds with continuing this proud and pious legacy. "Brave workers, go to your fields," Bishop Simpson said. "They are ripening to the harvest."[26] Benjamin Chidlaw used the same agricultural metaphor. "We are mustered out tonight from sowing that we may go to reaping," he said. "It is reaping time already."[27] Lemuel Moss had the final word. Like Demond, he was confident that this was just the beginning. "Wherever mention shall be made of the work it has accomplished," he predicted, "the quick, grateful, adoring response shall be, 'See what the Lord hath wrought.'"[28]

The final meeting, and its enthusiastic reception in the religious press, was only one small step in the postwar project of acclaiming the work of the USCC. Prominent USCC men toured Europe publicizing their experiences. Despite the death of his youngest son and his own failing health, George Stuart, the Commission president, embarked on a lengthy lecture tour of Britain and Ireland in 1866, speaking at various religious and society meetings about the organization's war work. In the final months of the war, Edward Parmelee Smith, secretary, wrote to key branch agents and dedicated delegates asking them to compile interesting anecdotes or incidents that illustrated the work of the Commission and its reception among both Union and Confederate troops. At the same time, Lemuel Moss began compiling an official history of the Christian Commission. These efforts resulted in the publication of two hefty, self-congratulatory volumes within only a few short years of the end of the war; Moss's *Annals of the United States Christian Commission* (1868) and Smith's *Incidents among Shot and Shell* (1870).[29] These were the last coordinated efforts to celebrate and memorialize the Commission's work, however. The delegates, diet kitchen managers, teachers, and station agents went home. The theological students resumed their studies. The aid societies turned to other social problems or disbanded altogether.

The afterlives of the Commission were disparate and defy neat categorization. Let me provide three brief examples to illustrate. Commission Secretary

Edward Parmelee Smith stayed in the South beyond the end of the war, assisting the American Missionary Association in their work setting up schools for freed people. In his reports from the field, printed in the monthly *American Missionary*, we can track the erosion of his initial optimism. In June 1867 he described the progress of the work as "remarkable" and praised his students' "great aptitude and anxiety for letters."[30] Just a year later, however, he reflected dejectedly on the huge structural and social obstacles that obstructed the work and the wider project of securing civic equality for African Americans as Reconstruction fell apart. "The whites are bitter in the extreme," he lamented, "and since the colored people have dared to vote, the bitterness has been increased. 'Nigger' is the common term, and if a man uses the word 'colored' he is at once known to have come from the North."[31]

The most prominent women in the Commission, Annie Wittenmyer, served from 1874 as the first president of the Women's Christian Temperance Union, lecturing up and down the country on the perils that drink posed to the morality and integrity of the nation and marshaling diffuse local actions into a powerful national lobby group with its own journal and the apparatus to gather huge petitions in favor of a prohibition amendment. Yet her presidency was shaped by a consistent political and social conservatism. She refused to endorse woman suffrage and echoed other nativist writers in identifying the most pressing threat to American sobriety, morality, and progress: "the foreign emigration" made up of "criminals flying from justice" and "paupers with infirmities of body and mind or idle and dissolute habits."[32] She was eventually ousted from the presidency in 1879 by the more radical Frances Willard, who turned the WCTU toward a broader raft of reform issues and made suffrage a central plank of the Union's goals and actions.[33] George Stuart, meanwhile, returned to the YMCA and Sunday School work that had occupied him before the war. In 1869 he was convinced by his wartime friend Ulysses S. Grant—by then in the White House—to join the newly created Board of Indian Commissioners. Although Stuart framed his involvement in sentimental, benevolent tones—his professed aim was "to do something to help the poor Indian"—the committee's attitudes and actions were grimly indicative of Native American policy after the Civil War, promoting Christianization schemes, endorsing the reservation system, and upholding the Grant administration's assimilationist line.[34]

Smith, Wittenmyer, Stuart, and many of their former colleagues navigated a changing philanthropic landscape in the years after the Commission concluded its work. Antebellum ideas about who constituted a "worthy" recipient of aid—and what that aid should look like—seemed to be passing away. On the surface, the voluntarism and sentimentalism of the USCC appeared increasingly outmoded, even obsolete. Charity was becoming professionalized. The "foundation" model of philanthropy built by Gilded Age titans of industry like Andrew Carnegie was not far away. Crucially, the task of saving America's souls remained distressingly incomplete. Yet the ideas and methods that underpinned the Commission's work did not vanish entirely. Traces of the optimism and sense of purpose that energized the gathering at the Hall of Representatives in February 1866 resurfaced in the decades following. The reforming zeal of the evangelicals who had founded the Christian Commission was evident in the programs and agendas of the late nineteenth-century Social Gospel movement (one leading figure, Washington Gladden, had served twice as a delegate of the USCC).[35] The evangelizing mission of the Christian Commission lived on too in the famous transatlantic revivals of the early 1870s, which were led by Dwight L. Moody, nine times a USCC delegate.[36] Meanwhile, the YMCA continued its proselytizing work, shifting its focus to foreign fields of endeavor and establishing missions in China and Japan at the end of the century.[37] The rugged athleticism and Christian manliness implicit in the USCC's insistence on physical fitness and vigor became more explicit in the YMCA's growing promotion of sports and physical activity as a means of regenerating individuals and communities.[38]

More importantly, the men and women who worked for and with the USCC during the war remembered its efforts—and the frequently life-changing experiences with which it had furnished them—with fondness and pride. It brought physical and mental comfort to thousands of Union troops. Its work demonstrated the continuing vitality and strength of evangelicalism as a social force in the mid-nineteenth century. The workers of the Commission, whether driven by pity, curiosity, or above all by an overwhelming sense of Christian duty, devoted their energies in the midst of a national crisis to making men think about the state of their souls, and to helping them wrestle against doubt and sin. The prayers and songs, the tracts and Bibles; the sewing kits and cups of coffee; the final conversations, the tears, the graves. All became part of the work of conversion. All were enlisted in the crusade to bring the Federal Army closer to salvation. The Second Coming of Christ was not yet a reality. But as they streamed out into the Washington night with Philip Phillips's sweet tenor still ringing in their ears, the war a fading memory, they must have felt it very close at hand.

NOTES

INTRODUCTION

1. Smith, *Incidents of the United States Christian Commission*, 289–92.

2. Lemuel Moss to Annie Wittenmyer, Feb. 1865, Letters Sent; United States Christian Commission Records, 1861–66; hereafter USCC.

3. Moss, *Annals*, 729.

4. Bernice D. Ames to "Brother Burnett," Nov. 3, 1864, Letters Sent, USCC.

5. Harper Bois, Report, Oct. 28, 1864, Delegates' Statistical Reports, USCC.

6. Fredrickson, *The Inner Civil War*, 107. For Fredrickson's influential discussion of the USSC see chap. 7 (98–112). William Quentin Maxwell also alludes to the Sanitary Commission's concerns about the "contagion of sentimentality" associated with the USCC. Maxwell, *Lincoln's Fifth Wheel*, 193. For more recent work on the Sanitary Commission, see Meier, "US Sanitary Commission Physicians and the Transformation of American Health Care," 19–40; L. A. Long, *Rehabilitating Bodies*, especially chap. 6 (84–112); and Schwalm, "A Body of 'Truly Scientific Work,'" 647–76. An important recent corrective to the image of the USSC as driven entirely by unsentimental, scientific approaches and ends is Gardner, "When Service Is Not Enough," 29–54.

7. Undated clipping, "Rev. Dr Bellows' Lecture on the Sanitary Commission," Scrapbooks, USCC. In reality, soldiers were often more than happy to accept writing paper, new clothing, or tasty little treats from whichever commission happened to establish a presence near their company.

8. As recent work on women's involvement in the Sanitary Commission has revealed, this rivalry extended to home front fundraising efforts spearheaded by female philanthropists. See, for instance, Giesberg, *Civil War Sisterhood;* and Attie, *Patriotic Toil.*

9. Works that focus on the Christian Commissions include: Cannon, "The United States Christian Commission," 61–80; Henry, "The United States Christian Commission during the

152 NOTES TO PAGES 6–9

Civil War," 375–87; McDevitt, "Fighting for the Soul of America"; and Raney, "In the Lord's Army." These works, while valuable, make limited use of archival material, and offer narrative accounts of the Commission's foundations and work, shedding relatively little light on the theological underpinnings and apocalyptic world view of the Commission. Some scholars have focused on particular aspects of the Commission's work: see, for instance, Bennett, "Saving Jack," 219–62, on the work of the USCC in the Union Navy; McDevitt, "'A Melody before Unknown," 105–36; and Leonard, *Yankee Women*, 51–102, on the diet kitchens established by the USCC in military hospitals; Hoisington, "'A Thousand Nameless Acts,'" 2–37, on the work of the Commission during and after the Battle of Gettysburg. The Christian Commission also appears in histories of the Civil War religion and of the lives of Civil War soldiers. See, for instance: R. J. Miller, *Both Prayed to the Same God*, 86–89; Rable, *God's Almost Chosen Peoples*, 213–20; Shattuck, *A Shield and Hiding Place*, 26–33, 85–92; Woodworth, *While God Is Marching On*, 167–70; and, most recently, B. L. Miller, *In God's Presence*.

10. Indicative of the "professionalization of charity" narrative is Greeley, *Beyond Benevolence*. Gardner, in "When Service Is Not Enough," suggests that the persistence of older ideas about charity also involved the survival of "a centuries old belief that not all suffering deserved to be relieved" (33). In Offiler and Williams, *American Philanthropy at Home and Abroad*, my coeditor and I stress the need to decenter "the foundation" from philanthropy history and to reexamine the persistence of older ideas about aid and its "worthy" recipients.

11. Interest in the theological history of the Civil War has gathered pace since the publication of Miller, Stout, and Wilson's important edited collection *Religion and the American Civil War* in 1998. Important works in this field include Noll, *The Civil War as a Theological Crisis*; Stout, *Upon the Altar of the Nation*; and Wright and Dresser, *Apocalypse and the Millennium*. An earlier but nonetheless valuable contribution is Moorhead, *American Apocalypse*.

12. Hall, "Introduction," in Hall, *Lived Religion in America*, vii.

13. Attie, *Patriotic Toil*, 33–38; Giesberg, *Civil War Sisterhood*, 23–25; Ginzberg, *Women and the Work of Benevolence*, 133–34.

14. McDevitt, "Fighting for the Soul of America," 103–10.

15. Colyer, *Report of the Christian Mission to the United States Army*, 4–5.

16. Moss, *Annals*, 75–116; Raney, "In the Lord's Army," 15–20. Other members of the original committee included John V. Farwell, a well-known Chicago merchant and philanthropist, John P. Crozer, a wealthy textile manufacturer; and Stephen H. Tyng, a popular New York preacher. McDevitt, "Fighting for the Soul of America," 112–13.

17. This delay extended to the documentation of the Christian Commission. Prior to mid-1863, as the secretary of the Commission later acknowledged, "the Commission did not preserve such complete and ample records of its operations as it did subsequently." Sparse and haphazard before this point, reports from delegates, and financial records, were far more meticulously kept in the last two years of the war. Moss, *Annals*, 725.

18. *United States Christian Commission, First Annual Report*, 105–9.

19. Although the earliest, largest, and most profitable branches were mostly located in New England, New York, and Pennsylvania, as the war progressed branches were established in the Northwest, on the Pacific Coast, and as far south as Kentucky, Maryland, and Missouri. See *United States Christian Commission, Second Annual Report*, iii–xii.

20. McDevitt, "Fighting for the Soul of America," 110–19; Moss, *Annals*, 122–33; Raney, "In the Lord's Army," 29–35. That the bulk of USCC activities—and hence records—postdate the

Emancipation Proclamation may explain the relative—and somewhat surprising—dearth of material relating to slavery and its abolition. As I discuss elsewhere, USCC delegates were often keen to engage with Black troops and were involved in efforts to aid freed people as the war drew to a close, but the Commission as an entity issued few public pronouncements condemning slavery or hailing the Federal Army as an emancipating force.

21. Hirrel, *Children of Wrath*, especially 9–25. See also Sutton, "Benevolent Calvinism and the Moral Government of God," 34–36.

22. Mullen, *The Chance of Salvation*, 27–31.

23. Goen, *Broken Churches, Broken Nation*, 47–48.

24. Griffin, *Their Brother's Keepers*, 64.

25. No summary of antebellum reform would be complete without wading into the debate over the "social control" theory, most famously articulated by Clifford Griffin and Charles Foster in the 1960s. Advocates of this interpretation characterized religious reform as a subtly coercive but deliberate campaign by upper class citizens—usually Whigs—who, responding to a perceived dwindling of their own cultural and political influence, attempted to impose their own conservative values on a rapidly changing society by bringing the population under the auspices of the Benevolent Empire. Foster, *An Errand of Mercy*; Griffin, *Their Brothers' Keepers*; and Griffin, "Religious Benevolence as Social Control, 1815–1860." See also Horlick, *Country Boys and Merchant Princes*. Useful early challenges to the classic social control thesis include Banner, "Religious Benevolence as Social Control," 23–41; Kohl, "The Concept of Social Control and the History of Jacksonian America," 21–34; and Howe, "The Evangelical Movement and Political Culture in the North," 1216–39, especially 1219–20. These scholars emphasize that antebellum reform organizations, while primarily promoting moral values determined and dictated by their middle- and upper-class leaders, were also committed to the liberating tenets of free spiritual agency, self-government and voluntarism, and sought to bring about the order they envisaged through self-discipline and self-help rather than through the imposition of institutional or legislative authority. We must remember, too, that the postmillennial eschatology that underpinned evangelical reform was part of a sincerely held belief system. Thus, the conscious goal of antebellum reformers was to achieve the preservation of a Christian republic held together by democracy, humility, self-reliance and voluntary association, and ultimately to bring about a utopian millennium, rather than to enact an elite conspiracy for material gain. I am most convinced by Steven Mintz, who rejects Foster, Griffin et al. as "excessively conspiratorial" and charts a course somewhere between "those who regard reform as a means of class-based social control and those who stress reformers' benevolent intentions." Mintz, *Moralists and Modernizers*, xvii. For a detailed historiographical survey see Harden, "Men and Women of Their Own Kind."

26. Abzug, *Cosmos Crumbling*, 124. See, for example, John, "Taking Sabbatarianism Seriously," 517–67; McCrossen, "Sabbatarianism," 134–51; Dannenbaum, *Drink and Disorder*, and Tyrrell, *Sobering Up*.

27. Joseph P. Ferrie estimates that as many as 20 percent of men living in rural areas in 1850 had moved to urban areas by 1860. Ferrie, "How Ya Gonna Keep 'Em down on the Farm [When They've Seen Schenectady]?" Hall and Ruggles address the cliometric challenges of precisely calculating migration rates in "'Restless in the Midst of Their Prosperity,'" 829–46.

28. Bremner, *From the Depths*, 42.

29. K. T. Long, *The Revival of 1857–58*, 61.

154 NOTES TO PAGES 10–14

30. Horlick, *Country Boys and Merchant Princes*, 232.

31. Boyer, *Urban Masses and Moral Order*, 111–20.

32. Lupkin, *Manhood Factories*, especially 1–35. Lupkin suggests that the early American YMCAs "occupied a site at the intersection of the Sunday school and the saloon . . . [offering] an alternative structure for leisure time, a religious reinterpretation of an elite men's club, with its masculine yet domestic comforts" (12).

33. Horlick, *Country Boys and Merchant Princes*, 236.

34. Richards, "Report of the President," 12. William Ballantyne, a prominent member of the Christian Commission, was Richards's vice-president.

35. Colyer, *Report of the Christian Mission*, 4–5.

36. Among those with prominent roles in the antebellum YMCAs who would go on to help shape the USCC were: John Farwell, Benjamin F. Jacobs, and Dwight L. Moody, all of Chicago; John Wanamaker of Philadelphia; and George Stuart himself. Stuart had met George Williams in London while on a business trip in 1851 and had helped establish the YMCA in Philadelphia in 1854, serving as its president in the early years of its existence. Boylan, *Sunday School*, 93; see also Francis, "The Religious Revival of 1858 in Philadelphia," 60–61.

37. See, for instance, Hoisington, *Gettysburg and the Christian Commission*, 1–4; K. T. Long, *The Revival of 1857–58*, 87–90, 119–20; Bremner, *The Public Good*, 57–70; and Paludan, *A People's Contest*, 352–54.

38. By 1859, after the intense religious enthusiasm of the past two years had subsided, 182 YMCAs were in existence across the United States, 98 of them formed in 1859. Raney, "In the Lord's Army," 12; Hopkins, *History of the YMCA in North America*, 83.

39. Moss, *Annals*, 66; see also Stuart, *The Life of George H. Stuart*, 106.

40. Historians continue to disagree over when the Second Great Awakening happened (the decades between 1790 to 1840 being the most popular answer), what it meant to the people involved and for American religion, or indeed whether it constitutes a useful historical label at all. The field is vast, but see, for instance, Conforti, "The Invention of the Great Awakening, 1795–1842," 99–118; C. D. Johnson, "The Protracted Meeting Myth," 349–83; and Rachel Cope's important excoriation of the omission of women's experiences from existing historiography in Cope, "From Smouldering Fires to Revitalising Showers," 25–49.

41. T. L. Smith, *Revivalism and Social Reform*, 43.

42. McLoughlin, *Revivals, Awakenings, and Reform*, 127.

43. K. T. Long, *The Revival of 1857–58*, 124. The Cane Ridge, Kentucky, revival of 1801 exemplified this democratization and foreshadowed the popular styles of the 1830s. Conkin, *Cane Ridge: America's Pentecost*; and Eslinger, *Citizens of Zion*, especially 202–14.

44. Hatch. *The Democratization of American Christianity*, 35.

45. Hopkins, *History of the YMCA*, 8.

46. P. E. Johnson, *A Shopkeeper's Millennium*, 98.

47. T. L. Smith, *Revivalism and Social Reform*, 60. For a succinct definition of what constituted a revival, see Bratt, "Religious Anti-Revivalism in Antebellum America," 65–106, 69.

48. Moorhead, "Between Progress and Apocalypse," 524–42, 527.

49. T. L. Smith, *Revivalism and Social Reform*, 65–68.

50. Hopkins, *History of the YMCA*, 81. Kathryn Long argues that the 1857–58 Revival was neither as novel in its interdenominational character nor as male in the makeup of its participants as contemporary newspaper coverage of the revival suggested. Earlier histories, which drew heavily upon this coverage, perpetuated an image of the revival as a male-

NOTES TO PAGES 17–21

dominated affair characterized by noon meetings of urban office workers—that is to say, as unprecedented and unique in the history of American revivalism by dint of both its methods and makeup (see, for instance, McLoughlin, *Revivals, Awakenings, and Reform,* 141; T. L. Smith, *Revivalism and Social Reform,* 64–77). Long suggests persuasively that this image is overly simplistic, and that in addition to downplaying the considerable interdenominational scrapping, it erases the involvement of countless women, as revivalists, converts, or anxious family members urging their relatives to repent and be saved. K. T. Long, *The Revival of 1857-58,* 11–92. It is not surprising, however, that the USCC delegates who were so keen to claim the 1857-58 Revival as their organization's natural progenitor embraced the orthodox account of events and emphasized the similarities between the male-dominated army camps in which they labored and the apparent "culture of masculine piety" generated by the revival. Hoisington, *Gettysburg and the Christian Commission,* 10.

51. *Rochester Democrat,* Dec. 12 1864; Scrapbooks, USCC.

1. CHRISTIAN MANLINESS AND THE VOLUNTEER DELEGATE SYSTEM

1. Attie, *Patriotic Toil,* 158–59; Bremner, *The Public Good,* 57–59; Shattuck, *A Shield and Hiding Place,* 26–27; Woodworth, *While God Is Marching On,* 168–70.

2. Moss, *Annals,* 551.

3. Attie, *Patriotic Toil,* 161.

4. David Raney details the names of USCC field agents and the departments they supervised in "In the Lord's Army," 30–33.

5. Moss, *Annals,* 541; "Commission no. 66," n.d., Scrapbooks, USCC.

6. J. R. Miller, "Circular," Mar. 30, 1864, Scrapbooks, USCC.

7. George Stuart, circular, Jan. 7, 1865, Scrapbooks, USCC.

8. Moss, *Annals,* 143.

9. Moss, *Annals,* 200.

10. Fea, *The Bible Cause,* 79–80.

11. For instance, William Fulton was "peculiarly impressed with the quietude, discipline, and moral order" of the freed people he encountered near Hampton. "The Gospel among the Colored Troops," *Presbyterian Standard,* Feb. 16, 1865. J. W. Harding said, "these colored soldiers have strong arms and strong hearts." Smith, *Incidents,* 358. In expressing surprise at Black soldiers' appetite for reading material and eagerness to learn to read and write, accounts like these betrayed the author's racist assumptions about the intellectual capacity of Black people. This is even more explicit in the recounting of other encounters with African Americans, where the Black interlocutor's speech was often rendered in a grotesque and exaggerated dialect. See, for instance, Smith, *Incidents,* 358–68.

12. Theodore Schnitzler, report, June 10, 1865, Weekly Reports of Delegates, USCC; Robert Patterson to George H. Stuart, Sept. 16, 1863, Reports, USCC.

13. *The American Freedmen's Aid Commission,* African American Pamphlet Collection, Library of Congress, 1865.

14. Levine, "Indian Fighters and Indian Reformers," 334.

15. *First Annual Report,* Feb. 1863, YMCA Archives.

16. Ulysses S. Grant, "Special Order No. 23," Dec. 12, 1863, quoted in "Authority" in *Christ in the Army,* 53.

156 NOTES TO PAGES 21–25

17. Sherman, quoted in Moss, *Annals*, 496.

18. Woodworth, *While God Is Marching On*, 169–70. "General Orders, No. 49," United States War Department, *The War of the Rebellion*, 1:382.

19. Maryniak, "Union Military Chaplains," 43–47; Shattuck, *Shield and Hiding Place*, 62; Wiley, *The Life of Billy Yank*, 263–64.

20. Maryniak, "Union Military Chaplains," 4.

21. Shattuck, *Shield and Hiding Place*, 52–54.

22. Woodworth, *While God Is Marching On*, 152.

23. Benjamin Waddle, diary entries, Mar. 3 and 16, 1864, Diaries, USCC. Waddle worked alongside Edward Phillips Payson, a Congregational minister with the 146th New York, and Joseph Mateer, a Presbyterian with the 155th Pennsylvania. G. H. Hall, "Religion in the Army," *Christian Advocate*, Feb. 23, 1865, Scrapbooks, USCC.

24. "B. H.," report dated Nov. 21, 1864, Reports, USCC.

25. N.a., "The US Christian Commission," *Congregationalist*, Jan. 20, 1865, Scrapbooks, USCC.

26. George Stuart to W. L. Tisdale, July 15, 1864, Letters Sent, USCC, RG94, NAB; George Stuart to Charles C. Clark, Dec. 12, 1864, Letters Sent, USCC.

27. I have written elsewhere about the problems and scandals created by delegate misbehavior. See Williams, "Heaping Coals of Fire on the Enemy's Head," 17–32.

28. George Stuart to W. J. King, Apr. 13, 1865, Letters Sent, USCC.

29. Lemuel Moss to Mary Chase, Feb. 14, 1865, Letters sent, USCC.

30. "Commission no. 66," n.d., Scrapbooks, USCC.

31. "Documents of the Christian Commission," 1862, Reports, USCC.

32. George Darius Downey, diary entry, July 19, 1862, United States Christian Commission Diary, 1862–circa 1865, Library of Congress, Miscellaneous Manuscripts Collection, Washington, DC.

33. William Boardman to J. E. Hall, Aug. 24, 1864, Letters sent, USCC.

34. William E. Boardman, "The Principles of the Christian Commission," in *Christ in the Army*, 25.

35. George Stuart and William Boardman, "United States Christian Commission: Information about Delegate Work," n.d., Reports, USCC.

36. Most scholarship on masculinity and the Civil War focuses on the experiences of soldiers and veterans. The best example of this is Lorien Foote's *The Gentlemen and the Roughs*. See also, for example, Blight, "No Desperate Hero," 55–75; Ramold, *Baring the Iron Hand;* and Thompson, *Friendly Enemies*.

37. See Griffen, "Reconstructing Masculinity," 183–204; Mangan and Walvin, "Introduction," 1–6; Rotundo, *American Manhood*, 10–30.

38. See Park, "Biological Thought, Athletics, and the Formation of a "Man of Character," 7–30; and Putney, *Muscular Christianity*.

39. Greenberg, *Manifest Manhood*, 10.

40. Vance, *The Sinews of the Spirit;* see also Hall, "Muscular Christianity," 3–13.

41. G. R. Bent to George H. Stuart, Sept. 14, 1863, Letters Sent, USCC.

42. Membership implied not only regular church attendance but also proof that congregants had undergone a moment of crisis through which they had subsequently been converted to Christ. Therefore members and, by extension, delegates, were the most zealous and committed sections of a congregation, which was further made up of "hearers" who professed

NOTES TO PAGES 25–31 157

belief or interest in Christ crucified but had yet to undergo this conversion process. See Carwardine, *Evangelicals and Politics,* 43; Finke and Stark, "Turning Pews into People," 186.

43. Conkin, *The Uneasy Center,* 114–15.

44. "Pacific Christian Commission," n.d., Scrapbooks, USCC. There were, of course, limits to this interdenominationality, which was confined to evangelical denominations. Catholics and Unitarians, needless to say, were absolutely verboten.

45. Griffin, *Their Brothers' Keepers,* 60.

46. Goen, *Broken Churches, Broken Nation.*

47. Moss, *Annals,* 575.

48. Henry G. Safford, report, Mar. 27, 1864, Delegates' Statistical Reports, USCC.

49. K. Atkinson, report, Sept. 7, 1863, Delegates' Statistical Reports, USCC.

50. *Information for Army Meetings, November 1864,* 12, 36; Lemuel Moss to A. K. Potter, Dec. 12, 1864, Letters Sent, USCC.

51. William Boardman to George Nair, Oct. 12, 1864, Letters Sent, USCC.

52. William Boardman to J. J. Abbott, Oct. 28, 1864, Letters Sent, USCC.

53. First Annual Report, 1863; Armed Services United States Christian Commission–related Records, Kautz Family YMCA Archives, Univ. of Minnesota.

54. J. P. Kennedy, report, Nov. 22, 1864, Delegates' Statistical Reports, USCC.

55. James L. Patton, report, Aug. 4, 1864, Delegates' Statistical Reports, USCC.

56. A. W. Knowlton, report, July 23, 1864, Weekly Reports of Delegates, USCC.

57. Registers of delegates, USCC.

58. George Stuart to M. S. Wells, Aug. 22, 1864, Letters Sent, USCC.

59. George Stuart to D. Harbison, Apr. 29, 1864, Letters Sent, USCC.

60. Moss, *Annals,* 591.

61. "The Christian Commission and Its Work," Nov. 11, 1864, Reports, USCC.

62. "Dinner and My Hosts," *Ripley Bee,* May 12, 1864, Gale Nineteenth Century Collections Online.

63. Ringel, "Thrills for Children," 77–91, 89.

64. Curtis, "Visions of Self, Success, and Society," 613–34; Horlick, *Country Boys and Merchant Princes.*

65. Mujic, "Save a School to Save a Nation," 110; Wongsrichanalai, *Northern Character.*

66. Wongsrichanalai, "College-Educated New Englanders in the Civil War," 71–72; for example, 56 percent of Harvard's class of 1861 and 42 percent of Yale's class of 1861 served in the Civil War. Andover's rolls went from 133 in 1860 to just 68 in 1864. Rowe, *History of Andover Theological Seminary,* 77; R. F. Miller, "Brahmins under Fire."

67. Mujic, "'Ours Is the Harder Lot,'" 33–67.

68. Bendroth, *A School of the Church,* 45–49.

69. Bendroth, *A School of the Church,* 438.

70. E. P. Smith, *Incidents,* 161–62.

71. Moss, *Annals,* 370; Faris, *The Life of J. R. Miller,* 25.

72. *Annual Catalogue of the Allegheny Theological Seminary,* 32.

73. William Boardman to Rev. J. S. Easton, Oct. 20, 1864, Letters Sent, USCC.

74. Wongsrichanalai, "'What Is a Person Worth at Such a Time,'" 49.

75. George Stuart to John Cole, Aug. 8, 1864, Letters Sent, USCC.

76. A. D. Morton, report dated spring 1864, Delegates' Statistical Reports, USCC.

158   NOTES TO PAGES 31–40

77. George Stuart to John L. McElroy, Aug. 11, 1864, Letters Sent, USCC.

78. Woodworth, *While God Is Marching On*, 148.

79. It must be pointed out that the USCC's president hardly conformed to this ideal: George Stuart's chronic asthma often saw him absent from the Philadelphia office, bedridden for long periods.

80. The primary proponent of this view is Ann Douglas, in *The Feminization of American Culture*. Douglas's thesis has not gone unchallenged (see, for instance, Schuyler, "Inventing a Feminine Past," 291–308; however, whether this process of feminization was real and identifiable is less important than fears among the clergy that their authority was being eroded. See also Welter, "The Feminization of American Religion: 1800–1860," 137–57.

81. Rotundo, *American Manhood*, 172; Shiels, "The Feminization of American Congregationalism, 1730–1835," 60. As I have suggested in the above note, whether American ministers were indeed "effeminate" is less important here than the perception of effeminacy, which drove attempts to energize and "masculinize" the clergy.

82. Rotundo, *American Manhood*, 173.

83. *Information for Army Meetings, June & July 1864*, 3.

84. *Information for Army Meetings, June & July 1864*, 6–7.

85. *Hymn Book for the Army and Navy*, 2.

86. *Hymn Book for the Army and Navy*, 3, 11.

87. Albright, *Civil War Diary of Louis Miller Albright*, Plate XI.

88. Leach, *History of the Bringhurst Family*, 80.

89. George Stuart, "Circular to Returned Delegates," Mar. 9, 1865, Scrapbooks, USCC.

90. George Bringhurst, sermon, n.d., Letters Received, USCC.

91. Hatch, *The Democratization of American Christianity*, 130–41. Preaching is discussed at greater length in chap. 4.

92. Roberts, *American Alchemy*, 160–65; Hendler, *Public Sentiment*, 36–38.

93. Mary Chapman and Glenn Hendler's important edited collection, *Sentimental Men*, is particularly useful in challenging what they call "the uncomplicated gendering of sentiment as feminine" in earlier scholarship. Chapman and Hendler, "Introduction," 7.

94. Moss, *Annals*, 252.

95. See, for example, Frank, *Life with Father*, 1–12; McDannell, *The Christian Home in Victorian America*, 108–16, 128–36; and Ryan, *Cradle of the Middle Class*, 157–62.

96. Mitchell, *The Vacant Chair*, 51–53, 75–80.

97. David, "The Politics of Emasculation," 329.

2. FEMALE WAR WORK AND THE CHRISTIAN COMMISSION

1. "Ladies Christian Commission," in *Christ in the Army*, 40.

2. Ryan, *Cradle of the Middle Class*, 83–98, 116–27; Shaver, *Beyond the Pulpit*; Hansen, *A Very Social Time*, 152–65; Cott, *The Bonds of Womanhood*, 126–59.

3. Blauvelt, "Women and Revivalism," 1:1–45.

4. Matthews, *The Rise of Public Woman*, 106.

5. Boylan, *Sunday School*, 114–26.

6. Mary Bingham to George Stuart, Apr. 20, 1864, Letters Received, USCC.

NOTES TO PAGES 40–46

7. Edward L. Clark to William Boardman, Nov. 13, 1864, Letters Received, USCC.

8. Registers of Delegates, 1863–65, USCC.

9. Roxanne Mountford argues that opposition to female preaching was built into the very architecture of American Protestant spaces, as pulpits, buildings, and church communities were deliberately designed to accommodate the (cis) male body. Mountford, *The Gendered Pulpit.*

10. Grammer, *Some Wild Visions,* 35. Lisa Shaver, in *Beyond the Pulpit,* has convincingly argued that focusing on the pulpit as the sole site from which religious rhetoric emanated is too simplistic, and risks overlooking and erasing other forms of rhetorical expression that were more accessible to women.

11. Brekus, *Strangers and Pilgrims,* 204–5.

12. Resolution proposed by Lucretia Mott, quoted in "Woman's Rights Convention, Held at Seneca Falls, 19–20 July 1848," in Gordon, *The Selected Papers of Elizabeth Cady Stanton and Susan B. Anthony,* 1:83. Zink-Sawyer, *From Preachers to Suffragists,* 18. Opponents of female preaching pointed to precedents laid out in the Pauline Epistles, in particular 1 Cor. 1434 ("Let your women keep silence in the churches: for it is not permitted unto them to speak; but they are commanded to be under obedience, as also saith the law.") and 1 Tim. 211–12 ("let the woman learn in silence under all subjection. But I suffer not a woman to teach, nor to usurp authority over the man, but to be in silence.").

13. George Stuart to Miss Ball, Aug. 12, 1864, Letters Sent, USCC.

14. Lemuel Moss to Hattie Jackson, Feb. 2, 1865, Letters Sent, USCC.

15. Moss, *Annals,* 315.

16. Rev. Dr. Kirk, "A National Movement for Organizing Ladies' Christian Commissions," in *Ladies Christian Commissions,* 3–10.

17. All USCC publications omit the possessive apostrophe in Ladies Christian Commission; I have done the same for consistency's sake.

18. Ginzberg, *Women and the Work of Benevolence,* 133–74; Giesberg, *Civil War Sisterhood;* and Attie, *Patriotic Toil.* On the links between consumption, patriotism, and emotion in Civil War home front production, see Cohen, "You Have No Flag out Yet?," 378–409.

19. Sarah Jones Weicksel stresses that Civil War home front production encompassed both industrial capitalist modes and the "family economy," and that the two modes were not discrete from one another. Weicksel, "'Make up a Box to Send Me,'" 67–86, 69.

20. Moss, *Annals,* 358.

21. Moss, *Annals,* 324.

22. *Ladies Christian Commissions,* 21; Moss, *Annals,* 357.

23. William Boardman to Reverend Wiswell, n.d., Letters Sent, USCC; Lemuel Moss to Mrs. Bannan, Dec. 15, 1864, Letters Sent, USCC; Zebley, *The Churches of Delaware,* 10; George Stuart, handwritten certificate, Dec. 20, 1864, and George Stuart to Mrs. Bannan, Dec. 20, 1864, Letters Sent, USCC.

24. Record of Contributions and Record of LCCs, USCC.

25. Luckingham, "Benevolence in Emergent San Francisco," 431–43.

26. Irwin, "'Going about and Doing Good,'" 41.

27. For more on the typical lineup and layout of Sanitary Commission fairs, which the LCC Fair closely modeled, see Madway, "Purveying Patriotic Pageantry," 268–301.

28. Huggins, "Women in Wartime," 261–66.

NOTES TO PAGES 46–53

29. Revolutionary and colonial "relics" were a staple of Civil War fundraising fairs and, Frances Clarke argues, both legitimized the Union as part of a noble, patriotic lineage stretching back to Washington and other Revolutionary heroes, and sanitized, simplified, and domesticated America's past, ultimately "fossilizing" it as a contrast to the modern, productive America of the 1860s. See Clarke, "Old-Fashioned Tea Parties," 294–312.

30. B. Gordon, *Bazaars and Fair Ladies*, 1, 9. For Sanitary Fairs, see especially 58–93.

31. As Joanna Cohen notes, censorious voices, though rare, were all too keen to condemn not only "raffling" but the unbecoming connection of wartime production to personal profit and aggrandisement. Cohen, "You Have No Flag out Yet?," 400–401.

32. "The Christian Commission Fair," *Evening Bulletin*, Aug. 25, 1864, Scrapbooks, USCC.

33. George Stuart to J. J. Johnston, Aug. 9, 1864, and George Stuart to E. N. Davis, Nov. 1, 1864, Letters Sent, USCC.

34. *History of the Hartsville Ladies Aid Society*, 17.

35. George Stuart to Mrs. C. F. Maurice, Oct. 22, 1864, and George Stuart to Melissa Snyder, Aug. 19, 1864, Letters Sent, USCC.

36. "Ladies Christian Commission," in *Christ in the Army*, 43–46.

37. "Ladies Christian Commission," in *Christ in the Army*, 46.

38. Bernice Ames to J. R. Miller, Oct. 29, 1864, Letters Sent, USCC.

39. George Stuart to Edwin Stanton, Apr. 1865, Letters Sent, USCC.

40. George Stuart to Abbie Doates, Aug. 2, 1864, Letters Sent, USCC.

41. George Stuart to Mrs. Harriet Webster, Sept. 15, 1864, Letters Sent, USCC.

42. George Stuart to Mrs. C. F. Maurice, Oct. 22, 1864, Letters Sent, USCC.

43. Moss, *Annals*, 644.

44. Olmsted, *To the Loyal Women of America*, 3.

45. Ginzberg, *Women and the Work of Benevolence*, 165.

46. Bernice Ames to Mary Rowe, Oct. 14, 1864, Letters Sent, USCC.

47. Attie, *Patriotic Toil*, 164, 160.

48. Giesberg, *Civil War Sisterhood*, 195n64.

49. *History of the Hartsville Ladies Aid Society*, 25.

50. *History of the Hartsville Ladies Aid Society*, 4.

51. Leonard, *Yankee Women*, 53–80. In fact, Robert Martin suggests, residual bitterness may explain why Wittenmyer chose to approach the USCC for support and collaboration rather than the better-resourced Sanitary Commission. R. F. Martin, "Annie Wittenmyer and the Twilight of Evangelical Reform," 141–61, 150–51.

52. Wittenmyer, *Under the Guns*, 260.

53. Wittenmyer, report, n.d., Communications Received, USCC; emphasis in original.

54. Wittenmyer, report, n.d., Communications Received, USCC; emphasis in original.

55. Moss, *Annals*, 670; Wittenmyer, report.

56. Moss, *Annals*, 670–71.

57. Moss, *Annals*, 682–84.

58. Schultz, *Women at the Front*, 45–50.

59. Wittenmyer, *A Collection of Recipes*, 7–8.

60. Wittenmyer, *A Collection of Recipes*, 39–40.

61. Wittenmyer, report.

62. "Diet Kitchens," in *Christ in the Army*, 86.

NOTES TO PAGES 54–58 161

63. Sklar, *Catharine Beecher;* Leavitt, *From Catharine Beecher to Martha Stewart,* 9–22.

64. Nightingale, *Notes on Nursing.*

65. Florence Nightingale, quoted in Wittenmyer, *Collection of Recipes,* frontispiece.

66. Nightingale, quoted in Wittenmyer, *Collection of Recipes,* 43–44.

67. Nightingale, quoted in Moss, *Annals,* 664.

68. Although Wittenmyer admired Nightingale and invoked her frequently in instructing the diet kitchen workforce, she did not consider managing diet kitchens a form of nursing. The contested status of "nurse" came with its own connotations, many of which were threatening to the Christian Commission's conservative interpretation of feminine respectability. For more on women nurses in the Civil War, see, for instance, Humphreys, *Marrow of Tragedy,* 63–75; and Schultz, *Women at the Front.*

69. Wittenmyer, *Under the Guns,* 259. This assessment was perhaps unduly (even deliberately) harsh. As James Robertson details, enlisted men, even those without prior cooking experience, had to become creative and basically competent chefs to make their meager and unappetizing field rations remotely palatable. Robertson Jr., *Soldiers Blue and Gray,* 64–74.

70. Surgeon in charge at New Albany, Indiana, quoted in Moss, *Annals,* 674–75.

71. Moss, *Annals,* 665.

72. Wittenmyer, *Under the Guns,* 261.

73. Schultz discusses how hospital roles (and labeling those roles) were influenced by class and race in *Women at the Front,* 21–23.

74. E. W. Jones to Wittenmyer, quoted in Moss, *Annals,* 678.

75. "The Work of the Christian Commission," *Daily Evening Bulletin,* Jan. 18, 1865, Gale Nineteenth Century Collections Online. Jones's account also suggests that the diet kitchens became unexpected sites of interracial encounter and cooperation. Among the register of seventy-six "lady managers" were seven women assigned to "colored" hospitals. Moss, *Annals,* 682–84.

76. Cheryl Wells has challenged the depiction of the Civil War hospital as a space controlled by men in "Battle Time," 409–28.

77. Leonard, *Yankee Women,* 67.

78. McDevitt, "A Melody before Unknown," 113.

79. McDevitt, "A Melody before Unknown," 92–93; Wittenmyer, "Instructions to Managers of Special Diet kitchens," n.d., Communications Received, USCC.

80. For example, Cook, *"Through Sunshine and Shadow,"* 31–32; Gusfield, *Symbolic Crusade,* 76–77.

81. Guinn, "Annie Wittenmyer and Nineteenth-Century Women's Usefulness," 351–77.

82. Burstyn, "Catharine Beecher and the Education of American Women," 386–403, 390–92.

83. Moss, *Annals,* 666.

84. Leonard, *Yankee Women,* 85.

85. Moss, *Annals,* 673.

86. Wittenmyer, *Collection of Recipes,* 39–40.

87. Wittenmyer, *Collection of Recipes,* 39–40.

88. Wittenmyer, *Collection of Recipes,* 39–40.

89. Henry L. W. Burrit to Annie Wittenmyer, Sept. 28, 1864, Communications Received, USCC.

90. Wittenmyer, report, n.d., Communications Received, USCC.

162   NOTES TO PAGES 58–63

91. Wittenmyer, report, n.d., Communications Received, USCC.

92. Mary Shelton to Edward Parmelee Smith, Apr. 25, 1865, Communications Received, USCC.

93. McDevitt, "A Melody before Unknown," 118.

94. McDevitt, "A Melody before Unknown," 118, 120.

3. EVANGELIZATION AND THE PRINTED WORD

1. "Religious Books for the Soldiers," *New York Evangelist,* Nov. 27, 1862, American Periodicals Series Online.

2. Foote, *Gentlemen and the Roughs,* 19–20.

3. Ramold, *Baring the Iron Hand.*

4. Giesberg, *Sex and the Civil War,* 37.

5. Foote, *Gentlemen and the Roughs,* 17–41; Lowry, *The Story the Soldiers Wouldn't Tell,* 61–88; Mitchell, *The Vacant Chair,* 39–55; Robertson Jr., *Soldiers Blue and Gray,* 81–102, 122–45; Wiley, *The Life of Billy Yank,* 247–62.

6. On the idealization of mother as moral guardian and educator, see Cott, *The Bonds of Womanhood,* 84–89; Epstein, *The Politics of Domesticity,* 67–87; McDannell, *The Christian Home in Victorian America,* 128–36; Ryan, *Cradle of the Middle Class,* 157–62.

7. Boyer, *Urban Masses and Moral Order in America,* 108–20; Horlick, *Country Boys and Merchant Princes,* 227–45.

8. Mitchell, *The Vacant Chair,* 19–39.

9. E. Colton, report, July 1, 1864, Delegates' Statistical Reports, USCC, 1861–1866.

10. W. C. Strong, report, Feb. 25, 1864, Delegates' Statistical Reports, USCC.

11. George H. Hesser, report, Aug. 1864, Delegates' Statistical Reports, USCC. The Christian Commission was particularly aggrieved at the level of profane language employed by troops, not only because this frequently involved blasphemous oaths but also because repeated swearing was believed to lead to mental, physical, and spiritual corruption. For nineteenth-century popular usage and attitudes of religious societies toward profanity, see, for instance, Montagu, *The Anatomy of Swearing,* 224–39; and McEnery, *Swearing in English,* 83–117.

12. A. D. Morton, report, spring 1864, Delegates' Statistical Reports, USCC.

13. William Winterbottom, report, Dec. 8, 1863, Delegates' Statistical Reports, USCC.

14. R. B. Godfrey, report, Nov. 12, 1863, Delegates' Statistical Reports, USCC.

15. Blum and Matsui, in *War Is All Hell,* argue that historians of religion have too often focused on how Americans articulated ideas about Jesus, God, and heaven at the expense of their obverse: Satan, hell, sin, and evil (4–9). While Christian Commission delegates rarely framed their understanding of the war in these terms, the specter of damnation underlay many of their writings.

16. Conkin, *The Uneasy Center,* 66, 114–15. The so-called "Bebbington quadrilateral" remains a useful distillation of the evangelical worldview. Bebbington, *Evangelicalism in Modern Britain,* 2–17.

17. Hatch, *The Democratization of American Christianity,* 15.

18. Most notable among these flourishing populist denominations was Methodism, which had a broad appeal among the poor and African Americans, and which witnessed

a sevenfold increase in membership between 1780 and 1790, from 8,504 to 57,631 members. Goen, *Broken Churches, Broken Nation*, 50. See also Conkin, *The Uneasy Center*, 78–89.

19. Johnson, *A Shopkeeper's Millennium*, 1–4; McLoughlin, "Charles Grandison Finney," 99–100; Mullen, *The Chance of Salvation*, 27–31; Sutton, "Benevolent Calvinism," 34–36.

20. Dorrien, *The Making of American Liberal Theology*, 114–16.

21. Mullen, *The Chance of Salvation*, 4.

22. Howe, *What Hath God Wrought*, 285–89. See also Moorhead, *World without End*, 1–18.

23. The most famous premillennialists were the followers of William Miller, a Baptist layman from New York state, who prophesied that Christ would return to Earth in 1843. For more on Millerism, see, for example, Numbers and Butler, *The Disappointed*.

24. Moorhead, *American Apocalypse*, 1–22; and Tuveson, *Redeemer Nation*, 186–214.

25. Tuveson, *Redeemer Nation*, 65; and Stout, *Upon the Altar of the Nation*, 35–38.

26. Tuveson, *Redeemer Nation*, 91–136. For more on interpretations of Providence during the Civil War, see Noll, *The Civil War as a Theological Crisis*, 75–94.

27. Bercovitch, *The American Jeremiad*, 174; Moorhead, *American Apocalypse*, 42–66; and Stout, *Upon the Altar of the Nation*, 72, 188–89.

28. "Impressions of a Visit to the Army of the Potomac," *Vermont Chronicle*, Apr. 2, 1864, Gale Nineteenth Century Collections Online.

29. "The Anniversary of the Christian Commission," *North American and United States Gazette*, Jan. 29, 1864, Gale Nineteenth Century Collections Online.

30. Patterson, "The Moral Results of the War," 136–40; emphasis in original.

31. Zboray, "Antebellum Reading," 180–97.

32. Wosh, *Spreading the Word*, 19.

33. Nord, "Free Grace, Free Books, Free Riders," 48–53.

34. Moore, *Selling God*, 18–22; and Mullen, *The Chance of Salvation*, 32–44.

35. Nord, "Benevolent Books," 2:221.

36. Brown, *The Word in the World*, 141–48.

37. Hovde, "The US Christian Commission's Library and Literacy Programs," 295–316.

38. Moss, *Annals*, 687.

39. Moss, *Annals*, 687. Delegates were asked to calculate and report weekly totals for the distribution of religious literature.

40. F. N. Pelobet, quoted in Moss, *Annals*, 706.

41. P. S. Pratt, report, Jan. 14, 1865, Weekly Reports of Delegates, USCC.

42. Work on Civil War soldiers' reading habits and tastes includes: Kaser, *Books and Libraries in Camp and Battle*; and, more recently, Steinroetter, "Soldiers, Readers," 5–28.

43. George Hesser, report, Aug. 1864, Delegates' Statistical Reports, USCC.

44. Despite condemning secular literature, the USCC did begin distributing secular magazines and periodicals in the Army of the Cumberland from 1864. The titles distributed reflected the Commission's commitment to pedagogy, with magazines such as the *North American Review, Scientific American,* and *Littell's Living Age* encouraging troops to dedicate themselves to intellectual, if not spiritual, self-improvement, a process that would eventually equip them with skills of inquiry and debate useful in the quest for grace. See Quenzel, "Books for the Boys in Blue," 222; and Moss, *Annals*, 715.

45. George Stuart, circular, Dec. 16, 1864, Scrapbooks, USCC.

46. McPherson, *What They Fought for, 1861–1865*, 4.

164 NOTES TO PAGES 67–71

47. "The Christian Commission," *Vermont Watchman and State Journal,* Aug. 14, 1863, Gale Nineteenth Century Collections Online.

48. Engelsing, *Der Bürger als Leser.*

49. Nord, "Religious Reading and Readers in Antebellum America," 241–72.

50. Francis H. Boynton, report, Apr. 23, 1864, Delegates' Statistical Reports, USCC.

51. "Temperance Tracts in the Army," *Congregationalist,* May 6, 1864, Gale Nineteenth Century Collections Online.

52. George H. Stuart to Amos L. Griffith, Aug. 2, 1864, Letters Sent, USCC.

53. W. H. H. Marsh, report, July 21, 1863, Delegates' Statistical Reports, USCC.

54. See, for example, Francis H. Boynton, report, Apr. 23, 1864, Delegates' Statistical Reports, USCC.

55. "Bible Study Outline," n.d., Folder 12, Box 4, Armed Services United States Christian Commission–Related Records.

56. "Bible Class in Camp," n.d., Letters Sent, USCC.

57. For the unpredictable demands placed on Civil War soldiers' time, see Wells, *Civil War Time,* especially 57–69.

58. Fahs, *The Imagined Civil War,* 19.

59. Wiley, *Life of Billy Yank,* 153.

60. Moss, *Annals,* 701–2.

61. List of Religious Newspapers Ordered, 1865, USCC. Most newspapers distributed were either New York– or Philadelphia-based, reflecting the northeastern, urban character of the Commission's most prominent personnel.

62. For more on newspapers during the Civil War, see Harris, "Newspapers," 193–202.

63. *United States Christian Commission: First Annual Report,* 120.

64. Nord, "Religious Reading," 251.

65. Mullen, *The Chance of Salvation,* 34–36. Mullen suggests that the brevity of the tracts collapsed the prolonged struggle for salvation into one moment, and transformed the act of reading itself into "the moment of grace, not just the means to grace" (36).

66. Moss, *Annals,* 707.

67. "The Lamp and the Ticket," n.d., Folder 12, Box 4, YMCA Archives.

68. Josiah Zimmerman, report, Dec. 12, 1863, Weekly Reports of Delegates, USCC.

69. E. T. Quimby, report, July 13, 1864, and L. W. Brinkwall, report, Aug. 31, 1864, Delegates' Statistical Reports, USCC.

70. And even, in some circumstances, some fighting for the Confederacy: in July 1864, in cooperation with the ABS, the USCC shipped twelve boxes of Bibles, Testaments, and portions of scripture to the Memphis and Shelby Bible Society, a rare occurrence that combined the Commission's evangelizing mission with its patriotic one—clearly, the distribution of these religious texts was meant to convert Southern recipients not only *to* evangelical Christianity, but *from* rebellion. George Stuart to J. H. Parsons, July 21, 1864, Letters Sent, USCC.

71. I. J. Burgess, report, Oct. 18, 1864, Weekly Reports of Delegates, USCC.

72. Miller, *In God's Presence,* 87–92; Hovde, "The US Christian Commission's Library and Literacy Programs," 302–5.

73. Moss, *Annals,* 712; Fea, *The Bible Cause,* 79–80.

74. Moss, *Annals,* 352.

75. This spasmodic work echoed, and sometimes overlapped with, ongoing efforts by

NOTES TO PAGES 71–76

other (white and Black) Northerners to provide systematic educational support for emancipated people during and after the Civil War. See, for instance, Butchart, *Schooling the Freed People;* Jones, *Soldiers of Light and Love;* Morris, *Reading, 'riting, and Reconstruction;* and Richardson, *Christian Reconstruction.*

76. Moss, *Annals,* 437–38.

77. Moss, *Annals,* 452. George Stuart to Benjamin Jones, Feb. 18, 1865, Letters Sent, USCC; George Stuart to Joseph Richards, Feb. 9, 1865, Letters Sent, USCC.

78. Wilson, *Campfires of Freedom;* 103–8.

79. Kytle, "From Body Reform to Reforming the Body Politics," 339–40. For more on white officers' frequently contradictory and ambivalent attitudes toward the Black troops under their command, see Glatthaar, *Forged in Battle,* especially chap. 4–6; and Berlin, Reidy, and Rowland, eds., *Freedom's Soldiers,* 31–32.

80. Moss, *Annals,* 712.

81. Moss, *Annals,* 712.

82. E. P. Smith, *Incidents,* 358.

83. Z. R. Farrington, Report, Apr. 20, 1864, Delegates' Statistical Reports, USCC.

84. Moss, *Annals,* 453.

85. Moss, *Annals,* 711–12.

86. E. P. Smith, *Incidents,* 467–68. Jeremiah Porter similarly reported: "among the colored soldiers, we found many strange notions and perverted, physical ways of looking at spiritual realities, which did not however prevent a precious and beautiful simplicity of trust in Christ." E. P. Smith, *Incidents,* 475.

87. H. H. Houghton, placard, n.d., Scrapbooks, USCC.

88. Bennett, "Saving Jack," 255.

89. Moss, *Annals,* 711.

90. Raney, "In the Lord's Army," 275; Quenzel, "Books for the Boys in Blue," 226.

91. "The Hospitals," in *Christ in the Army,* 69.

92. Loan Library Catalogue, Memorandum Books, USCC.

93. B. L. Brisbane, report from library 70, quoted in Moss, *Annals,* 722.

94. Charles Wiener, quoted in Moss, *Annals,* 722.

95. Loan Library Catalogue, Memorandum Books, USCC.

96. W. A. Kelton, report, May 17, 1865, Memorandum Books, USCC; emphases in original.

97. William Winterbottom, report, Dec. 8, 1863, Delegates' Statistical Reports, USCC.

98. J. A. Hough, report, June 28, 1864, Delegates' Statistical Reports, USCC.

99. "Religious Readings Blessed," n.d., Letters Sent, USCC.

100. M. P. Brown, *The Pilgrim and the Bee;* Cressy, "Books as Totems," 92–106; Davis, "Beyond the Market," 69–88; Knight, "'Furnished' for Action," 37–73; Watson, "Some Nontextual Uses of Books," 48–92.

101. Nord, "Religious Reading and Readers," 260–62.

102. Fahs, *The Imagined Civil War,* 54.

103. William S. Schaeffer, report, Aug. 13, 1864, Delegates' Statistical Reports, USCC.

104. M. H. Liebenau, "Testaments vs Cards," n.d., Letters Sent, USCC.

105. B. Crist, report, Jan. 21, 1865, Weekly Reports of Delegates, USCC.

106. J. A. Hough, report, June 28, 1864, Delegates' Statistical Reports, USCC.

107. E. Colton, report, July 1, 1864, Delegates' Statistical Reports, USCC.

166 NOTES TO PAGES 78–84

4. PREACHING AND PRAYING

1. George H. Stuart, "Instructions to Delegates," Sept. 15, 1862, Reports, USCC.

2. B. H., "The Christian Commission and Its Work," Nov. 21, 1864, Reports, USCC.

3. B. H., "The Christian Commission and Its Work," Nov. 21, 1864, Reports, USCC.

4. B. H., "The Christian Commission and Its Work," Nov. 21, 1864, Reports, USCC. B. H. also believed delegates often compared favorably to chaplains, who might be worn down by lengthy service, and who might struggle to find new material to interest the troops.

5. Cyril Pearl, "Six Weeks with the Soldiers of the Union," letter to G. S. Griffiths, n.d., Delegates' Statistical Reports, USCC.

6. George Marc Smith, report, May 3, 1864, Delegates' Statistical Reports, USCC.

7. E. P. Lewis, report, July 30, 1863, Delegates' Statistical Reports, USCC.

8. E. P. Lewis, report, July 30, 1863, Delegates' Statistical Reports, USCC.

9. "Information for Those Wishing to Be Delegates," Wisconsin USCC circular, n.d., Scrapbooks, USCC.

10. "Commission," n.d., Scrapbooks, USCC.

11. George H. Stuart, "Instructions to Delegates," Sept. 15, 1862, Reports, 1862–66, USCC.

12. George H. Stuart, "Instructions to Delegates," Sept. 15, 1862, Reports, 1862–66, USCC.

13. Delegates' Statistical Reports, 1863–65, USCC.

14. Weekly Reports of Delegates, 1864–64, and Day Book, Nashville Station, 1865, USCC.

15. A. Tobey, report, Nov. 17, 1863, Delegates' Statistical Reports, USCC.

16. *Nineteenth Annual Report of the American Tract Society,* 17.

17. Cyril Pearl, "Six Weeks with the Soldiers of the Union," letter to G. S. Griffiths, n.d., Delegates' Statistical Reports, USCC.

18. Reynolds, "From Doctrine to Narrative," 481; and Mountford, *The Gendered Pulpit,* 42.

19. Hatch, *The Democratization of American Christianity,* 50.

20. Reynolds, "From Doctrine to Narrative," 485; and Nord, *Faith in Reading,* 113–30.

21. Buell, "The Unitarian Movement and the Art of Preaching," 167.

22. Reynolds, "From Doctrine to Narrative," 491.

23. Coleman, "The Antebellum American Sermon," 521–54.

24. Coleman, "The Antebellum American Sermon," 552.

25. As discussed in the second chapter, female preachers were few and far between and were often treated with suspicion, and the USCC consequently subscribed to a firmly masculine image of the preacher.

26. Mountford, *The Gendered Pulpit,* 41, 53.

27. Hatch, *Democratization of American Christianity,* 132–39.

28. Coleman, "Antebellum American Sermon," 545.

29. Diary entry, Apr. 10, 1864, Diaries, USCC.

30. Albright, *Civil War Diary,* 23.

31. Robert Love, "A Lay Sermon to the Soldiers," n.d., Weekly Reports of Delegates, 1864–65, USCC. Love was not a great believer in punctuation.

32. Shattuck, *A Shield and Hiding Place,* 60; Woodworth, *While God Is Marching On,* 161, 182–83, 205.

33. B. L. Miller, *In God's Presence,* especially chap. 3, 39–69.

34. H. H. White, report, n.d., Delegates' Statistical Reports, USCC.

NOTES TO PAGES 84-89

35. Henry G. Safford, report, Mar. 27, 1864, Delegates' Statistical Reports, USCC.

36. Henry G. Safford, report, Mar. 27, 1864, Delegates' Statistical Reports, USCC.

37. Moss, *Annals*, 175–76.

38. Lemuel Moss to Charles (?), Dec. 14, 1864, and George Stuart to Charles N. Todd, Jan. 10, 1865, Letters Sent, USCC. George Stuart to G. Farnsworth, Dec. 14, 1864, and Lemuel Moss to Charles (?), Dec. 14, 1864, Letters Sent, USCC. "List of Stock Purchased for the Christian Commission," memorandum, n.d., Memorandum Books, USCC. The chapel tents were not without their drawbacks; their canvas structures meant bad weather could hinder erection and disrupt services. E. P. Willard suffered multiple setbacks at his station at Vienna, Virginia, describing how high winds prevented the delegates from putting up their tent, and how inclement weather further discouraged soldiers from attending services once it was erected. E. P. Willard, reports, Mar. 18, 1865; Mar. 25, 1865; and Apr. 1, 1865, Weekly Reports of Delegates, USCC.

39. George Stuart to G. Farnsworth, Dec. 14, 1864, USCC; and Moss, *Annals*, 180.

40. G. Stuart to G. Farnsworth, Dec. 14, 1864, USCC; and Moss, *Annals*, 180; "The Gospel in the Army," Thanksgiving supplement, Nov. 1864, USCC.

41. B. H., "The Christian Commission and Its Work," Nov. 21, 1864, Reports, USCC.

42. Moss, *Annals*, 181.

43. Lemuel Moss to Charles Kellogg, Feb. 28, 1865, USCC.

44. W. W. Condit, report, May 20, 1864, USCC.

45. "Intelligence from the Army," *Vermont Chronicle*, Mar. 12, 1864, Gale Nineteenth Century Collections Online.

46. Moss, *Annals*, 184–85.

47. *United States Christian Commission: Second Annual Report*, 19.

48. Woodworth, *While God Is Marching On*, 210–11.

49. E. P. Smith, *Incidents*, 230.

50. George Stuart, "Instructions to Delegates," Sept. 15, 1862, Reports, USCC.

51. George Stuart, "US Christian Commission: Information about Delegate Work," n.d., Reports, USCC.

52. See Carwardine, "The Second Great Awakening," 327–40; P. E. Johnson, *A Shopkeeper's Millennium*, 94–102; and McLoughlin, *Revivals, Awakenings, and Reform*, 121–27.

53. Ostrander, *Life of Prayer in a World of Science*, 10.

54. Kirk, "A National Movement for Organizing Ladies' Christian Commissions," 8.

55. Kirk, "A National Movement for Organizing Ladies' Christian Commissions," 8.

56. B. H., "The Christian Commission and Its Work," Nov. 21, 1864, Reports, USCC. The revival meeting, set up by layman Jeremy Lanphier at the Fulton Street Dutch Reformed church in New York City during the 1857–58 Revival, was held up by the religious press as a prime example of interdenominational cooperation and harmony, and lauded by contemporaries for the emphasis on prayer and piety as a means of regeneration and reform. Kathryn Long argues that the Fulton Street revivals were inherently conservative for their emphasis on prayerful regeneration rather than political/social activism, for their strict rules on the length and subject matter of prayers, and for their deliberate exclusion of African Americans, immigrants, and, to a lesser extent, women. This conservatism found expression in many aspects of the USCC's work and mission. Long, *The Revival of 1857–58*, 103–7.

57. Stephen Ives, report, Feb.—Apr. 1864, Delegates' Statistical Reports, USCC.

58. B. H., "The Christian Commission and Its Work," Nov. 21, 1864, Reports, USCC.

59. *United States Christian Commission: First Annual Report*, 17.

60. "Address of the Christian Commission," Jan. 13, 1864, Reports, USCC.

61. "Address to the Young Men's Christian Association," Sept. 17, 1862, Reports, USCC.

62. A. B. Clough, entry, Apr. 16, 1865, and R. A. Foster, entry, Feb. 19, 1865, Day Book, Nashville Station, USCC.

63. E. P. Smith, *Incidents*, 230.

64. Asa Farwell, report, Apr. 22, 1864, Delegates' Statistical Reports, USCC.

65. A. S. Fuller, report, Feb. 29, 1864, Delegates' Statistical Reports, USCC.

66. A. B. Chase, report, Dec. 3, 1864, Weekly Reports of Delegates, USCC.

67. S. W. Turney, reports, Mar. 26, 1864, and Apr. 5, 1864, Weekly Reports of Delegates, USCC.

68. As well as finding sufficient space, other obstacles also hindered the delegates' attempts to lead men to Christ through prayer. Secular preoccupations often distracted men from the USCC's message—M. Fisk conceded that the question occupying the troops in Washington was not a spiritual one but rather "wherewithal shall we be clothed." M. Fisk, report, May 13, 1865, Weekly Reports of Delegates, USCC. Occasionally, army officers hostile to the presence of civilian/religious personnel forbade delegates from holding evangelical services, and delegates were obliged by oath to comply with these orders. See William Thayer, report, n.d., Weekly Reports of Delegates, USCC. Troop movement during the war also caused disruption to Christian Commission prayer meetings, reducing congregation sizes and interrupting the routine of the camp. "I do not expect that our meetings will be as interesting hereafter, the Camp has been so reduced," William Jewell lamented in May 1864 after ten regiments left Camp Barry, where he was stationed. William Jewell, report, May 28, 1864, Weekly Reports of Delegates, USCC. The cessation of hostilities proved particularly difficult for the Commission as the threat of death—a great motivator for religious reflection—was removed and replaced with the seemingly more pressing concern of homecoming. J. B. Adams found the troops at his station more preoccupied with earthly than heavenly homecoming, and concluded, "there is an unsettled state of mind occasioned by the expectation of discharge that is unfavourable to religious influence." J. B. Adams, report, May 13, 1865, Weekly Reports of Delegates, USCC.

69. George Marc Smith, report, May 3, 1864, Delegates' Statistical Reports, USCC.

70. Bratt, "Religious Anti-Revivalism in Antebellum America," 11–17. Long argues that this deradicalization was to some extent exaggerated and constructed by contemporary accounts.

71. Asa Farwell, report, Apr. 22, 1864, Delegates' Statistical Reports, USCC.

72. Asa Farwell, report, Apr. 22, 1864, Delegates' Statistical Reports, USCC. For Farwell's career as principal of Abbot Academy and prominent Andover Congregational minister, see McKeen and McKeen, *Annals of Fifty Years*, 39–45.

73. H. H. White, report, n.d., Delegates' Statistical Reports, USCC.

74. Delegates were, as a rule, more likely to express pessimistic sentiments in their weekly reports to Philadelphia rather than in their lengthier exit reports, which tended not to focus on individual frustrations and failures but on a grander narrative of progress and success. This trend reflects both the greater amount of time delegates had to reflect when writing exit reports and their desire to contribute a positive history of the USCC, especially once it became clear that the Executive Committee planned to publish such material in public volumes.

75. Thomas A. Lewis, report, June 29, 1863, Delegates' Statistical Reports, USCC.

76. Asa Farwell, report, Apr. 22, 1864, Delegates' Statistical Reports, USCC; S. S. Cummings, report, Jan. 25, 1865, Weekly Reports of Delegates, USCC.

NOTES TO PAGES 93–99

77. S. D. Holman, report, May 14, 1864, Delegates' Statistical Reports, USCC.

78. Charles Tarbell, diary entry, Dec. 12, 1864, United States Christian Commission Journals.

79. Albright, *Civil War Diary*, 21.

80. James Cooper, report, Feb. 21, 1864, Delegates' Statistical Reports, USCC.

81. I have discussed the "manly" potential of tears in chapter 1. For more on crying as a physical manifestation of spiritual striving in antebellum revivalism and conversion narratives, see Clark, "'The Sacred Rights of the Weak,'" 476–77; Hatch, *The Democratization of American Christianity*, 105; and Corrigan, *Business of the Heart*, 221–22.

82. Hatch, *The Democratization of American Christianity*, 105; and Corrigan, *Business of the Heart*, 221–22.

83. "Work among the Soldiers," *Vermont Chronicle*, Apr. 30, 1864, Gale Nineteenth Century Collections Online.

84. A. B. Dascomb, quoted in E. P. Smith, *Incidents*, 101.

5. CLOTHING THE UNION SOLDIER'S BODY

1. Dressed, *The Hospital on Seminary Ridge*.

2. Charles W. Torrey, report, Sept. 10, 1863, Delegates' Statistical Reports, USCC.

3. Charles W. Torrey, report, Sept. 10, 1863, Delegates' Statistical Reports, USCC.

4. See, for instance, Cannon, "The United States Christian Commission," 73–74; R. J. Miller, *Both Prayed to the Same God*, 86–98; and Henry, "The United States Christian Commission during the Civil War," 375–87.

5. Stuart, *The Life of George Hay Stuart*, 129.

6. The parable of the sheep and the goats also demonstrates how displays of kindness and compassion toward fellow human beings are also, by their very nature, displays of love for God: Jesus tells the righteous, "inasmuch as ye have done it unto one of the least of these my brethren, ye have done it unto me" (Matthew 25:40).

7. "Local Agents' and Delegates' Weekly Report," preamble on sample undated form, Scrapbooks, USCC.

8. See, for instance, Cannon, "The United States Christian Commission," 73–74; Paludan, *A People's Contest*, 352–54; Shattuck Jr., *A Shield and Hiding Place*, 27–29; and Woodworth, *While God Is Marching On*, 168–71.

9. Isaac S. Smyth, "To the Friends of the US Christian Commission in the Mississippi Valley," circular, Apr. 20, 1864, Scrapbooks, USCC.

10. Henry F. Lee, report, Sept. 26, 1862, Delegates' Statistical Reports, USCC.

11. W. J. Park, report, July 6, 1863, Delegates' Statistical Reports, USCC.

12. B. F. Woolston, report, July 16, 1863, Delegates' Statistical Reports, USCC. See also Charles H. Richards, report, Nov. 10, 1863, Delegates' Statistical Reports, USCC.

13. Minnesota YMCA Annual Report, Jan. 8, 1865, Scrapbooks, USCC.

14. W. P. Weyman, "Receiver's Report," Scrapbooks, USCC.

15. "Warehouse Manifest of Stores and Publications," Scrapbooks, USCC.

16. Sylvester Wolle, circular, Apr. 1864, Scrapbooks, USCC.

17. Lemuel Moss to Mary Brewer, May 22, 1865, Letters Sent, USCC.

18. George Stuart to E. W. Rogers, Feb. 2, 1865, Letters Sent, USCC.

19. Lemuel Moss to Mrs. R. Stoddart, Mar. 11, 1865, Letters Sent, USCC.

170 NOTES TO PAGES 99–104

20. E. Clark Cline, report, Sept. 7, 1863, Delegates' Statistical Reports, USCC.

21. A. M. Palmer, report, July 20, 1863, Delegates' Statistical Reports, USCC.

22. John French, report, Oct. 4, 1864, Weekly Reports of Delegates, USCC.

23. N. R. Peck, "Appeal of the Sacramento Committee," circular, June 23, 1864, Scrapbooks, USCC.

24. Moss, *Annals*, 34.

25. Robertson Jr., *Soldiers Blue and Gray*, 14.

26. Wiley, *The Life of Billy Yank*, 16.

27. Weicksel, "Confederate Cultures of Military Clothing Production," 32–53. See also Zakim, *Ready-Made Democracy*; and Cohen, *Luxurious Citizens*, 200–218.

28. Robertson, *Soldiers Blue and Gray*, 155.

29. Robertson, *Soldiers Blue and Gray*, 77.

30. Roche, *The Culture of Clothing*, 228–29.

31. Roche, *The Culture of Clothing*, 239.

32. Roche, *The Culture of Clothing*, 229.

33. Eicher and Roach-Higgins, "Definition and Classification of Dress," 12.

34. Weitz, "Drill, Training, and the Combat Performance of the Civil War Soldier," 263–89.

35. The masculine meanings of uniform were troubled most explicitly by the hundreds of "distaff soldiers" who fought on both sides of the conflict; that is, women who disguised themselves as men in order to enlist and serve. While more work remains to be done to explore how disguise allowed individuals to queer the gender binary, Blanton and Cook's *They Fought Like Demons* remains a useful text on how this allowed women to escape the confines of socially prescribed gender roles, lay claim to full citizenship, and appropriate male power and independence, as well as discussion of how women adapted their uniforms and their daily routines in order to keep passing as men. I have found no evidence that any USCC delegate knowingly encountered a woman soldier, nor any evidence that the Commission was aware of such transgression.

36. Foote, *The Gentlemen and the Roughs*, 150–52.

37. As Wendy Parkins suggests, dress can both "contest or legitimate the power of the state and the meaning of citizenship." Parkins, "Introduction: (Ad)dressing Citizens," 2.

38. Moss, *Annals*, 34.

39. Moss, *Annals*, 161; Zombek, "Paternalism and Imprisonment at Castle Thunder," 221–52.

40. For more on the meaning of amputation and prosthesis in the Civil War, see Clarke, "'Honorable Scars,'" 361–94; Herschbach, "Prosthetic Reconstructions," 22–57; O'Connor, "'Fractions of Men,'" 742–77.

41. Walter S. Carter, circular, n.d., Scrapbooks, USCC.

42. "Instructions to Delegates," 1862, Reports, USCC.

43. C. C. Coffin, quoted in Moss, *Annals*, 582.

44. J. Edward Dwight, for instance, claimed, "I repeatedly received an officer's salute, tho' I wore no article of military dress, and I am confident that such salutes were given not through ignorance but from respect to the badge which I wore." Dwight, report, July 12, 1864, Delegates' Statistical Reports, USCC.

45. We can also see the symbolic and contradictory power of clothing in early colonial encounters with indigenous people; nudity or near-nudity was variously associated by European settlers with superior innocence and humility, or with weakness and lack of civiliza-

NOTES TO PAGES 104–108 171

tion, and swiftly became synonymous with "savagery." See, for example, Kupperman, *Indians & English,* 48–55.

46. See, for instance, Moss, *Annals,* 313, 391, 416.

47. Most famously, Abraham Lincoln emphasized the nationalist implications of the phrase when he evoked Psalm 147 in his second inaugural address ("let us strive on to finish the work we are in, to bind up the nation's wounds, to care for him who shall have borne the battle and for his widow and his orphan"). Lincoln, "Second Inaugural Address," 449.

48. See, for instance, Bercovitch, *American Jeremiad;* Cherry, *God's New Israel,* 25–29.

49. "The Present Campaign in Virginia," circular, July 1864, Scrapbooks, USCC.

50. LaBarre, "The American Housewife Goes to War," 5.

51. Smith-Rosenberg, "The Female World of Love and Ritual," 1–29; and Cott, *The Bonds of Womanhood,* especially 63–100. For a critique of the "separate spheres" rhetoric, which investigates how labor in the home (including sewing) did not always conform to prescribed gender roles, and varied greatly from household to household, see, for instance, Osterud, "'She Helped Me Hay It as Good as a Man,'" 87–97.

52. Beaudry, *Findings,* 173–76; and Hansen, "'Helped Put in a Quilt,'" 334–54. Hansen argues that the division of labor was often less absolute and gender-determined in rural areas in comparison with urban areas.

53. Roche, *Culture of Clothing,* 231. This theory met with only limited success, both in the prerevolutionary French armies discussed by Roche, and the Civil War armies under scrutiny here; Civil War armies traveled with an extensive array of "camp followers," many of them female, including laundresses, prostitutes, servants, and relatives.

54. Roche, *The Culture of Clothing,* 232.

55. Cleveland branch circular to Sabbath schools, Jan. 1865, Scrapbooks, USCC.

56. Isaac Smyth, "Housewives Wanted for Soldiers," circular, Nov. 1864, Scrapbooks, USCC.

57. Isaac Smyth, "Housewives Wanted for Soldiers," circular, Nov. 1864, Scrapbooks, USCC.

58. George Stuart to Samuel Willard, Nov. 3, 1864, Letters Sent, USCC.

59. Moss, *Annals,* 652.

60. Charles Demond, "Comfort-Bag," circular, n.d., Scrapbooks, USCC.

61. W. J. Park, report, July 6, 1863, Delegates' Statistical Reports, USCC.

62. Samuel Griffin, letter, Sept. 28, 1864, quoted in "Comfort-Bag," circular, n.d., Scrapbooks, USCC. These letters were later reproduced in Moss, *Annals,* 652–53.

63. E. A. Taylor to First Presbyterian Church Sabbath School, St. Louis, July 27, 1864, quoted in Smyth, "Housewives Wanted for Soldiers," Nov. 1864, Scrapbooks, USCC.

64. E. A. Taylor to First Presbyterian Church Sabbath School, St. Louis, July 27, 1864, quoted in Smyth, "Housewives Wanted for Soldiers," Nov. 1864, Scrapbooks, USCC.

65. E. A. Taylor to anonymous child, July 27, 1864, quoted in Smyth, "Housewives Wanted for Soldiers," Nov. 1864, Scrapbooks, USCC.

66. W. J. Park, report, July 6, 1863, Delegates' Statistical Reports, USCC.

67. They could thus serve to alleviate homesickness, which was a persistent problem among soldiers during the Civil War. See Mitchell, *The Vacant Chair,* 25–26, 135–36; and Robertson, *Soldiers Blue and Gray,* 102–4. For more on contemporary understandings of homesickness, see Anderson, "Dying of Nostalgia," 247–82; and Clarke, "So Lonesome I Could Die," 253–82.

68. For more on the involvement of children in war work and fundraising, see Marten, *The Children's Civil War,* 178–85.

NOTES TO PAGES 108–113

69. George Stuart to Samuel Willard, Nov. 3, 1864, Letters Sent, USCC.

70. Cleveland branch circular to Sabbath schools, Jan. 1865, Scrapbooks, USCC.

71. Cleveland branch circular to Sabbath schools, Jan. 1865, Scrapbooks, USCC.

72. Lemuel Moss to Mrs. Bigelow, Dec. 12, 1864, Letters Sent, USCC, RG94, NAB; and the Cleveland branch circular to Sabbath schools, Jan. 1865, Scrapbooks, USCC.

73. Charles Demond, "Comfort-Bag," circular, n.d., Scrapbooks, USCC.

74. "The Present Campaign in Virginia," circular, July 1864, Scrapbooks, USCC.

6. THE GOSPEL OF THE LOAF

1. W. P. Tritsworth, report, Dec. 5, 1863, Delegates' Statistical Reports, USCC.

2. E. P. Lewis, report, July 30, 1863, Delegates' Statistical Reports, USCC.

3. Joshua Cowpland, report, Aug. 6, 1863, Delegates' Statistical Reports, USCC.

4. "How to Do It," *Congregationalist*, July 29, 1864, Gale Nineteenth Century Collections Online.

5. For more on how ideas about class, gender, and race inflected the aims, targets, methods, and rhetoric of the antebellum temperance movement(s), see Tyrrell, *Sobering Up*; S. C. Martin, *Devil of the Domestic Sphere*; and Parsons, *Manhood Lost*.

6. Spencer, *The Heretic's Feast*, 273.

7. Nissenbaum, *Sex, Diet and Debility in Jacksonian America*, 19.

8. Nissenbaum, *Sex, Diet and Debility in Jacksonian America*, 98–99.

9. Nissenbaum, *Sex, Diet and Debility in Jacksonian America*, 3.

10. Spencer, *Heretic's Feast*, 272–74. Vegetarianism in this period focused mostly on the gluttony and overindulgence associated with animal diet. The welfare and suffering of animals were not primary concerns, though some early vegetarians argued that butchering animals and feasting on bloody meat brought out violent and "uncivilized" impulses in the consumer.

11. Spencer, *Heretic's Feast*, 273; and Nissenbaum, *Sex, Diet and Debility*, 49.

12. Shprintzen, *The Vegetarian Crusade*, 4.

13. As David Sack has noted, nineteenth-century dietary reformers' views on the right way for a Christian to eat corresponded closely with how white, middle- and upper-class Americans ate, rejecting the perceived excesses and overstimulation of indigenous, Black, and immigrant foodways. Sack, *Whitebread Protestants*, 186–97.

14. Scholarship on food and the Civil War has primarily focused on food shortage and politics, including the impact of the Union blockade on Confederate food supplies and the Richmond bread riots as expressions of women's political agency (for example, Smith, *Starving the South*; and Cashin, "Hungry People in the Wartime South," 160–75). William C. Davis's *A Taste for War* remains the most recent and comprehensive book-length study on soldiers' rations, but see also Humphreys, "'We Made up Soup as Fast as Possible,'" 330–38.

15. Wiley, *The Life of Billy Yank*, 224, 237.

16. Wiley, *The Life of Billy Yank*, 127–8; and Robertson Jr., *Soldiers Blue and Gray*, 70.

17. Robertson Jr., *Soldiers Blue and Gray*, 65; and Wiley, *Life of Billy Yank*, 234.

18. W. C. Davis, *Taste for War*, xvi.

19. Attie, *Patriotic Toil*; and Ginzberg, *Women and the Work of Benevolence*.

20. Moss, *Annals*, 640. Characteristically, Moss overstated this shift: individual families

NOTES TO PAGES 113–117   173

persisted in sending private packages to their sons for the duration of the war, undeterred by delays, breakages, and fluctuating freight costs.

21. Moss, *Annals,* 643.

22. "Plan of Cooperation between the Executive Committee and the Several Army Committees in Pittsburgh, Cincinnati, Chicago, St. Louis, and Peoria, Adopted Oct. 16th 1863," Reports, USCC.

23. Sylvester Wolle, Bethlehem Branch circular, Apr. 1864, Scrapbooks, USCC.

24. Moss, *Annals,* 649.

25. "The Christian Commission," *Vermont Watchman and State Journal,* Aug. 14, 1863, Gale Nineteenth Century Collections Online.

26. Charles W. Lorry, report, Aug. 1863, Delegates' Statistical Reports, USCC.

27. John Rhodes, report, June 3, 1865, Weekly Reports of Delegates, USCC.

28. Moss, *Annals,* 654.

29. Isaac Jacobus, report, May 24, 1864, Weekly Reports of Delegates, USCC.

30. W. A. Lawrence, quoted in Moss, *Annals,* 655.

31. "Rev. Dr. Bomberger's Report from the Late Battlefields to the Christian Commission," *German Reformed Messenger,* Oct. 29, 1862, American Periodicals Series Online.

32. "A Summer's Day Treat for the Wounded," 28. See also William Boardman to W. P. Weyman, Sept. 7, 1864, Letters Sent, USCC.

33. W. C. Davis, *Taste for War,* 26.

34. Moss, *Annals,* 527.

35. Stuart, *The Life of George H. Stuart,* 141.

36. Robert Bellah's suggestion that ostensibly secular festivals became increasingly essential ritualistic components of an American "civil religion" during and after the Civil War still carries weight. Bellah, "Civil Religion in America," 1–21.

37. Abraham Lincoln, "By the President of the United States of America: A Proclamation," Oct. 3, 1865, quoted in Baker, *Thanksgiving,* 71.

38. W. C. Davis, *Taste for War,* 115–24.

39. John Scott, report, n.d., Delegates' Statistical Reports, USCC.

40. John Scott, report, n.d., Delegates' Statistical Reports, USCC.

41. "US Christian Commission," *Milwaukee Daily Sentinel,* Aug. 27, 1863, Gale Nineteenth Century Collections Online.

42. *Cincinnati Presbyter,* Nov. 23, 1864, Scrapbooks, USCC.

43. "Christmas Dinner for the Soldiers," circular, n.d., Scrapbooks, USCC.

44. For more on alcohol and soldiers in the Civil War, see S. C. Martin, "'A Soldier Intoxicated Is Far Worse Than No Soldier at All,'" 66–87; and Bever, *At War with King Alcohol.*

45. Foote, *The Gentlemen and the Roughs,* 29–39.

46. Lande, *Madness, Malingering, and Malfeasance,* 81.

47. Raney, "In the Lord's Army: The United States Christian Commission, Soldiers, and the Union War Effort," 277.

48. "Plan of Cooperation between the Executive Committee and the Several Army Committees in Pittsburgh, Cincinnati, Chicago, St. Louis, and Peoria," Oct. 16, 1863, Reports, USCC.

49. Wittenmyer, *A Collection of Recipes,* 31–32.

50. Michael A. Flannery discusses medicinal uses and abuses of alcohol during the Civil War in *Civil War Pharmacy.*

174 NOTES TO PAGES 117–126

51. Flannery, *Civil War Pharmacy*, 31.

52. George Stuart to Rev. John Thurston, Aug. 11, 1864, Letters Sent, USCC.

53. Bernice Ames to G. C. Thompson, Oct. 13, 1864, Letters Sent, USCC.

54. Tyrrell, *Sobering Up*, 33–37.

55. Tyrrell, *Sobering Up*, 70.

56. W. H. Hayward, report, Feb.–Apr. 1864, Delegates' Statistical Reports, USCC.

57. William Jewell, report, May 28, 1864, Weekly Reports of Delegates, USCC.

58. Henry G. Safford, report, Mar. 27, 1864, Delegates' Statistical Reports, USCC.

59. See also Williams, "Heaping Coals of Fire," 17–32.

60. Smith, *Incidents*, 157–58.

61. W. W. Condit, report, May 20, 1864, Delegates' Statistical Reports, USCC.

62. Robert Patterson to "Jacob," Apr. 13, 1865, Letters Sent, USCC.

63. Lemuel Moss to Robert Patterson, May 29, 1865, Letters Sent, USCC.

64. Smith, *Incidents*, 180.

65. R. Patterson, "At the Front," 91.

66. E. P. Smith, *Incidents*, 384.

67. E. P. Smith, *Incidents*, 177.

68. E. P. Smith, *Incidents*, 283.

69. *United States Christian Commission: Second Annual Report*, 78.

70. *United States Christian Commission: First Annual Report*, 13.

71. *United States Christian Commission: First Annual Report*, 178.

72. A. L. Pratt, report, Dec. 24, 1864, Weekly Reports of Delegates, USCC.

73. William Robinson, report, Nov. 18, 1864, Delegates' Statistical Reports, USCC.

74. William C. Learned, report, Aug. 6, 1864, Delegates' Statistical Reports, USCC.

75. George Stuart to C. M. Reed, Apr. 13, 1865, Letters Sent, USCC.

76. C. H. Richards, quoted in Moss, *Annals*, 446.

77. While the Commission's distribution of food has been widely neglected by scholars, some have alluded to the importance of physical ministry in providing opportunities for spiritual conversation. See Bremner, *The Public Good*, 59; Rable, *God's Almost Chosen Peoples*, 213–25; and T. L. Smith, *Revivalism and Social Reform*, 175.

78. N. S. Burton, report, July 2, 1864, Delegates' Statistical Reports, USCC.

79. J. P. Stryker, report, Apr. 14, 1865, Weekly Reports of Delegates, USCC.

80. H. G. Thomas, report, July 1863, Delegates' Statistical Reports, USCC.

81. W. W. Condit, report, May 20, 1864, Delegates' Statistical Reports, USCC.

82. Wittenmyer, report, n.d., Communications Received, USCC.

83. Barbara Hamer discusses the diet kitchen recipe book in *From Hardtack to Home Fries*, 34–60.

84. Wittenmyer, *Collection of Recipes*, 38–40.

85. McDevitt, "'A Melody before Unknown,'" 121.

86. E. W. Jones to Annie Wittenmyer, Jan. 10, 1865, quoted in Moss, *Annals*, 678.

87. Edward Parmelee Smith to George Stuart, Jan. 6, 1865, quoted in Moss, *Annals*, 667.

88. Minnesota YMCA Annual Report, Jan. 8, 1865, Scrapbooks, USCC.

89. A. S. Fuller, report, Feb. 29, 1864, Delegates' Statistical Reports, USCC.

NOTES TO PAGES 128–133

7. DEATH, SALVATION, AND THE CHRISTIAN COMMISSION

1. Hacker, "A Census-Based Count of the Civil War Dead," 307–48.

2. Nicholas Marshall points out that, after a steady rise through the eighteenth century, average life expectancy fell from fifty-six in 1790 to forty-eight by 1860, possibly as a result of increased population mobility, and that before the advent of germ theory, the medical profession was largely powerless to alleviate affliction in this period. Marshall, "'In the Midst of Life We Are in Death,'" 176–78. See also Saum, "Death in the Popular Mind of Pre–Civil War America," 479–81.

3. Linderman, *Embattled Courage,* 126.

4. For instance, see Scott, "'Earth Has No Sorrow That Heaven Cannot Cure,'" 843–66; Faust, *This Republic of Suffering;* Smith, *Heaven in the American Imagination;* Sommerville, *Aberration of Mind;* Berry, "The Historian as Death Investigator," 176–88; Finseth, *The Civil War Dead and American Modernity;* and Schantz, *Awaiting the Heavenly Country.* Together, this body of work has often been identified as part of a wider "dark turn" in Civil War studies. See Sternhell, "Revisionism Reinvented?," 239–56; and Jordan, "The Future of Civil War History."

5. Scott, "Earth Has No Sorrow," 850–52; Faust, *This Republic of Suffering,* 6–17. Faust is the only scholar to explore USCC attitudes to death and dying in any detail, but she focuses solely on the IRD and does not consider the responses of ordinary delegates.

6. Moss, *Annals,* 261.

7. Faust, *This Republic of Suffering,* 108–10.

8. "United States Christian Commission: Individual Relief Department," cover of ledger, n.d., Abstract of Letters, USCC.

9. Individual Relief Department form (exemplar, n.d.), Record of Letters Written, USCC.

10. Moss, *Annals,* 409.

11. Faust, *This Republic of Suffering,* 109.

12. Clarke, *War Stories,* 6.

13. Abstracts of Letters Written for Sick and Wounded Soldiers, USCC.

14. Abstracts of Letters Written for Sick and Wounded Soldiers, USCC.

15. James B. Whitten, report, Oct. 26, 1864, Abstracts of Letters Written, USCC.

16. John Davidson, report, Oct. 24, 1864, Abstracts of Letters Written, USCC.

17. Laderman, *The Sacred Remains,* 134.

18. E. P. Smith, *Incidents,* 74. In this case and in many others, mother became the home incarnate, representing the care and emotional sustenance ideally provided within the domestic sphere.

19. E. Clarke Cline, report, Sept. 7, 1863, Delegates' Statistical Reports, USCC.

20. Mitchell, *The Vacant Chair,* 141.

21. G. S. Smith, *Heaven in the American Imagination,* 78. Smith demonstrates that antebellum ministers were at great pains to prove the theory of heavenly recognition; that although heavenly bodies would be reformed and perfected at their resurrection, family members would be able to recognize each other by their internal qualities (80–83). See also Faust, *This Republic of Suffering,* 178–88; Schantz, *Awaiting the Heavenly Country,* 60–68; Scott, "Earth Has No Sorrow," 853–56.

22. Scott, "Earth Has No Sorrow," 845. Scott focuses primarily on the attitudes of civilians on the home front and their hopes and anxieties for their menfolk on the battlefront. He therefore fails to consider the experiences and attitudes of civilians in closer proximity to the fighting, such as the agents of the Christian Commission.

23. Faust, *This Republic of Suffering*, 180.

24. Samuel Wright, report, Aug. 4, 1864, Delegates' Statistical Reports, USCC.

25. E. P. Smith, *Incidents*, 354. The anticipation of reunion, not with beloved family members but with Jesus Christ, was a recurrent theme in USCC deathbed narratives. While Gary Scott Smith indicates that nineteenth-century ideas about heaven focused on human intercourse and reunion, USCC narratives suggest that God had not been entirely decentered in the heavenly landscape. G. S. Smith, *Heaven in the American Imagination*, 70.

26. Schantz, *Awaiting the Heavenly Country*, 46.

27. E. P. Smith, *Incidents*, 83. Even the delegates themselves could be vessels of light: after the war, Charles Demond praised the work of the Christian Commission as "the means of shedding the light of heaven into the dark valley." Moss, *Annals*, 255.

28. E. P. Smith, *Incidents*, 318.

29. Adams, *Living Hell*, 84–107.

30. E. P. Smith, *Incidents*, 403.

31. Woodworth, *While God Is Marching On*, 106–8.

32. *United States Christian Commission: Second Annual Report*, 176.

33. Saum, "Death in the Popular Mind," 488.

34. William S. Schaeffer, report, Aug. 13, 1864, Delegates' Statistical Reports, USCC.

35. Charles M. Hyde, report, Nov. 16, 1864, Abstracts of Letters Written, USCC.

36. Laderman, *The Sacred Remains*, 133.

37. Jack Smock, report, May 6, 1864, Delegates' Statistical Reports, USCC.

38. J. M. Rookwood, report, Oct. 30, 1864, Abstracts of Letters Written, USCC.

39. E. P. Smith, *Incidents*, 257.

40. E. P. Smith, *Incidents*, 318; emphasis in original.

41. Moorhead, *American Apocalypse*, 148.

42. Stout, *Upon the Altar of the Nation*, 52. This rhetoric became even more pronounced after Lincoln issued the Emancipation Proclamation in September 1862, effectively transforming the war into a struggle to free the slaves, rather than solely to preserve the Union.

43. "Soldier's Hymns," Armed Services United States Christian Commission–Related Records.

44. "Mass Meeting at Platt's Hall in Behalf of the Christian Commission," *Daily Evening Bulletin*, May 23, 1864, Gale Nineteenth Century Collections Online.

45. Stout, *Upon the Altar of the Nation*, 115.

46. Shattuck, *A Shield and Hiding Place*, 60, 87.

47. "Evening Prayers," in *Christ in the Army*, 83.

48. "The Pastoral Letter," *Congregationalist*, July 29, 1864, Gale Nineteenth Century Collections Online. See also Williams, "Civil War Relief Agencies," 39–52.

49. *United States Christian Commission: Second Annual Report*, 122.

50. E. P. Smith, *Incidents*, 429–30.

51. E. P. Smith, *Incidents*, 429.

52. E. P. Smith, *Incidents*, 76.

NOTES TO PAGES 139–146

53. Faust, *This Republic of Suffering*, 65–76; Linderman, *Embattled Courage*, 126–27, 248; Mitchell, *Civil War Soldiers*, 62–64; Patterson, *Debris of Battle*, 28–31, 121–23.

54. Faust, *This Republic of Suffering*, 87–89.

55. K. Atkinson, report, Sept. 7, 1863, Delegates' Statistical Reports, USCC; William Jewell, report, May 1864, Weekly Reports of Delegates, USCC.

56. George Bringhurst, sermon, n.d., Letters Received, USCC.

57. Scott, "Earth Has No Sorrow," 852.

58. George Bringhurst, sermon, n.d., Letters Received, USCC.

59. George Bringhurst, sermon, n.d., Letters Received, USCC.

60. Grant, "Raising the Dead," 509–29.

61. Bellah, "Civil Religion in America," 1–21.

62. For more on the efforts of local communities to memorialize and monumentalize their war dead, see, for instance, R. V. Wells, *Facing the "King of Terrors,"* 126–33.

63. R. G. Johnson, report, Feb. 26, 1864, Weekly Reports of Delegates, USCC; E. P. Smith, *Incidents*, 429–30.

64. E. P. Smith, *Incidents*, 76; Thomas Lightbody, report, Apr. 1, 1865, Weekly Reports of Delegates, USCC.

65. E. Clark Cline, report, Sept. 7, 1863, Delegates' Statistical Reports, USCC.

66. Schantz, *Awaiting the Heavenly Country*, 80. Sarah J. Purcell has recently explored the role of public funerals of high-profile figures—conducted with much more pomp and circumstance than the hasty, private affairs described in this chapter—in (re)constructing national identity and revealing the emerging fault lines of Civil War memory during and after the war. Purcell, *Spectacle of Grief.*

67. Faust, *This Republic of Suffering*, 107–10.

68. USCC identification tag, n.d., Scrapbooks, USCC.

EPILOGUE

1. "Untitled," *Bradford Reporter,* Feb. 15, 1866, Chronicling America.

2. "From Washington," *Baltimore Daily Commercial,* Feb. 12, 1866, Chronicling America.

3. Charles Henry Howard to Lizzie Howard, Feb. 12, 1866, Series 3: Correspondence, Freedmen's Bureau period, May 1865–Spring 1874, Box 3, Folder 74, Oliver Otis Howard Papers, George J. Mitchell Department of Special Collections & Archives, Bowdoin College Library, Brunswick, ME, https://library.bowdoin.edu/arch/mss/ooh-pdf/M91b03f074.pdf. Howard was the brother of Gen. Oliver Otis Howard, a longtime supporter of the USCC.

4. Julia Wilbur, Feb. 11, 1866, Julia Wilbur papers (HC.MC.1158) Quaker and Special Collections, Haverford College, Haverford, PA, https://digitalcollections.tricolib.brynmawr.edu/object/hc62645.

5. Minutes of the Reformed Presbytery, June 13, 1866, https://www.covenanter.org/reformed/2017/6/3/1866.

6. Moss, *Annals*, 229–79. Transcriptions of the addresses delivered over the course of the evening were published in several religious newspapers in the following days.

7. Hutchinson, *Story of the Hutchinsons,* 1:430–31.

8. Butterworth and Brown, *The Story of the Hymns and Tunes,* 256, 150, 240.

178   NOTES TO PAGES 146–150

9. Butterworth and Brown, *The Story of the Hymns and Tunes*, 239, 257.

10. "Closing Anniversary of the Christian Commission," *New York Herald*, Feb. 12, 1866, Chronicling America; Butterworth and Brown, *The Hymns and Tunes*, 257.

11. Hutchinson, *Story of the Hutchinsons*, 431.

12. Stuart, *The Life of George H. Stuart*, 167–68.

13. "Closing Anniversary of the Christian Commission."

14. Moss, *Annals*, 278.

15. Moss, *Annals*, 235.

16. Moss, *Annals*, 260.

17. Moss, *Annals*, 239.

18. Moss, *Annals*, 241.

19. Moss, *Annals*, 237.

20. Moss, *Annals*, 235.

21. Moss, *Annals*, 250.

22. Moss, *Annals*, 259.

23. Moss, *Annals*, 260.

24. Moss, *Annals*, 265.

25. Moss, *Annals*, 255.

26. Moss, *Annals*, 279.

27. Moss, *Annals*, 271.

28. Moss, *Annals*, 233, 736.

29. Frances Clarke argues that these volumes were part of a concerted effort by Northern reformers to rescue and promote the international reputation of the United States in the wake of the Civil War. Speaking tours, too, suggested "Northerners believed they had rekindled God's favor and thus passed successfully through the scourge of war," and that they sought public vindication on the world stage (67). Clarke, "'Let All Nations See,'" 66–93. See also Gardner, "When Service Is Not Enough," 29–54.

30. "Meeting for the Freedmen," *American Missionary* 11, no. 6 (1867), 124. The AMA's president was Edward Norris Kirk, whom the USCC frequently enlisted to address their galas and annual meetings.

31. "Our Boston Anniversary," *American Missionary* 12, no. 7 (1868), 158.

32. Wittenmyer, *Under the Guns*, 270.

33. Epstein, *The Politics of Domesticity*, 115–47. See also Slagell, "The Rhetorical Structure of Frances E. Willard's Campaign," 1–23; and Tyrrell, *Woman's World/Woman's Empire*.

34. Stuart, *Life of George H. Stuart*, 241; Levine, "Indian Fighters and Indian Reformers," 329–52; Stockwell, *Interrupted Odyssey*, 79–82; and Prucha, *American Indian Policy in Crisis*, 35–46.

35. White and Hopkins, *The Social Gospel*.

36. Evens, *God's Man for the Gilded Age*.

37. Davidann, *A World of Crisis and Progress*; and Xing, *Baptized in the Fire of Revolution*.

38. E. Johnson, *The History of YMCA Physical Education*; Putney, *Muscular Christianity*.

BIBLIOGRAPHY

All Bible references are taken from the King James Bible.

ONLINE PRIMARY SOURCES

American Periodicals Series Online
Cornell Univ. Library, Making of America Digital Collection
Gale Nineteenth-Century Collections Online
Julia Wilbur Papers, Quaker and Special Collections, Haverford College, Haverford, PA
Library of Congress, Chronicling America: Historic American Newspapers
Minutes of the Reformed Presbytery
Oliver Otis Howard Papers, George J. Mitchell Department of Special Collections & Archives, Bowdoin College Library, Brunswick, ME

UNPUBLISHED PRIMARY SOURCES

Armed Services United States Christian Commission–Related Records. Kautz Family YMCA Archives, Univ. of Minnesota, Minneapolis.
United States Christian Commission Journals, 1865. Miscellaneous Manuscripts, Library of Congress Manuscript Division, Washington, DC.
United States Christian Commission Records, 1861–66. Records of the Adjutant General's Office, Record Group 94, National Archives Building, Washington, DC.

180 BIBLIOGRAPHY

PUBLISHED PRIMARY SOURCES

Albright, Louis Miller. *Civil War Diary of Louis Miller Albright.* Edited by Paul M. Duke. Medina, OH: Belding Publishing, 2005.

Annual Catalogue of the Allegheny Theological Seminary of the United Presbyterian Church of North America, 1890–91. Pittsburgh: Murdoch, Kerr, & Co., 1891.

Butterworth, Hezekiah, and Theron Brown. *The Story of the Hymns and Tunes.* New York: American Tract Society, 1906.

Christ in the Army: A Selection of Sketches of the Work of the US Christian Commission. Philadelphia: Ladies Christian Commission, 1865.

Colyer, Vincent. *Report of the Christian Mission to the United States Army.* New York: George A. Whitehorne, 1862.

Fehrenbacher, Don E., ed. *Abraham Lincoln: Selected Speeches and Writings.* New York: Vintage, 1992.

First Annual Report of the Washington City Young Men's Christian Association. Washington, DC: Association, 1854.

Gordon, Ann D., ed. *The Selected Papers of Elizabeth Cady Stanton and Susan B. Anthony.* Vol. 1, *In the School of Anti-Slavery, 1840–1866.* New Brunswick, NJ: Rutgers Univ. Press, 2001.

History of the Hartsville Ladies Aid Society. Doylestown: W. W. H. Davis, 1867.

Hutchinson, John Wallace. *Story of the Hutchinsons (Tribe of Jesse).* Vol. 1. Boston: Lee and Shepard, 1896.

Hymn Book for the Army and Navy. New York: American Tract Society, 1863.

Information for Army Meetings, June & July 1864. Philadelphia: J. B. Rodgers, 1864.

Information for Army Meetings, November 1864. Philadelphia: J. B. Rodgers, 1864.

Ladies Christian Commissions. Philadelphia: C. Sherman and Sons, 1864.

Lincoln, Abraham. "Second Inaugural Address." In *Abraham Lincoln: Selected Speeches and Writings,* edited by Don E. Fehrenbacher, 449. New York: Vintage, 1992.

Kirk, Edward Norris. "A National Movement for Organizing Ladies' Christian Commissions." In *Ladies Christian Commissions,* 3–10. Philadelphia: C. Sherman and Sons, 1864.

McKeen, Philena, and Phebe F. McKeen. *Annals of Fifty Years: A History of Abbot Academy, Andover, Mass., 1829–1879.* Andover, MA: Warren F. Draper, 1880.

Moss, Lemuel, *Annals of the United States Christian Commission.* Philadelphia: J. B. Lippincott & Co., 1868.

Nightingale, Florence. *Notes on Nursing: What It Is and What It Is Not.* London: Harrison and Sons, 1859.

Nineteenth Annual Report of the American Tract Society. Boston: Perkins and Marvin, 1833.

Olmsted, Frederick Law. *To the Loyal Women of America.* Washington, DC: Commission, 1861.

Patterson, Joseph. "The Moral Results of the War." In *Christ in the Army: A Selection of Sketches of the Work of the US Christian Commission,* 136–40. Philadelphia: Ladies Christian Commission, 1865.

Patterson, Robert. "At the Front." In *Christ in the Army: A Selection of Sketches of the Work of the US Christian Commission,* 89–100. Philadelphia: Ladies Christian Commission, 1865.

Richards, Zalmon. "Report of the President." In *First Annual Report of the Washington City Young Men's Christian Association.* Washington, DC: Association, 1854.

Smith, Edward Parmelee. *Incidents among Shot and Shell.* Philadelphia: J. B. Lippincott, 1869.

BIBLIOGRAPHY 181

Stuart, George H. *The Life of George H. Stuart.* Philadelphia: J. M. Stoddart & Co., 1890.

"A Summer's Day Treat for the Wounded." In *Information for Army Meetings, September 1864.* Philadelphia: James B. Rodgers, 1864.

United States Christian Commission: First Annual Report. Philadelphia: Commission, 1863.

United States Christian Commission: Second Annual Report. Philadelphia: Commission, 1864.

United States War Department. *The War of the Rebellion: A Compilation of the Official Records of the Union and Confederate Armies.* Washington, DC: Government Printing Office, 1880–1901.

Wittenmyer, Annie. *A Collection of Recipes for the Use of Special Diet Kitchens in Military Hospitals.* St. Louis: E. P. Studley & Co., 1864.

———. *Under the Guns: A Woman's Reminiscences of the Civil War.* Boston: E. B. Stillings & Co, 1895.

SECONDARY SOURCES

Abzug, Robert H. *Cosmos Crumbling: American Reform and the Religious Imagination.* Oxford: Oxford Univ. Press, 1994.

Adams, Michael C. C. *Living Hell: The Dark Side of the Civil War.* Baltimore: Johns Hopkins Univ. Press, 2014.

Anderson, David. "Dying of Nostalgia: Homesickness in the Union Army during the Civil War." *Civil War History* 56, no. 3 (2010): 247–82.

Attie, Jeanie. *Patriotic Toil: Northern Women and the American Civil War.* Ithaca, NY: Cornell Univ. Press, 1998.

Baker, James W. *Thanksgiving: The Biography of an American Holiday.* Lebanon: Univ. of New Hampshire Press, 2009.

Banner, Lois W. "Religious Benevolence as Social Control: A Critique of an Interpretation." *Journal of American History* 60, no. 1 (1973): 23–41.

Beaudry, Mary Carolyn. *Findings: The Material Culture of Needlework and Sewing.* New Haven, CT: Yale Univ. Press, 2006.

Bebbington, David. *Evangelicalism in Modern Britain: A History from the 1730s to the 1980s.* London: Unwin Hyman, 1989.

Bellah, Robert N. "Civil Religion in America." *Daedalus* 96, no. 1 (1967): 1–21.

Bendroth, Margaret Lamberts. *A School of the Church: Andover Newton across Two Centuries.* Grand Rapids, MI: William B. Eerdmans Publishing Company, 2008.

Bennett, Michael J. "Saving Jack: Religion, Benevolent Organizations, and Union Sailors during the Civil War." In *Union Soldiers and the Northern Home Front: Wartime Experiences, Postwar Adjustments,* edited by Randall Miller and Paul Cimbala, 253–62. New York: Fordham Univ. Press, 2002.

Bercovitch, Sacvan. *The American Jeremiad.* Rev. ed. Madison: Univ. of Wisconsin Press, 2012.

Berlin, Ira, Joseph P. Reidy, and Leslie S. Rowland, eds. *Freedom's Soldiers: The Black Military Experience in the Civil War.* Cambridge: Cambridge Univ. Press, 1998.

Berry, Stephen. "The Historian as Death Investigator." In *Weirding the War: Tales from the Civil War's Ragged Edges,* edited by Stephen Berry, 176–88. Athens: Univ. of Georgia Press, 2011.

BIBLIOGRAPHY

Bever, Megan L. *At War with King Alcohol: Debating Drinking and Masculinity in the Civil War.* Chapel Hill: Univ. of North Carolina Press, 2022.

Blanton, DeAnne, and Lauren M. Cook. *They Fought Like Demons: Women Soldiers in the American Civil War.* Baton Rouge: Louisiana State Univ. Press, 2002.

Blauvelt, Martha Tomhave. "Women and Revivalism." In *Women and Religion in America.* Vol. 1, *The Nineteenth Century,* edited by Rosemary Radford Ruether and Rosemary Skinner Keller, 1–45. San Francisco: Harper & Row, 1981.

Blight, David W. "No Desperate Hero: Manhood and Freedom in a Union Soldier's Experience." In *Divided Houses: Gender and the Civil War,* edited by Catherine Clinton and Nina Silber, 55–75. Oxford: Oxford Univ. Press, 1992.

Blum, Edward J., and John H. Matsui. *War Is All Hell: The Nature of Evil and the Civil War.* Philadelphia: Univ. of Pennsylvania Press, 2021.

Boyer, Paul. *Urban Masses and Moral Order in America, 1820–1920.* Cambridge, MA: Harvard Univ. Press, 1978.

Boylan, Anne M. *Sunday School: The Formation of an American Institution, 1790–1880.* New Haven, CT: Yale Univ. Press, 1988.

Bratt, James D. "Religious Anti-Revivalism in Antebellum America." *Journal of the Early Republic* 24, no. 1 (2004): 65–106.

Brekus, Catherine A. *Strangers and Pilgrims: Female Preaching in America, 1740–1845.* Chapel Hill: Univ. of North Carolina Press, 1998.

Bremner, Robert H. *From the Depths: The Discovery of Poverty in the United States.* New York: New York Univ. Press, 1956.

———. *The Public Good: Philanthropy and Welfare in the Civil War Era.* New York: Alfred A. Knopf, 1980.

Brown, Candy Gunther. *The Word in the World: Evangelical Writing, Publishing, and Reading in America, 1789–1880.* Chapel Hill: Univ. of North Carolina Press, 2004.

Brown, Matthew P. *The Pilgrim and the Bee: Reading Rituals and Book Culture in Early New England.* Philadelphia: Univ. of Pennsylvania Press, 2007.

Buell, Lawrence. "The Unitarian Movement and the Art of Preaching in 19th-Century America." *American Quarterly* 24, no. 2 (1972): 166–90.

Burstyn, Joan N. "Catharine Beecher and the Education of American Women." *New England Quarterly* 47, no. 3 (1974): 386–403.

Butchart, Ronald. *Schooling the Freed People: Teaching, Learning, and the Struggle for Black Freedom, 1861–1876.* Chapel Hill: Univ. of North Carolina Press, 2010.

Cannon, M. Hamlin. "The United States Christian Commission." *Mississippi Valley Historical Review* 38, no. 1 (1951): 61–80.

Carwardine, Richard. *Evangelicals and Politics in Antebellum America.* Knoxville: Univ. of Tennessee Press, 1997. First published 1993.

———. "The Second Great Awakening in the Urban Centers: An Examination of Methodism and the 'New Measures.'" *Journal of American History* 59, no. 2 (1972): 327–40.

Cashin, Joan E. "Hungry People in the Wartime South: Civilians, Armies, and the Food Supply." In *Weirding the War: Stories from the Civil War's Ragged Edges,* edited by Stephen Berry, 160–75. Athens: Univ. of Georgia Press, 2011.

Chapman, Mary, and Glenn Hendler, eds. *Sentimental Men: Masculinity and the Politics of Affect in American Culture.* Berkeley: Univ. of California Press, 1999.

Cherry, Conrad, ed. *God's New Israel: Religious Interpretations of American Destiny.* Chapel Hill: Univ. of North Carolina Press, 1998.

Clark, Elizabeth B. "'The Sacred Rights of the Weak': Pain, Sympathy, and the Culture of Individual Rights in Antebellum America." *Journal of American History* 82, no. 2 (1995): 476–77.

Clarke, Frances M. "Honorable Scars: Northern Amputees and the Meaning of Civil War Injuries." In *Union Soldiers and the Northern Home Front: Wartime Experiences, Postwar Adjustments,* edited by Paul Cimbala and Randall M. Miller, 361–94. New York: Fordham Univ. Press, 2002.

———. "'Let All Nations See': Civil War Nationalism and the Memorialization of Wartime Voluntarism." *Civil War History* 52, no. 1 (2006): 66–93.

———. "Old-Fashioned Tea Parties: Revolutionary Memory in Civil War Sanitary Fairs." In *Remembering the Revolution: Memory, History, and Nation-Making from Independence to the Civil War,* edited by Michael McDonnell, Clare Corbould, Frances M. Clarke, and W. Fitzhugh Brundage, 294–312. Boston: Univ. of Massachusetts Press, 2013.

———. "So Lonesome I Could Die: Nostalgia and Debates over Emotional Control in the Civil War North." *Journal of Social History* 41, no. 2 (2007): 253–82.

———. *War Stories: Suffering and Sacrifice in the Civil War North.* Chicago: Univ. of Chicago Press, 2011.

Cohen, Joanna. *Luxurious Citizens: The Politics of Consumption in Nineteenth-Century America.* Philadelphia: Univ. of Pennsylvania Press, 2017.

———. "You Have No Flag out Yet?: Commercial Connections and Patriotic Emotion in the Civil War North." *Journal of the Civil War Era* 9, no. 3 (2019): 378–409.

Coleman, Dawn. "The Antebellum American Sermon as Lived Religion." In *A New History of the Sermon: The Nineteenth Century,* edited by Robert H. Ellison, 521–54. Boston: Koninklijke Brill, 2010.

Conforti, Joseph. "The Invention of the Great Awakening, 1795–1842." *Early American Literature* 26, no. 2 (1991): 99–118.

Conkin, Paul K. *Cane Ridge: America's Pentecost.* Madison: Univ. of Wisconsin Press, 1990.

———. *The Uneasy Center: Reformed Christianity in Antebellum America.* Chapel Hill: Univ. of North Carolina Press, 1995.

Cook, Sharon Anne. *"Through Sunshine and Shadow": The Woman's Christian Temperance Union, Evangelicalism, and Reform in Ontario, 1874–1930.* Montreal: McGill-Queen's Univ. Press, 1995.

Cope, Rachel. "From Smouldering Fires to Revitalising Showers: A Historiographical Overview of Revivalism in Nineteenth-Century New York." *Wesley and Methodist Studies* 4 (2012): 25–49.

Corrigan, John. *Business of the Heart: Religion and Emotion in Nineteenth-Century America.* Berkeley: Univ. of California Press, 2002.

Cott, Nancy F. *The Bonds of Womanhood: "Woman's Sphere" in New England, 1780–1835.* 2nd ed. New Haven, CT: Yale Univ. Press, 1997.

Cressy, David. "Books as Totems in Seventeenth-Century England and New England." *Journal of Library History (1974–1987)* 12, no. 1, Libraries, Books, & Culture 1 (Winter 1986): 92–106.

Curtis, Heather D. "Visions of Self, Success, and Society among Young Men in Antebellum Boston." *Church History* 73, no. 3 (2004): 613–34.

BIBLIOGRAPHY

Dannenbaum, Jed. *Drink and Disorder: Temperance Reform in Cincinnati from the Washingtonian Revival to the WCTU.* Urbana: Univ. of Illinois Press, 1984.

David, James C. "The Politics of Emasculation: The Caning of Charles Sumner and Elite Ideologies of Manhood in the Mid-Nineteenth Century United States." *Gender & History* 19, no. 2 (2007): 324–45.

Davidann, Jon Thares. *A World of Crisis and Progress: The American YMCA in Japan, 1890–1930.* Cranbury, NJ: Associated Univ. Presses, 1998.

Davis, Natalie Zemon. "Beyond the Market: Books as Gifts in Sixteenth-Century France: The Prothero Lecture." *Transactions of the Royal Historical Society* 33 (1983): 69–88.

Davis, William C. *A Taste for War: The Culinary History of the Blue and the Gray.* Mechanicsburg, PA: Stackpole Books, 2003.

Dorrien, Gary J. *The Making of American Liberal Theology: Imagining Progressive Religion, 1805–1900.* Louisville, KY: Westminster John Knox Press, 2001.

Douglas, Ann. *The Feminization of American Culture.* New York: Alfred A. Knopf, 1977.

Dressed, Michael A. *The Hospital on Seminary Ridge at the Battle of Gettysburg.* Jefferson, NC: McFarland, 2002.

Eicher, Joanne B., and Mary Ellen Roach-Higgins. "Definition and Classification of Dress: Implications for Analysis of Gender Roles." In *Dress and Gender: Making and Meaning in Cultural Contexts,* edited by Ruth Barnes and Joanne B. Eicher, 8–28. Oxford: Berg, 1992.

Engelsing, Rolf. *Der Bürger als Leser: Lesegeschichte in Deutschland, 1500–1800.* Stuttgart: Metzlersche, 1973.

Epstein, Barbara L. *The Politics of Domesticity: Women, Evangelism, and Temperance in Nineteenth-Century America.* Middletown, CT: Wesleyan Univ. Press, 1981.

Eslinger, Ellen. *Citizens of Zion: The Social Origins of Camp Meeting Revivalism.* Knoxville: Univ. of Tennessee Press, 1999.

Evens, Bruce J. *God's Man for the Gilded Age: D. L. Moody and the Rise of Modern Mass Evangelism.* Oxford: Oxford Univ. Press, 2003.

Fahs, Alice. *The Imagined Civil War: Popular Literature of the North and South 1861–1865.* Chapel Hill: Univ. of North Carolina Press, 2001.

Faris, John T. *The Life of J. R. Miller: "Jesus and I Are Friends."* Philadelphia: Presbyterian Board of Publications, 1912.

Faust, Drew Gilpin. *This Republic of Suffering: Death and the American Civil War.* New York: Vintage Books, 2008.

Fea, John. *The Bible Cause: A History of the American Bible Society.* Oxford: Oxford Univ. Press, 2016.

Ferrie, Joseph P. "How Ya Gonna Keep 'Em down on the Farm [When They've Seen Schenectady]?: Rural-to-Urban Migration in 19-Century America, 1850–70." Unpublished working paper, https://faculty.wcas.northwestern.edu/fe2r/papers/urban.pdf.

Finke, Roger, and Rodney Stark. "Turning Pews into People: Estimating 19th-Century Church Membership." *Journal for the Scientific Study of Religion* 25, no. 2 (1986): 180–92.

Finseth, Ian. *The Civil War Dead and American Modernity.* Oxford: Oxford Univ. Press, 2018.

Flannery, Michael A. *Civil War Pharmacy.* 2nd ed. Carbondale: Southern Illinois Univ. Press, 2011.

Foote, Lorien. *The Gentlemen and the Roughs: Violence, Honor, and Manhood in the Union Armies.* New York: New York Univ. Press, 2010.

BIBLIOGRAPHY

Foster, Charles I. *An Errand of Mercy: The Evangelical United Front, 1790–1837.* Chapel Hill: Univ. of North Carolina Press, 1960.

Francis, Russell E. "The Religious Revival of 1858 in Philadelphia." *Pennsylvania Magazine of History and Biography* 70 (1946): 52–77.

Frank, Stephen M. *Life with Father: Parenthood and Masculinity in the Nineteenth-Century American North.* Baltimore: Johns Hopkins Univ. Press, 1998.

Fredrickson, George M. *The Inner Civil War: Northern Intellectuals and the Crisis of the Union.* New York: Harper Torchbooks, 1965.

Gardner, Sarah E. "When Service Is Not Enough: Charity's Purpose in the Immediate Aftermath of the Civil War." *Journal of the Civil War Era* 9, no. 1 (Mar. 2019): 29–54.

Giesberg, Judith. *Sex and the Civil War: Soldiers, Pornography, and the Making of American Morality.* Chapel Hill: Univ. of North Carolina Press, 2017.

Giesberg, Judith Ann. *Civil War Sisterhood: The US Sanitary Commission and Women's Politics in Transition.* Boston: Northeastern Univ. Press, 2000.

Ginzberg, Lori D. *Women and the Work of Benevolence: Morality, Politics and Class in the Nineteenth-Century United States.* New Haven, CT: Yale Univ. Press, 1990.

Glatthaar, Joseph T. *Forged in Battle: The Civil War Alliance of Black Soldiers and White Officers.* Baton Rouge: Louisiana State Univ. Press, 2000. First published 1990.

Goen, C. C. *Broken Churches, Broken Nation: Denominational Schisms and the Coming of the American Civil War.* Macon, GA: Mercer Univ. Press, 1985.

Gordon, Beverly. *Bazaars and Fair Ladies: The History of the American Fundraising Fair.* Knoxville: Univ. of Tennessee Press, 1998.

Grammer, Elizabeth Elkin. *Some Wild Visions: Autobiographies by Female Itinerant Evangelists in Nineteenth-Century America.* Oxford: Oxford Univ. Press, 2003.

Grant, Susan-Mary. "Raising the Dead: War, Memory, and American National Identity." *Nations and Nationalism* 11, no. 4 (2005): 509–29.

Greeley, Dawn M. *Beyond Benevolence: The New York Charity Organization Society and the Transformation of American Social Welfare, 1882–1935.* Bloomington: Indiana Univ. Press, 2022.

Greenberg, Amy S. *Manifest Manhood and the Antebellum American Empire.* Cambridge: Cambridge Univ. Press, 2005.

Griffen, Clyde. "Reconstructing Masculinity from the Evangelical Revival to the Waning of Progressivism: A Speculative Synthesis." In *Meanings for Manhood: Constructions of Masculinity in Victorian America,* edited by Mark C. Carnes and Clyde Griffen, 183–204. Chicago: Univ. of Chicago Press, 1990.

Griffin, Clifford S. "Religious Benevolence as Social Control, 1815–1860." *Mississippi Valley Historical Review* 44, no. 3 (Dec. 1957): 423–44.

———. *Their Brothers' Keepers: Moral Stewardship in the United States, 1800–1865.* Reprint, Westport, CT: Greenwood Press, 1983.

Guinn, Lisa. "Annie Wittenmyer and Nineteenth-Century Women's Usefulness." *Annals of Iowa* 74, no. 4 (2015): 351–77.

Gusfield, Joseph R. *Symbolic Crusade: Status Politics and the American Temperance Movement.* 2nd ed. Chicago: Univ. of Illinois Press, 1986.

Hacker, J. David. "A Census-Based Count of the Civil War Dead." *Civil War History* 57, no. 4 (2011): 307–48.

Hall, David D., ed. *Lived Religion in America: Toward a History of Practice.* Princeton, NJ: Princeton Univ. Press, 1997.

Hall, Donald E. "Muscular Christianity: Reading and Writing the Male Social Body." In *Muscular Christianity: Embodying the Victorian Age,* edited by Donald E. Hall, 3–13. Cambridge: Cambridge Univ. Press, 1994.

Hall, Patricia Kelly, and Steven Ruggles. "'Restless in the Midst of Their Prosperity': New Evidence on the Internal Migration of Americans, 1850–2000." *Journal of American History* 91, no. 3 (2004): 829–46.

Hamer, Barbara. *From Hardtack to Home Fries: An Uncommon History of American Cooks and Meals.* New York: Free Press, 2002.

Hansen, Karen V. "'Helped Put in a Quilt': Men's Work and Male Intimacy in Nineteenth-Century New England." *Gender and Society* 3, no. 3 (1989): 334–54.

———. *A Very Social Time: Crafting Community in Antebellum New England.* Berkeley: Univ. of California Press, 1994.

Harden, Glenn M. "Men and Women of Their Own Kind: Historians and Antebellum Reform." PhD diss., George Mason Univ., 2001.

Harris, Brayton. "Newspapers." In *Civil War America: A Social and Cultural History,* edited by Maggi M. Morehouse and Zoe Trodd, 193–202. New York: Routledge, Taylor & Francis Group, 2013.

Hatch, Nathan O. *The Democratization of American Christianity.* New Haven, CT: Yale Univ. Press, 1989.

Hendler, Glenn. *Public Sentiment: Structures of Feeling in Nineteenth-Century American Literature.* Chapel Hill: Univ. of North Carolina Press, 2001.

Henry, James O. "The United States Christian Commission during the Civil War." *Civil War History* 6, no. 4 (1960): 374–88.

Herschbach, Lisa. "Prosthetic Reconstructions: Making the Industry, Re-making the Body, Modelling the Nation." *History Workshop Journal* 44, no. 1 (1997): 22–57.

Hirrel, Leo P. *Children of Wrath: New School Calvinism and Antebellum Reform.* Lexington: Univ. of Kentucky Press, 1998.

Hoisington, Daniel John. *Gettysburg and the Christian Commission.* Roseville, MN: Edinborough Press, 2002.

———. "'A Thousand Nameless Acts': The Christian Commission at Gettysburg." In Hoisington, *Gettysburg and the Christian Commission,* 2–37.

Hopkins, C. Howard. *History of the YMCA in North America.* New York: Association Press, 1951.

Horlick, Allan Stanley. *Country Boys and Merchant Princes: The Social Control of Young Men in New York.* Lewisburg, PA: Bucknell Univ. Press, 1975.

Hovde, David M. "The US Christian Commission's Library and Literacy Programs for the Union Military Forces in the Civil War." *Libraries and Culture* 24, no. 3 (1989): 295–316.

Howe, Daniel Walker. "The Evangelical Movement and Political Culture in the North during the Second Party System." *Journal of American History* 77, no. 4 (1991): 1216–39.

———. *What Hath God Wrought: The Transformation of America, 1815–1848.* Oxford: Oxford Univ. Press, 2007.

Huggins, Dorothy H. "Women in Wartime, San Francisco, 1864: The Ladies' Christian Commission Fair." *California Historical Society Quarterly* 24, no. 3 (1945): 261–66.

BIBLIOGRAPHY

Humphreys, Margaret. *Marrow of Tragedy: The Health Crisis of the American Civil War.* Baltimore: Johns Hopkins Univ. Press, 2013.

———. "'We Made up Soup as Fast as Possible': Nutrition and the Nineteenth-Century Male Body." In *Civil War Medicine: A Surgeon's Diary,* edited by Robert D. Hicks, 330–38. Bloomington: Indiana Univ. Press, 2019.

Irwin, Mary Ann. "'Going About and Doing Good': The Lady Managers of San Francisco, 1850–1880." In *California Women and Politics: From the Gold Rush to the Great Depression,* edited by Robert W. Cherry, Mary Ann Irwin, and Ann Marie Wilson, 27–58. Lincoln: Univ. of Nebraska Press, 2011.

John, Richard R. "Taking Sabbatarianism Seriously: The Postal System, the Sabbath, and the Transformation of American Political Culture." *Journal of the Early Republic* 10, no. 4 (1990): 517–67.

Johnson, Curtis D. "The Protracted Meeting Myth: Awakenings, Revivals, and New York State Baptists, 1789–1850." *Journal of the Early Republic* 34, no. 3 (2014): 349–83.

Johnson, Elmer. *The History of YMCA Physical Education.* Chicago: Association Press, 1979.

Johnson, Paul E. *A Shopkeeper's Millennium: Society and Revivals in Rochester, New York, 1815–1837.* New York: Hill and Wang, 1978.

Jones, Jacqueline. *Soldiers of Light and Love: Northern Teachers and Georgia Blacks, 1865–1873.* Athens: Univ. of Georgia Press, 1992. First published 1980.

Jordan, Brian Matthew. "The Future of Civil War History." *Emerging Civil War.* https://emergingcivilwar.com/2016/06/23/the-future-of-civil-war-history-brian-matthew-jordan/.

Kaser, David. *Books and Libraries in Camp and Battle: The Civil War Experience.* Westport, CT: Greenwood Press, 1984.

Knight, Jeffrey Todd. "'Furnished' for Action: Renaissance Books as Furniture." *Book History* 12 (2009): 37–73.

Kohl, Lawrence Frederick. "The Concept of Social Control and the History of Jacksonian America." *Journal of the Early Republic* 5 (1985): 21–34.

Kupperman, Karen Ordahl. *Indians & English: Facing Off in Early America.* Ithaca, NY: Cornell Univ. Press, 2000.

Kytle, Ethan J. "From Body Reform to Reforming the Body Politics: Transcendentalism and the Military Antislavery Career of Thomas Wentworth Higginson." *American Nineteenth-Century History* 8, no. 3 (2007): 325–50.

LaBarre, Steven M. "The American Housewife Goes to War: Sewing Kits That Accompanied the American Soldier to the Front, 1776–1976." MA diss., Univ. of Nebraska–Kearney, 2020.

Laderman, Gary. *The Sacred Remains: American Attitudes toward Death, 1799–1883.* New Haven, CT: Yale Univ. Press, 1996.

Lande, R. Gregory. *Madness, Malingering, and Malfeasance: The Transformation of Psychiatry and the Law in the Civil War Era.* Washington, DC: Brassey's, Inc., 2003.

Leach, Josiah Granville. *History of the Bringhurst Family.* Philadelphia: J. B. Lippincott and Co., 1901.

Leavitt, Sarah A. *From Catharine Beecher to Martha Stewart: A Cultural History of Domestic Advice.* Chapel Hill: Univ. of North Carolina Press, 2003.

Leonard, Elizabeth D. *Yankee Women: Gender Battles in the Civil War.* New York: W. W. Norton & Co., 1994.

Levine, Richard R. "Indian Fighters and Indian Reformers: Grant's Indian Peace Policy and the Conservative Consensus." *Civil War History* 31, no. 4 (1985): 329–52.

Linderman, Gerald F. *Embattled Courage: The Experience of Combat in the American Civil War.* New York: Free Press, 1987.

Long, Kathryn Teresa. *The Revival of 1857–58: Interpreting an American Religious Awakening.* Oxford: Oxford Univ. Press, 1998.

Long, Lisa A. *Rehabilitating Bodies: Health, History, and the American Civil War.* Philadelphia: Univ. of Pennsylvania Press, 2004.

Lowry, Thomas W. *The Story the Soldiers Wouldn't Tell: Sex in the Civil War.* Mechanicsburg, PA: Stackpole Books, 1994.

Luckingham, Bradford. "Benevolence in Emergent San Francisco: A Note on Immigrant Life in the Urban Far West." *Southern California Quarterly* 55, no. 4 (1973): 431–43.

Lupkin, Paula. *Manhood Factories: YMCA Architecture and the Making of Modern Urban Culture.* Minneapolis: Univ. of Minnesota Press, 2010.

Madway, Lorraine. "Purveying Patriotic Pageantry: The Civil War Sanitary Fairs in New York." *New York History* 93, no. 4 (2012): 268–301.

Mangan, J. A., and James Walvin. "Introduction." In *Manliness and Morality: Middle-Class Masculinity in Britain and America, 1800–1940,* edited by J. A. Mangan and James Walvin, 1–6. Manchester: Manchester Univ. Press, 1987.

Marshall, Nicholas. "'In the Midst of Life We Are in Death': Affliction and Religion in Antebellum New York." In *Mortal Remains: Death in Early America,* edited by Nancy Isenberg and Andrew Burstein, 176–86. Philadelphia: Univ. of Pennsylvania Press, 2002.

Marten, James. *The Children's Civil War.* Chapel Hill: Univ. of North Carolina Press, 1998.

Martin, Robert F. "Annie Wittenmyer and the Twilight of Evangelical Reform." In *Varieties of Southern Religious History: Essays in Honor of Donald G. Mathews,* edited by Regina D. Sullivan and Monte Harrell Hampton, 141–61. Columbia: Univ. of South Carolina Press, 2015.

Martin, Scott C. *Devil of the Domestic Sphere: Temperance, Gender, and Middle-Class Ideology, 1800–1860.* DeKalb: Northern Illinois Univ. Press, 2008.

———. "'A Soldier Intoxicated Is Far Worse Than No Soldier at All': Intoxication and the American Civil War." *The Social History of Alcohol and Drugs* 25, no. 1–2 (2011): 66–87.

Maryniak, Benedict. "Union Military Chaplains." In *Faith in the Fight: Civil War Chaplains,* edited by John W. Brinsfield, Williams C. Davis, Benedict Maryniak, and James I. Robertson Jr., 43–47. Mechanicsburg, PA: Stackpole Books, 2003.

Matthews, Glenna. *The Rise of Public Woman: Woman's Power and Woman's Place in the United States, 1630–1970.* Oxford: Oxford Univ. Press, 1992.

Maxwell, William Quentin. *Lincoln's Fifth Wheel: The Political History of the United States Sanitary Commission.* New York: Longmans, Green & Co., 1956.

McCrossen, Alexis. "Sabbatarianism: The Intersection of Church and State in the Orchestration of Everyday Life in Nineteenth-Century America." In *Religious and Secular Reform in America: Ideas, Beliefs, and Social Change,* edited by David K. Adams and Cornelius Van Minnen, 134–51. New York: New York Univ. Press, 1999.

McDannell, Colleen. *The Christian Home in Victorian America, 1840–1900.* Bloomington: Indiana Univ. Press, 1994. First published 1986.

McDevitt, Theresa. "'A Melody before Unknown': The Civil War Experiences of Mary and Amanda Shelton." *Annals of Iowa* 63 (2004): 105–36.

BIBLIOGRAPHY

McDevitt, Theresa R. "Fighting for the Soul of America: A History of the United States Christian Commission." PhD diss., Kent State Univ., 1997.

McEnery, Tony. *Swearing in English: Bad Language, Purity and Power from 1586 to the Present*. New York: Routledge, 2006.

McLoughlin, William G. *Revivals, Awakenings, and Reform: An Essay on Religion and Social Change in America, 1607–1977*. Chicago: Univ. of Chicago Press, 1978.

McPherson, James. *What They Fought for, 1861–1865*. New York: Anchor Books, 1995.

Meier, Kathryn Shively. "US Sanitary Commission Physicians and the Transformation of American Health Care." In *So Conceived and So Dedicated: Intellectual Life in the Civil War-Era North*, edited by Kanisorn Wongsrichanalai and Lorien Foote, 19–40. New York: Fordham Univ. Press, 2015.

Miller, Benjamin Lee. *In God's Presence: Chaplains, Missionaries, and Religious Space during the American Civil War*. Lawrence: Univ. Press of Kansas, 2019.

Miller, Randall M., Harry S. Stout, and Charles Reagan Wilson, eds. *Religion and the American Civil War*. Oxford: Oxford Univ. Press, 1998.

Miller, Richard F. "Brahmins under Fire: Peer Courage and the Harvard Regiment." *Historical Journal of Massachusetts* 30 (2002): online. https://www.westfield.ma.edu/historical-journal/wp-content/uploads/2018/06/Miller-Winter-2002-complete.pdf

Miller, Robert J. *Both Prayed to the Same God: Religion and Faith in the American Civil War*. Lanham, MD: Lexington Books, 2007.

Mintz, Steven. *Moralists and Modernizers: America's Pre-Civil War Reformers*. Baltimore: Johns Hopkins Univ. Press, 1995.

Mitchell, Reid. *Civil War Soldiers*. Rev. ed. New York: Penguin, 1997.

———. *The Vacant Chair: The Northern Soldier Leaves Home*. Oxford: Oxford Univ. Press, 1993.

Montagu, Ashley. *The Anatomy of Swearing*. Philadelphia: Univ. of Pennsylvania Press, 1967.

Moore, Robert Laurence. *Selling God: American Religion in the Marketplace of Culture*. Oxford: Oxford Univ. Press, 1995.

Moorhead, James H. *American Apocalypse: Yankee Protestants and the Civil War, 1860–1869*. New Haven, CT: Yale Univ. Press, 1978.

———. "Between Progress and Apocalypse: A Reassessment of Millennialism in American Religious Thought, 1800–1880." *Journal of American History* 71 (1984): 524–42.

———. *World without End: Mainstream American Protestant Visions of the Last Things, 1880–1925*. Bloomington: Indiana Univ. Press, 1999.

Morris, Robert C. *Reading, 'riting, and Reconstruction: The Education of Freedmen in the South, 1861–1870*. Chicago: Univ. of Chicago Press, 1981.

Mountford, Roxanne. *The Gendered Pulpit: Preaching in American Protestant Spaces*. Carbondale: Southern Illinois Univ. Press, 2003.

Mujic, Julie. "'Ours Is the Harder Lot': Student Patriotism at the University of Michigan during the Civil War." In *Union Heartland: The Midwestern Homefront during the Civil War*, edited by Ginette Aley and Joseph L. Anderson, 33–67. Carbondale: Southern Illinois Univ. Press, 2013.

———. "Save a School to Save a Nation: Faculty Responses to the Civil War at Midwestern Universities." In *So Conceived and So Dedicated: Intellectual Life in the Civil War–Era North*, edited by Lorien Foote and Kanisorn Wongsrichanalai, 110–28. New York: Fordham Univ. Press, 2015.

Mullen, Lincoln A. *The Chance of Salvation: A History of Conversion in America.* Cambridge, MA: Harvard Univ. Press, 2017.

Nissenbaum, Stephen. *Sex, Diet and Debility in Jacksonian America: Sylvester Graham and Health Reform.* Westport, CT: Greenwood Press, 1980.

Noll, Mark A. *The Civil War as a Theological Crisis.* Chapel Hill: Univ. of North Carolina Press, 2006.

Nord, David. "Religious Reading and Readers in Antebellum America." *Journal of the Early Republic* 15 (1995): 241–72.

Nord, David Paul. "Benevolent Books: Printing, Religion, and Reform." In *A History of the Book in America,* edited by Robert A. Gross and Mary Kelley. Vol. 2, *An Extensive Republic: Print, Culture, and Society in the New Nation, 1790–1840,* 221–46. Chapel Hill: Univ. of North Carolina Press, 2004.

———. *Faith in Reading: Religious Publishing and the Rise of Mass Media in America.* Oxford: Oxford Univ. Press, 2004.

———. "Free Grace, Free Books, Free Riders: The Economics of Religious Publishing in Early Nineteenth-Century America." In *Religion, Media, and the Marketplace,* edited by Lynn Schofield Clark, 48–53. New Brunswick, NJ: Rutgers Univ. Press, 2007.

Numbers, Ronald L., and Jonathan M. Butler, eds. *The Disappointed: Millerism and Millenarianism in the Nineteenth Century.* 2nd ed. Knoxville: Univ. of Tennessee Press, 1993.

O'Connor, Erin. "Fractions of Men: Engendering Amputation in Victorian Culture." *Comparative Studies in Society and History* 39 (1997): 742–77.

Offiler, Ben, and Rachel Williams, eds. *American Philanthropy at Home and Abroad: New Directions in the History of Giving.* London: Bloomsbury, 2022.

Osterud, Nancy Grey. "'She Helped Me Hay It as Good as a Man': Relations among Women and Men in an Agricultural Community." In *To Toil the Livelong Day: America's Women at Work, 1780–1980,* edited by Carol Groneman and Mary Beth Norton, 87–97. Ithaca, NY: Cornell Univ. Press, 1987.

Ostrander, Rick. *Life of Prayer in a World of Science: Protestants, Prayer, and American Culture, 1870–1930.* Oxford: Oxford Univ. Press, 2000.

Paludan, Phillip Shaw. *A People's Contest: The Union & Civil War, 1861–1865.* 2nd ed. Lawrence: Kansas Univ. Press, 1996.

Park, Roberta J. "Biological Thought, Athletics, and the Formation of a 'Man of Character,' 1830–1900." In *Manliness and Morality: Middle-Class Masculinity in Britain and America, 1800–1940,* edited by J. A. Mangan and James Walvin, 7–30. Manchester: Manchester Univ. Press, 1987.

Parkins, Wendy, ed. *Fashioning the Body Politic: Dress, Gender, Citizenship.* Oxford: Berg, 2002.

Parsons, Elaine Frantz. *Manhood Lost: Fallen Drunkards and Redeeming Women in the Nineteenth-Century United States.* Baltimore: Johns Hopkins Univ. Press, 2003.

Patterson, Gerald A. *Debris of Battle: The Wounded of Gettysburg.* Mechanicsburg, PA: Stackpole Books, 1997.

Prucha, Francis Paul. *American Indian Policy in Crisis: Christian Reformers and the Indian, 1865–1900.* Norman: Univ. of Oklahoma Press, 1976.

Purcell, Sarah J. *Spectacle of Grief: Public Funerals and Memory in the Civil War Era.* Chapel Hill: Univ. of North Carolina Press, 2022.

BIBLIOGRAPHY

Putney, Clifford. *Muscular Christianity: Manhood and Sports in Protestant America, 1880–1920.* Cambridge, MA: Harvard Univ. Press, 2003.

Quenzel, Carrol H. "Books for the Boys in Blue." *Journal of the Illinois State Historical Society (1908–1984)* 44 (1951): 218–30.

Rable, George C. *God's Almost Chosen Peoples: A Religious History of the American Civil War.* Chapel Hill: Univ. of North Carolina Press, 2010.

Ramold, Steven J. *Baring the Iron Hand: Discipline in the Union Army.* DeKalb: Northern Illinois Univ. Press, 2010.

Raney, David. "In the Lord's Army: The United States Christian Commission in the Civil War." PhD diss., Univ. of Illinois at Urbana-Champaign, 2001.

———. "In the Lord's Army: The United States Christian Commission, Soldiers, and the Union War Effort." In *Union Soldiers and the Northern Home Front: Wartime Experiences, Postwar Adjustments,* edited by Randall Miller and Paul Cimbala, 263–92. New York: Fordham Univ. Press, 2002.

Reynolds, David S. "From Doctrine to Narrative: The Rise of Pulpit Storytelling in America." *American Quarterly* 32 (1980): 479–98.

Richardson, Joe M. *Christian Reconstruction: The American Missionary Association and Southern Blacks, 1861–1890.* Tuscaloosa: Univ. of Alabama Press, 1986.

Ringel, Paul B. "Thrills for Children: The *Youth's Companion,* the Civil War, and the Commercialization of American Youth." In *Children and Youth during the Civil War Era,* edited by James Marten, 77–91. New York: NYU Press, 2012.

Roberts, Brian. *American Alchemy: The California Gold Rush and Middle-Class Culture.* Chapel Hill: Univ. of North Carolina Press, 2000.

Robertson Jr., James I. *Soldiers Blue and Gray.* Columbia: Univ. of South Carolina Press, 1988.

Roche, Daniel. *The Culture of Clothing: Dress and Fashion in the "Ancien Regime."* Translated by Jean Birrell. Cambridge: Cambridge Univ. Press, 1994.

Rotundo, E. Anthony. *American Manhood: Transformations in Masculinity from the Revolution to the Modern Era.* New York: Basic Books, 1993.

Rowe, Henry K. *History of Andover Theological Seminary.* Boston: Thomas Todd Co., 1933.

Ryan, Mary P. *Cradle of the Middle Class: The Family in Oneida County, New York, 1790–1865.* Cambridge: Cambridge Univ. Press, 1981.

Sack, David. *Whitebread Protestants: Food and Religion in American Culture.* New York: St. Martin's Press, 2000.

Saum, Lewis O. "Death in the Popular Mind of Pre-Civil War America." *American Quarterly* 26 (1974): 479–81.

Schantz, Mark. *Awaiting the Heavenly Country: The Civil War and America's Culture of Death.* Ithaca, NY: Cornell Univ. Press, 2008.

Schultz, Jane. *Women at the Front: Hospital Workers in Civil War America.* Chapel Hill: Univ. of North Carolina Press, 2004.

Schuyler, David. "Inventing a Feminine Past." *The New England Quarterly* 51, no. 3 (Sept. 1978): 291–308.

Schwalm, Leslie A. "A Body of 'Truly Scientific Work': The US Sanitary Commission and the Elaboration of Race in the Civil War Era." *Journal of the Civil War Era* 8, no. 4 (2018): 647–76.

Scott, Sean A. "'Earth Has No Sorrow That Heaven Cannot Cure': Northern Civilian Perspectives on Death and Eternity during the Civil War." *Journal of Social History* 41 (2008): 843–66.

Shattuck, Gardiner H. *A Shield and Hiding Place: The Religious Life of the Civil War Armies.* Macon, GA: Mercer Univ. Press, 1987.Shaver, Lisa J. *Beyond the Pulpit: Women's Rhetorical Roles in the Antebellum Religious Press.* Pittsburgh: Univ. of Pittsburgh Press, 2012.

Shiels, Richard D. "The Feminization of American Congregationalism, 1730–1835." *American Quarterly* 33, no. 1 (Spring 1981): 46–62.

Shprintzen, Adam D. *The Vegetarian Crusade: The Rise of an American Reform Movement, 1817–1921.* Chapel Hill: Univ. of North Carolina Press, 2013.

Sklar, Kathryn Kish. *Catharine Beecher: A Study in American Domesticity.* New Haven, CT: Yale Univ. Press, 1973.

Slagell, Amy R. "The Rhetorical Structure of Frances E. Willard's Campaign for Woman Suffrage, 1876–1896." *Rhetoric and Public Affairs* 4, no. 1 (2001): 1–23.

Smith, Andrew F. *Starving the South: How the North Won the Civil War.* New York: St. Martin's Press, 2011.

Smith, Gary Scott. *Heaven in the American Imagination.* Oxford: Oxford Univ. Press, 2011.

Smith, Timothy L. *Revivalism and Social Reform: American Protestantism on the Eve of the Civil War.* New York: Harper Torchbooks, 1965. First published 1957.

Smith-Rosenberg, Carroll. "The Female World of Love and Ritual: Relations between Women in Nineteenth-Century America." *Signs* 1 (1975): 1–29.

Sommerville, Diane Miller. *Aberration of Mind: Suicide and Suffering in the Civil War-Era South.* Chapel Hill: Univ. of North Carolina Press, 2011.

Spencer, Colin. *The Heretic's Feast: A History of Vegetarianism.* Hanover, MA: Univ. Press of New England, 1993.

Steinroetter, Vanessa. "Soldiers, Readers, and the Reception of Victor Hugo's *Les Misérables* in Civil War America." *Reception: Texts, Readers, Audiences, History* 8 (2016): 5–28.

Sternhell, Yael A. "Revisionism Reinvented? The Antiwar Turn in Civil War Scholarship." *Journal of the Civil War Era* 3, no. 2 (2013): 239–56.

Stockwell, Mary. *Interrupted Odyssey: Ulysses S. Grant and the American Indians.* Carbondale: Southern Illinois Univ. Press, 2018.

Stout, Harry S. *Upon the Altar of the Nation: A Moral History of the Civil War.* London: Penguin, 2006.

Sutton, William R. "Benevolent Calvinism and the Moral Government of God: The Influence of Nathaniel W. Taylor on Revivalism in the Second Great Awakening." *Religion and American Culture: A Journal of Interpretation* 2 (1992): 23–47.

Thompson, Lauren K. *Friendly Enemies: Soldier Fraternization throughout the American Civil War.* Lincoln: Univ. of Nebraska Press, 2020.

Tuveson, Ernest Lee. *Redeemer Nation: The Idea of America's Millennial Role.* Chicago: Univ. of Chicago Press, 1968.

Tyrrell, Ian. *Woman's World/Woman's Empire: The Woman's Christian Temperance Union in International Perspective, 1880–1930.* Chapel Hill: Univ. of North Carolina Press, 1991.

Tyrrell, Ian R. *Sobering Up: From Temperance to Prohibition in Antebellum America, 1800–1860.* Westport, CT: Greenwood Press, 1979.

Vance, Norman. *The Sinews of the Spirit: The Ideal of Christian Manliness in Victorian Literature and Religious Thought.* Cambridge: Cambridge Univ. Press, 1985.

Watson, Rowan. "Some Non-textual Uses of Books." In *A Companion to the History of the Book,* edited by Simon Eliot and Jonathan Rose, 48–92. Oxford: Blackwell Publishing, 2007.

Weicksel, Sarah Jones. "Confederate Cultures of Military Clothing Production." In *Clothing and Fashion in Southern History,* edited by Ted Ownby and Becca Walton, 32–53. Columbia: Univ. Press of Mississippi, 2020.

———. "'Make up a Box to Send Me': Consumer Culture and Camp Life in the American Civil War." In *The Military and the Market,* edited by Jennifer Mittelstadt and Mark R. Wilson, 67–86. Philadelphia: Univ. of Pennsylvania Press, 2022.

Weitz, Mark A. "Drill, Training, and the Combat Performance of the Civil War Soldier: Dispelling the Myth of the Poor Soldier, Great Fighter." *Journal of Military History* 62, no. 2 (1998): 263–89.

Wells, Cheryl. "Battle Time: Gender, Modernity, and Confederate Hospitals." *Journal of Social History* 35, no. 2 (2001): 409–28.

Wells, Cheryl A. *Civil War Time: Temporality and Identity in America, 1861–1865.* Athens: Univ. of Georgia Press, 2012. First published 2005.

Wells, Robert V. *Facing the "King of Terrors": Death and Society in an American Community, 1750–1990.* Cambridge: Cambridge Univ. Press, 2000.

Welter, Barbara. "The Feminization of American Religion: 1800–1860." In *Clio's Consciousness Raised: New Perspectives on the History of Women,* edited by Mary S. Hartman and Lois W. Banner, 137–57. New York: Harper and Row, 1974.

White, Ronald Cedric, and C. Howard Hopkins. *The Social Gospel: Religion and Reform in Changing America.* Philadelphia: Temple Univ. Press, 1976.

Wiley, Bell Irvin. *The Life of Billy Yank: The Common Soldier of the Union.* 2nd ed. Indianapolis: Charter Books, 1962.

Williams, Rachel. "Civil War Relief Agencies, the Union Soldier, and Healing the Union." In *The Health of the Nation: European Views of the United States,* vol. 6, edited by Meldan Tanrisal and Tanfer Emin Tunç, 39–52. Heidelberg: Universitätsverlag, 2014.

———. "Heaping Coals of Fire on the Enemy's Head: The Political Uses of Benevolence in the Civil War." In *American Philanthropy at Home and Abroad: New Directions in the History of Giving,* edited by Ben Offiler and Rachel Williams, 17–32. London: Bloomsbury, 2022.

Wilson, Keith P. *Campfires of Freedom: The Camp Life of Black Soldiers during the Civil War.* Kent, OH: Kent State Univ. Press, 2002.

Wongsrichanalai, Kanisorn. "College-Educated New Englanders in the Civil War." *Massachusetts Historical Review* 13 (2011): 67–95.

———. *Northern Character: College-Educated New Englanders, Honor, Nationalism, and Leadership in the Civil War Era.* New York: Fordham Univ. Press, 2016.

———. "'What Is a Person Worth at Such a Time': New England College Students, Sectionalism, and Secession." In *Children and Youth in the Civil War Era,* edited by James Marten, 46–62. New York: NYU Press, 2012.

Woodworth, Steven E. *While God Is Marching On: The Religious World of Civil War Soldiers.* Lawrence: Univ. Press of Kansas, 2001.

Wosh, Peter. *Spreading the Word: The Bible Business in Nineteenth-Century America.* Ithaca, NY: Cornell Univ. Press, 1994.

Wright, Ben, and Zachary W. Dresser, eds. *Apocalypse and the Millennium in the American Civil War Era.* Baton Rouge: Louisiana State Univ. Press, 2013.

Xing, Jun. *Baptized in the Fire of Revolution: The American Social Gospel and the YMCA in China, 1919–1937.* Cranbury, NJ: Associated Univ. Presses, 1996.

Zakim, Michael. *Ready-Made Democracy: A History of Men's Dress in the American Republic, 1760–1860.* Chicago: Univ. of Chicago Press, 2003.

Zboray, Ronald J. "Antebellum Reading and the Ironies of Technological Innovation." In *Reading in America: Literature and Social History,* edited by Cathy N. Davidson, 180–97. Baltimore: Johns Hopkins Univ. Press, 1989.

Zebley, Frank R. *The Churches of Delaware.* N.p.: Privately published, 1947.

Zink-Sawyer, Beverly. *From Preachers to Suffragists: Woman's Rights and Religious Conviction in the Lives of Three Nineteenth-Century American Clergywomen.* Louisville, KY: Westminster John Knox Press, 2003.

Zombek, Angela M. "Paternalism and Imprisonment at Castle Thunder: Reinforcing Gender Norms in the Confederate Capital." *Civil War History* 63, no. 3 (2017): 221–52.

Index

abolitionism, 20, 29, 112, 153n20
alcohol, 10, 61, 111, 116–18. *See also* temperance
Alcott, Bronson, 112
Allegheny Theological Seminary, 29, 30
American Bible Society, 9, 20, 65, 70–71, 118
American Missionary Association, 149
American Sunday School Union, 9
American Tract Society, 9, 65–66, 70–71
Ames, Bernice, 5, 47, 49, 117–18
Andover Theological Seminary, 29
antebellum reform, 9–10, 26, 39, 65–66, 69, 111–12, 153n25. *See also* benevolence; "Benevolent Empire"; temperance
apocalypse. *See* postmillennialism
Arminianism, 63–64, 88
army camps, 11, 36, 61–62, 77–79, 84–85, 89, 109, 115. *See also* soldiers
Arthur, T. S., 72
Auburn Theological Seminary, 146
Augur, Christopher, 144

Ballantyne, William, 6
Bancroft, George, 146
Bangor Theological Seminary, 29
baptism, 26, 126
Baptists, 4, 25, 82
Barnes, Joseph K., 52
Beecher, Catharine, 54, 57
Bellows, Henry Whitney, 5
benevolence, 48–49, 82, 113, 149–50, 152n10
"Benevolent Empire," 9–10, 13. *See also* antebellum reform

Bible, 46, 71, 73, 75, 96; as object, 65–68. *See also* American Bible Society; books; religious literature; scriptural teaching
blood, 100, 102; symbolic properties of, 1–2, 121, 129, 135, 137–38, 141, 143
Board of Indian Commissioners, 149
Boardman, William, 26–27, 30, 45, 56, 95
bodies, 96–98, 118, 126–27, 138–40; as conduit to the soul, 15–16, 126–27; delegates' ministry toward, 15, 16, 33, 35–36; manual labor and, 36, 40, 53; nourishment of, 111–12; nudity of, 95, 103; physical discomfort of, 37, 95; symbolic properties of, 43, 93, 96, 103–4, 139–40. *See also* death
books, 65–68, 76; hymnbooks, 7, 33, 137; secular, 48, 163; as talismans, 74–75. *See also* Bible; libraries; literacy; religious literature
Boston, MA, 42, 108, 148
Bowman, Elizabeth, 45
Bringhurst, George, 33–37, 140–41
Bull Run, First Battle of, 11
Burnell, Kay, 116, 139
"Businessman's Revival." *See* 1857–58 Revival

California, 4, 5, 40, 45–46
Calvinism, 9, 63, 133. *See also* predestination
Cameron, Simon, 85
Carnegie, Andrew, 150
Catholicism, 10, 157n44
Chamberlain, John Calhoun, 29
chapel tents, 79, 84–86, 96, 167n38
chaplains, 19, 22–24, 31, 57, 58, 78–79, 140, 166n4

195

charity. *See* philanthropy
Chase, Salmon P., 144, 147
Chicago, IL, 7, 40
Chidlaw, Benjamin, 146, 148
children, 4, 36, 106–8. *See also* youth
Christ. *See* Jesus
Christmas, 115–16, 123
church membership, 14, 25, 26, 39, 156n42. *See also* congregations
City Point, VA, 5, 27, 70, 83, 124
clothing, 16; distribution of, 98–100, 104; donation of, 44, 47, 53, 85; repair of, 108–9; restorative properties of, 96–97, 102. *See also* bodies: nudity of; sewing kits; shirts; uniforms
coffee, 110, 114, 119, 123
Cole, John, 31
Colfax, Schuyler, 144, 146
colleges, 28–29, 31. *See also* students
Colyer, Vincent, 7, 9, 11
combat, 11, 34–35, 61, 68, 101–2, 128, 132, 135, 139
Confederate soldiers, 6, 100, 119–22, 164n70
Confederate States of America, 42–43, 62, 119, 139
Congregationalists, 4, 13, 25, 92
congregations, 20, 37, 77, 90, 107, 144–46, 150
contrabands. *See* freed people
conversion, 4, 14–15, 25, 37, 41, 60, 73–74, 88–89, 94. *See also* evangelicalism; revivalism; soul crying, 35–36, 76, 93, 121, 150

Davis, Charles, 147
death, 2–3, 17, 27, 35; "Good Death," 129, 132; and hope of eternal life, 132–35; and mourning, 130; scholarship about, 129; toll of Civil War, 128, 132, 135, 137. *See also* funerals
delegates: competence and skills of, 22–23, 31, 36, 146–47; death of, 27; instructions to, 23–24, 32–33, 76, 79, 96–97; and masculinity, 15, 24, 30, 32–33, 34, 102–3; misbehavior of, 23, 26, 31; motivations of, 15, 31; observations and testimony of, 62–63, 90–93, 123–24, 132–35; and relationship with officers, 23–24; service of, 8, 12, 19–20, 27, 34–37, 71, 83–84, 99–100, 113–14; as soldiers of Christ, 31–33, 146–47
Demond, Charles, 108, 109, 147, 148, 176n27
diet kitchens, 15, 38, 50–59, 124–26; conflict within, 56–58–59; lady managers of, 51, 52, 55–59, 125
discipline: military 36, 61–62, 71, 89, 118; self-, 25, 31, 153n25
domesticity, 39–40, 46, 50–51, 54, 56, 125, 133, 175n18. *See also* femininity
donors, 4, 21, 26, 49–50, 98–99, 106, 116. *See also* fundraising; northern home front
Doolittle, James, 146, 148
Dow, Lorenzo, 82

education. *See* literacy; Sunday schools
1857–58 Revival, 12–15, 88, 92, 154n50, 167n56

Emancipation Proclamation, 20
Episcopalians, 4, 33, 44, 147
evangelicalism, 4, 9, 25, 126; conservatism of, 41; delegate commitment to, 25, 37, 134–35; and interpretations of Civil War, 2–3, 103, 119, 128, 136–37; and reform activity, 9–10, 41, 150; and secession crisis, 26; theology of, 63–65, 76, 87, 89; and women, 39–40, 49. *See also* interdenominationality; postmillennialism; revivalism; Second Great Awakening

Faust, Drew Gilpin, 129, 175n5
femininity, 39, 41–42, 47, 105
field agents, 8, 19, 29. *See also* delegates: instructions to; delegates: service of
fighting. *See* combat
Finney, Charles Grandison, 9, 63, 91
food, 16, 34; cultural ideas about, 54–55, 111–12, 173n13; distribution of, 3, 16, 96, 120, 123–24; home front production of, 43–44, 48, 50, 112–13; preparation in diet kitchens of, 52, 124–25; restorative properties of, 110–11, 126–27; shortages of, 112, 172n14; as social lubricant, 115–16
Fredericksburg, Battle of, 32
freed people, 20–21, 71–72, 149, 164n75. *See also* slavery; United States Colored Troops (USCT)
fundraising, 5, 6, 9, 23, 44, 46, 48–49, 85–86. *See also* donors; Ladies Christian Commissions; northern home front
funerals, 35, 133, 139–43. *See also* death

gambling, 46, 61, 67, 74, 75
Gates, Ellen H., 146
Gettysburg, Battle of, 30, 95, 99, 121
Gladden, Washington, 150
God: duty of Christians to, 21, 61; gratitude of delegates to, 35, 70, 90–91, 115; love for humanity, 84, 142–43; power to save, 13, 64–65, 75, 135; relationship between humans and, 14, 68, 87–88, 107; wrath of, 3, 42, 61, 64, 137. *See also* Jesus
"Good Samaritanism," 2, 96, 106, 119, 121, 126
Graham, Sylvester, 54, 111–12
Grant, Susan-Mary, 141
Grant, Ulysses S., 21, 51, 144, 147, 149
Griffiths, G. S., 78

Harpers Ferry, VA, 40, 72–73
Hatch, Nathan, 13, 81
health, 16, 110–13, 148; of delegates, 27–28, 31, 126; of soldiers, 101, 126–27
heaven, 93, 133–34, 136, 137, 141–42, 175n21, 176n25
Higginson, Thomas Wentworth, 71
Holy Communion, 26, 121
Holy Spirit, 13–14, 63–64, 91, 93, 96
homesickness, 36, 116

INDEX

hospitals, 1–2, 5, 51–53, 55–58, 98, 113–14, 133–34, 140
Howe, Julia Ward, 138
hymns, 2, 13, 16, 33, 116, 137, 144–46

illness, 67–68, 111, 114, 135
immigration, 10. *See also* soldiers: immigrant
interdenominationality, 4, 12, 15, 25–26, 90; conflict between denominations, 26, 91

Jacobs, Benjamin F., 7, 40, 139, 154n36
Jesus, 33, 37, 90, 96, 137, 139; biblical teaching about, 103–4, 138; delegates as ambassadors for, 109, 111, 147; focus of prayer, 106, 133; sacrifice of, 142–43
Johnson, Herrick, 129, 146, 147

Keeney, Mary, 45
Kirk, Edward Norris, 42–43, 45, 87–88

Laderman, Gary, 132–33
Ladies Christian Commissions, 15, 38, 43–50, 59, 99, 113. *See also* domesticity; fundraising; northern home front; women
libraries, 72–74. *See also* books; religious literature
Lincoln, Abraham, 8, 46, 115, 171n47; death of, 146; support for USCC, 52, 146
literacy, 16, 71. *See also* books; religious literature

masculinity: and Christianity, 18, 32, 34; and effeminacy, 31–32, 37, 40–41, 105; and morality, 98; and "muscular Christianity," 24–25; northern models of, 30, 98, 101–2, 105, 150; and physicality, 32, 40–41, 102, 139
material culture, 16, 19, 101, 109–10
McClellan, George, 8
Meade, George, 147
mending, 105–6. *See also* sewing kits; uniforms
Methodists, 82, 92
Miller, James Russell, 23, 28, 29–30
Moody, Dwight L., 7, 9, 40, 42, 150
Moorhead, James, 64
mortality, 78–79, 89–90, 106, 136. *See also* death
Moss, Lemuel, 3, 7, 148; advice to donors, 86, 99; attitude to Black troops, 72; as Commission secretary, 26, 41, 44, 120–21; postwar writings of, 18, 48, 100, 106, 109, 148

newspapers, 16, 21, 66, 71, 106–7, 113, 132; distribution of, 68–69, 164n61
New York City, NY, 7
Nightingale, Florence, 54–55
northern home front, 6, 21, 46–47, 50, 85–86, 90, 99, 109, 112–13. *See also* donors; fundraising; Ladies Christian Commissions
nursing, 36, 52, 56, 161n68

Olivet College, 29

patriotism, 17, 54, 86, 108–9, 115, 135; conflated with piety by USCC, 17, 24, 29, 136, 138, 141, 144; female expressions of, 15, 38–39, 42–43; limits of, 119–20
Patterson, John, 6
Patterson, Joseph, 65
Patterson, Robert, 45, 120
Pearl, Cyril, 78, 80
Philadelphia, PA, 7, 33, 45. *See also* United States Christian Commission (USCC): headquarters of
philanthropy, 5–7, 12, 19, 45, 59, 150. *See also* antebellum reform; benevolence
Phillips, Philip, 146, 150
postmillennialism, 2–4, 12, 64–65, 137; and America as "redeemer nation," 3, 17, 34, 60, 65; and Second Coming of Christ, 10, 64, 96, 150
prayer, 14, 87–88, 107; meetings for, 12, 16, 77, 87–94
preaching, 78–79, 80–83. *See also* sermons
predestination, 64, 133. *See also* Calvinism
Presbyterians, 13, 29
prisoners of war, 102, 119–20, 122, 134
proselytization. *See* conversion

reading. *See* religious literature
Reconstruction, 21, 148–49
refugees, 20, 119. *See also* freed people
religious literature: antebellum proliferation of, 65–66, 82; appetite of soldiers for, 66–67, 74–75; bibliotherapeutic properties of, 67–68, 72; distribution of, 11–12, 16, 67–70, 76; in languages other than English, 70–71; reading practices involving, 67, 73–74; targeted at Black soldiers, 71. *See also* Bible; books; libraries; newspapers; tracts
revivalism, 12–14, 32, 82, 90–92, 137. *See also* conversion; 1857–58 Revival; Second Great Awakening
Richmond, VA, 120–21
Roman Catholicism. *See* Catholicism

scriptural teaching: on God's punishment for sin, 42; on Jesus's sacrifice for mankind, 143–44; on justification for charitable acts, 36–37, 96, 121; militaristic imagery in, 33; on nudity, 103–4; on places of worship, 85; on treatment of one's enemies, 121; on water as a cleansing force, 126–27; on women's role in the church, 41; use in delegates' sermons of, 83
Second Great Awakening, 12–15, 32, 39, 82, 88. *See also* revivalism
secularism, 24, 86, 137; and literature, 66, 69, 72, 82, 163n44; of Union troops, 168n68
sermons, 34, 83–84. *See also* preaching
sewing kits, 4, 104–9. *See also* mending; uniforms
Shelton, Amanda, 53, 58–59, 126

Shelton, Mary, 53, 58, 126

Sherman, William Tecumseh, 1, 21, 147

shirts, 29, 96, 98, 99, 102–3, 109

Simpson, Matthew, 144, 146, 148

sin, 11, 60, 64, 94, 138

slavery, 20–21, 42, 119, 137, 153n20. *See also* abolitionism; freed people

Smith, Edward Parmelee, 20, 86, 90, 138, 148

Smith, Hannah, 53

Social Gospel, 150

soldiers, 28, 32, 37, 55, 61–62, 89, 100, 107–8; behavior of, 28, 61–62; Black (*see* United States Colored Troops [USCT]); Confederate (*see* Confederate soldiers); immigrant, 71, 73; perceived martyrdom of, 17, 128, 132, 136–38, 141

soul, 4, 63–64, 76, 103–4, 110, 135, 142–43. *See also* conversion

South. *See* Confederate States of America; Confederate soldiers

Spiritualism, 133

Stuart, George Hay: advice to delegates, 25, 31, 67, 78, 96, 106; advice to donors, 48, 99; concern for reputation of USCC, 23, 47, 117–18, 148; fundraising efforts of, 114–15; poor health of, 148, 158n79; postwar career of, 148–49; relationship with Abraham Lincoln, 146; relationship with Edwin Stanton, 48; role as USCC president, 7–8, 21, 33–34, 123

students, 4, 28–31. *See also* colleges; youth

Sunday schools, 7, 10, 11, 39, 41, 51, 149. *See also* American Sunday School Union

swearing, 61

Swedenborg, Emmanuel, 133

Taylor, Nathaniel William, 9, 63

temperance, 72, 111, 117–18. *See also* alcohol; Women's Christian Temperance Union

Testaments, 67–68, 139

Thanksgiving, 115

tracts, 69–70. *See also* American Tract Society

treason, 119–22

uniforms: military, 16, 43, 98, 100–101, 105, 109, 170n35; of USCC delegates, 102–3

Union cause, 6, 21, 42, 101–2, 119; contribution of USCC to, 34, 40, 74, 108–9; religious interpretations of, 16, 62–65, 104, 136–38. *See*

also postmillennialism: and America as "redeemer nation"; United States Army; United States government

United States Army, 3, 7, 60–61, 101, 102, 112. *See also* soldiers

United States Christian Commission (USCC): attitudes of officers toward, 21, 33, 57; bureaucratic procedures of, 19, 44, 47, 73, 80, 132; concern for public reputation, 23–24, 27, 41; Executive Committee, 7, 18, 47; headquarters of, 7, 43; hopes for future 147–52; ideas about race, 20, 56; Individual Relief Department, 129–32; and local branches, 8–9, 19, 44, 90, 98, 148, 152n19; meeting rooms, 12, 19, 72, 86; rivalry with USSC, 4–5, 46, 48–49, 97; theological ideas of, 49, 63–65; and women (*see* diet kitchens; Ladies Christian Commissions); workers (*see* delegates)

United States Colored Troops (USCT), 20–21, 71–72, 153n20, 155n11

United States government, 7, 21–22, 23, 139–40

United States Navy, 72–73, 114

United States Sanitary Commission (USSC), 7, 19, 46, 140, 147, 151n6; rivalry with Christian Commission, 4–5, 48–50, 97

universities. *See* colleges

vegetarianism, 111–12

Washington, DC, 6, 11, 113, 144–47

water, 34, 97, 114, 123, 126–27

Willard, Frances, 57, 149

Williams, E. F., 71, 119–20

Wittenmyer, Annie, 3, 51–59, 117, 125–26, 149, 160n51

women, 4, 32; advice of USCC to, 40, 42, 48, 53, 57; business acumen and professionalization of, 46, 51, 56–57; contribution to Union war effort of, 6, 43, 46–47, 50, 113; and evangelical religion, 39–40, 45; and piety, 43, 54, 59; and preaching, 41; rejected as USCC delegates, 40–41. *See also* domesticity; femininity; Ladies Christian Commissions; northern home front

Women's Christian Temperance Union, 57, 149

Young Men's Christian Associations (YMCAs), 6, 10–12, 19, 24, 62, 88, 149–50, 154n36

youth, 11, 27–29